Parenting Plan & Child Custody Evaluations

Using Decision Trees to Increase Evaluator Competence & Avoid Preventable Errors

Leslie M. Drozd
Nancy W. Olesen
Michael A. Saini

Professional Resource Press
Sarasota, Florida

Published by Professional Resource Press
(An Imprint of Professional Resource Exchange, Inc.)
Post Office Box 3197
Sarasota, FL 34230-3197

For ease in reading, this book is published in APA style with the following exception: when a citation in the text has four or more authors, the first author's name is followed by "et al."

Library of Congress Cataloging-in-Publication Data

Drozd, Leslie.
  Parenting plan & child custody evaluations : using decision trees to increase competence and avoid preventable errors / Leslie Drozd, Nancy Olesen, Michael Saini.
    pages cm.
  Includes bibliographical references and index.
  ISBN-13: 978-1-56887-148-6 (alk. paper)
  ISBN-10: 1-56887-148-1
  1. Custody of children--United States. 2. Divorced parents--Legal status, laws, etc.--United States. 3. Expert testimony--United States. I. Olesen, Nancy, date. II. Saini, Michael. III. Title.
  HV741.D76 2013
  346.7301'73--dc23
                                                                        2013008143

Acknowledgments

Writing this book has been a wonderful process of exploring ideas and refining our thinking. Many people have provided enormous help in reviewing drafts, making suggestions, or challenging us where we were not clear or were wrong. We cannot thank them enough: Jennifer Curtis (copy editor), Milford "Bud" Dale (psychologist-attorney), Jonathan Gould (diplomate in forensic psychology), The Honorable Mark Juhas, Stacey Kinney (Marriage and Family Therapist), Kathryn Kuehnle (psychologist), Lorraine Martin (social worker), David Martindale (diplomate in forensic psychology), Jeffrey Perlman (editor), Sarah Olesen (graphic designer), and The Honorable Marjorie Slabach.

Preface

"Everything should be made as simple as possible, but not simpler."
Albert Einstein

We were drawn to write this book by our shared interest in the recent flowering of books and articles about cognitive error and flawed decision making. All three authors are active child custody evaluators, and we teach workshops for and review the reports of other evaluators. We are aware of the flaws that appear in some evaluations, despite the development of standards and guidelines, the ongoing continuing education, and the increasing demands from the courts and attorneys for evaluations of the highest quality.

The authors also share an interest in visual ways to organize information in these evaluations: charts, decision trees, and grids. We have noticed an increase in the use of checklists and tools across other professional systems and industries (e.g., the health care system, the airline industry) to reduce human biases and errors and to improve the accuracy of decision making. This book is about developing systematic ways to improve the ways evaluators create and test hypotheses, collect information, organize the information they have, and analyze the data in a transparent and comprehensive way. We believe that the processes that we describe may even mirror the process used by judicial officers in sorting and weighing evidence, creating clusters of factors around issues, and generating decisions based on the overall evidence presented in court. These tools have been "field tested" in our practices and teaching, and we believe that we have increased the consistency and transparency of decision making with the aid of these tools.

Throughout the book, our deliberate use of the term parenting plan evaluation (PPE) rather than child custody evaluation is more than just semantics or an attempt to further confuse the field with yet another new term. We strongly believe that it is critical for those who work with families to emphasize the importance of parenting over the ownership implications of determining custody. Although we use both terms interchangeably throughout the book to be consistent with previous writings, we utilize the term parenting plan evaluations in the development of the resources that we have created to make better parenting plan decisions.

The first chapter will describe the current paradigm that exists in most PPEs and the shift proposed by the authors, and then it will describe several common cognitive errors that are also common sources of bias in child custody evaluations. We then begin developing the decision tree for creating systematic PPEs in Chapter 2, followed by a case example in Chapter 3 to guide evaluators on how best to use our approach. In Chapter 3 we will describe a process for the generation of hypotheses and ways to keep them in mind and test them throughout the process.

In Chapters 4 and 5, we present and demonstrate the use of a data matrix in which the evaluator can organize by source the information gathered. Using the hypothetical case, tools for weighing and clustering the facts into themes are presented in Chapter 6. Chapter 7 addresses considerations in the creation of parenting plans and demonstrates the use of the data matrices to help the evaluator make recommendations that take all of the important factors into account. In Chapter 8 we return to the proposed paradigm shift as we present ways to review and revise one's evaluation and tips on report writing, based on the themes of this book.

Appendix A contains a chapter on the use of social science research as well as additional resources for evaluators to use in their own work.

Table of Contents

Appendices *(continued)*

Parenting Plan & Child Custody Evaluations

Using Decision Trees to Increase Evaluator Competence & Avoid Preventable Errors

Chapter 1

Cognitive Errors and Paradigm Shifts

This book was written out of the authors' interest in the recent developments in cognitive science and the determination to help make child custody evaluations more competently and comprehensively done. The authors recognized the ways that the voluminous research on cognitive error, used to describe decision-making success and failure in other settings, is relevant for child custody evaluations as well. More than a generation of that research has demonstrated that there are predictable errors in cognitive processing and decision making, and some of those results will be presented here with examples of the ways that flawed child custody evaluations can be understood in terms of the cognitive errors of the evaluators. The authors propose in this book a paradigm shift in custody evaluation processes with a goal of minimizing preventable errors.

A paradigm shift is a "radical change in underlying beliefs or theory" (Collins Dictionary of English, "paradigm shift" 2012). Thomas Kuhn coined the term in his 1962 book, in which he referred to revolutions in scientific thinking. Kuhn described large shifts, such as the change from seeing the earth as the center of the universe to seeing the sun as the center with the earth as one of several planets orbiting it. Kuhn described the ways that such grand shifts in thought were marked by conflict and even bloodshed and by periods of great instability until the new paradigm was accepted by the majority. But the term can also apply to radical shifts in thinking on smaller, more contained levels.

Other authors have described paradigm shifts in divorce and family law (Elrod & Dale, 2008; Singer, 2008). Singer described the shift from adversarial, legal means of settling divorce disputes to cooperative, collaborative, and interdisciplinary methods. Elrod and Dale described the history of multiple, major paradigm shifts over the previous 50 years in the ways that families, children, and divorce are viewed and dealt with in legislation, in the courts, and in the social sciences. They note that the legal system has been moving over time to redefine its own role, the definition of a successful outcome in custody disputes, and expectations of mental health professionals who serve as evaluators. Gould and D. A. Martindale (2007) described the development of specialized and sophisticated methods for child custody evaluation as a paradigm shift as the methods and procedures were made more standard and forensically defensible. This book proposes a methodology and tools that are part of another paradigm shift—one that is concerned with avoiding preventable errors in thinking by child custody evaluators.

This book is focused on the work of parenting plan evaluators who are appointed by courts in adversarial matters, with a focus on ways to increase evaluators' competence and reduce preventable errors in their evaluation work products. This book looks at what is known about human cognitive errors and errors in decision making, and proposes a paradigm shift in the work of child custody evaluators who are operating "in the shadow of the court" (R. H. Mnookin & Kornhauser, 1979). The potential flaws in child custody evaluations are many and will be described, along with methods to offset or correct the flaws.

As Elrod and Dale (2008) point out, the early child custody evaluators tended to be traditional clinical practitioners, but over time through many efforts to standardize and regulate the practice of child custody evaluation, a specific set of procedures and skills was developed. Various professional organizations published guidelines and standards to outline the procedures that should be used (see Table 1.1), and many excellent books have been published outlining the best practices for child custody evaluations. These authors and books are described at the end of the chapter in the Annotated Bibliography section.

Table 1.1 Published Standards and Guidelines for Evaluating Child Custody Disputes

---

Association of Family and Conciliation Courts (AFCC)
http://www.afccnet.org/ResourceCenter/PracticeGuidelinesandStandards

> AFCC Model Standards of Practice for Child Custody Evaluation (PDF) (2006)
>
> Guidelines for Court-Involved Therapy (PDF) (2010)
>
> Guidelines for Brief Focused Assessment (PDF) (2009)
>
> Model Standards of Practice for Child Custody Evaluation (PDF) (2006)
>
> Guidelines for Parenting Coordination (PDF) (2005)
>
> Model Standards of Practice for Family and Divorce Mediation Symposium on Standards of Practice Convened by AFCC (2000)

American Bar Association

> Standards of Practice for Lawyers Representing Children in Custody Cases
> American Bar Association Section of Family Law (August 2003)
> http://www.americanbar.org/groups/family_law/resources/standards_of_practice_reports_recommendations.html
>
> Standards of Practice for Lawyers Who Represent Children in Abuse and Neglect Cases (February 5, 1969) (PDF)
> http://www.americanbar.org/groups/family_law/resources/standards_of_practice_reports_recommendations.html

Supervised Visitation Network

> Supervised Visitation Network (Rev. 2006) Standards and Guidelines for Supervised Visitation Practice
> http://svnworldwide.org/attachments/standards.pdf

American Academy of Matrimonial Lawyers

> Child Custody Evaluation Standards (2011)
> http://www.aaml.org/library/publications/21621/child-custody-evaluationstandards/introduction-summary

American Psychological Association

> APA Ethical Principles of Psychologists and Code of Conduct (2002)
> http://www.apa.org/ethics/code/index.aspx
>
> *American Psychologist*, Vol. 65(5), July/August 2010, 493
> APA Ethical Principles of Psychologists and Code of Conduct: 2010 Amendments (2010)
> http://www.apa.org/news/press/releases/2010/02/ethics-code.aspx
>
> APA Guidelines for Child Custody Evaluations in Family Law Proceedings (2009)
> www.apapracticecentral.org/news/guidelines.pdf
>
> APA Guidelines for Psychological Evaluations in Child Protection Matters (2011)
> www.apa.org/practice/guidelines/child-protection.pdf
>
> Guidelines for the Practice of Parenting Coordination (February 2011)
> www.apa.org/practice/guidelines/parenting-coordination.pdf
>
> Specialty Guidelines for Forensic Psychologists (2011)
> http://www.ap-ls.org/aboutpsychlaw/SpecialtyGuidelines.php
>
> APA Record Keeping Guidelines (2007)
> www.apa.org/practice/recordkeeping.pdf
>
> AERA, APA, and NCME, Standards for Educational and Psychological Testing (1999)
> http://www.apa.org/science/programs/testing/standards.aspx

Almost all of the books, guidelines, and standards have emphasized the need to use forensically informed methods rather than clinical judgment in the evaluation process. While the authors of this book agree with those statements, it is their observation that more is needed to improve the ways that child custody evaluators approach the complex task they face. The authors have conducted many child custody evaluations and have reviewed many evaluations conducted by other professionals. The flaws and errors found in so many evaluation reports can be seen as the result of predictable and universal cognitive errors as have been described in the research literature mentioned above.

The paradigm shift that is proposed here is movement from the approach in which evaluators think of the psycholegal questions in binary terms—as "yes/no" questions—often general in their terms. For example, the question may be framed, "Has this father committed domestic violence?" or "Is this mother alienating?" When such questions are couched in that form, evaluators tend to focus on them in that form. They think about the families in terms of singular, unidimensional, linear causes and paradoxically often in terms of relatively global concepts. For example, the evaluator may attempt to frame the question as "Is the father a domestic violence perpetrator or not?" or "Is the mother alienating or not?"

The authors propose that evaluators shift to an approach that is multidimensional, multilevel, multicausal, and interactive to see the answers to the court's questions as yes/no/both/and. Such a process requires that the evaluator holds in mind all of the possible explanations throughout the course of the evaluation. The proposed approach provides tools for the evaluator to do this, and it also provides tools to help the evaluator generate hypotheses that are operational and answerable and tools to use to test those hypotheses in the course of their evaluation. In addition, the proposed approach pushes the evaluator to organize his or her observations as separate from inferences, inferences as separate from opinions, and then opinions as separate from recommendations, as originally described by Tippins and Wittmann (2005).

Using the methods proposed in this book, an evaluator should be able to keep in mind many different facts and factors, to weigh them, to analyze them, and to reach conclusions about them, all while using rational analysis. The systematic method proposed will not completely protect an evaluator from making errors because, of course, a human being is doing the analysis. But the method will help make transparent the evaluator's procedures of data gathering and the process of thinking about the issues and facts. Such transparency, as will be discussed later, is central to forensic work as it allows the attorneys, the families, and the court to make independent judgments about the issues in the case based on alternative interpretations or on additional information not available to the evaluator.

Common Errors

One way to look at the common errors in evaluations is to separate them into procedural errors, systematic errors in thinking, and errors in the assertions of relationships based on research.

Procedural Errors

Procedural errors are "methodological shortcuts" for conducting evaluations that omit or distort certain steps or procedures that can impact the overall results (e.g., not conducting an observation with one of the parents and the child; failing to learn the relevant statutes, case law, and rules of court that govern in the particular jurisdiction; or altering the standard administration of psychological assessment instruments). As mentioned, many writers have described the best practices and procedures, and these are not the primary focus of this book although there will be some consideration of some procedural errors and ways to counteract them in Chapter 2. Here we provide a brief overview of important writing in procedural matters.

There are currently a number of books and articles for understanding specific issues regarding child custody disputes (e.g., M. J. Ackerman, 1995, 2001, 2006; Benjamin & Gollan, 2003; Bradley, 2004; Butterfield, 2003; Emery, 1994, 2011; Evans, 1997; R. M. Galatzer-Levy & Ostrov, 1999; R. M. Galatzer-Levy, Kraus, & J. Galatzer-Levy, 2009; Goldstein et al., 1984; Gould, 2006; Gould & D. A. Martindale, 2007;

Grisso, 1987; Gunsberg & Hymowitz, 2005; Hynan, 2003; Johnston, Roseby, & Kuehnle, 2009; Knapp & Keller, 1993; Kuehnle, 1996; Kuehnle & Connell, 2009; Lebow, Walsh, & Rolland, 1999; D. A. Martindale, J. L. Martindale, & Broderick, 1991; Mooney & Nelson, 1989; Otto, Buffington-Vollum, & Edens, 2003; Rohrbaugh, 2007; Schaul, 2005; Schutz et al., 1989; Stahl, 1994, 1999, 2002, 2010; Tumas, 2005). Although each of these books or articles provides further awareness of some specific issues in isolation, there is currently no book that provides a comprehensive and systematic approach for the integration of the factors as assessed. In addition to these sources, there are other publications in which people have written limited, ideologically driven views of these complex problems that can further polarize practitioners in family law.

Systematic Errors

Systematic errors are "thinking shortcuts" in which people think too fast and thus react too fast or too unconsciously, or they become blind to some of the hypotheses by overfocusing on one or two other proposed explanations. These errors are the focus of this chapter and the next. Evaluators taking shortcuts in thinking do not allow themselves to consider alternatives systematically, and they get stuck in their original ideas about the situation, event, or person. Evaluators who prematurely focus on one or two explanations for the family difficulties they observe also remain blind to other possible explanations.

Even more important than outlining the cognitive errors, this book will follow the lead in medicine and in safety regulations for air travel and nuclear power stations and will provide systematic tools for child custody evaluators to use to counteract the human tendencies to make the errors described. These tools, developed by the authors, include a decision tree showing an overview of the entire evaluation procedure, decision trees specific to case issues, and matrices both to organize the data gathered and to set out ways the data is analyzed and synthesized. Throughout the book the reader will find tools for record keeping and for self-reflection.

Assertion Errors

Assertion errors based on the misuse or overuse of research are "application shortcuts," the overgeneralization of research findings to particular cases without considering the potential limits of transferability based on sample, design, methods, and/or results. An example of an assertion error is saying that the research says that young children must be in the sole custody of the primary caregiver to protect their attachment status with that parent. Another example of an assertion error is the belief that all children benefit from joint custody. The first example is an assertion error because, whereas attachment is an important element to consider when choosing a parenting plan for young children, it is not solely determinative given there are circumstances in which keeping the child in the care of the same parent is not in the best interest of the child (e.g., when that parent's functioning is impaired due to major depression with psychotic features combined with dependence on Oxycontin). In the later example, whereas it is true that children in general benefit from the sharing of parenting, it is an assertion error to state that joint custody is best for all children given some children do not benefit from joint custody when there is coercive control intimate partner violence or substance abuse. Assertion errors will be further addressed in the Research chapter (Appendix A).

Cognitive Errors and Biases

There is a growing popular awareness of research on cognitive errors—errors that are specific and predictable and lead to biased decisions in many areas of life. They also can lead to a myriad of biases in PPEs.

Research on Cognitive Errors

Twenty years ago, Kleinmuntz and Schkade (1993, p. 221) noted, "Two decades of research have emphasized the shortcomings of human judgement and decision-making processes." Many others have worked in these lines of cognitive research, which have been described in the popular press over the past 5 years.

There is much for evaluators to learn from this important literature that could help them see complex cases differently.

Readers can demonstrate cognitive error proneness to themselves with a simple problem to solve (Kahneman, 2011): A bat and a ball cost a dollar and 10 cents. The bat costs a dollar more than the ball. How much does the ball cost? Most people will say 10 cents quickly and without thinking, and in fact a majority of students at Harvard and MIT will say 10 cents. It is only after thinking about it more closely that you realize it must be 5 cents. Here's the math: If you go with the quick answer and say that the ball costs 10 cents, you are wrong because if the bat costs a dollar more than the 10-cent ball, then the bat would cost $1.10, leaving the bat and ball altogether costing $1.20, not $1.10. Daniel Kahneman and others have described the phenomenon underlying this common mental error and have researched such predictable errors for more than 5 decades.

Kahneman refers to intuitive, rapid, and unconscious processing as "fast thinking" or "System 1 thinking," while others call it intuition. This book will use the term intuition to describe this thinking process, although intuition is a word that has other meanings in common usage. Intuition or intuitive thinking requires very little effort and conveys no sense of voluntary control. General intuition and rapid clinical judgment would be examples of this type of decision-making process. It is based in the emotional centers of the brain; it is necessary and goes on all the time outside of consciousness, allowing humans to make quick and necessary judgments without thinking about them. Examples of these useful cognitive functions include judgments about other people and their potential to harm us, judgments about the speed of a car heading our way, and judgments about many other situations requiring quick, automatic decision making (Gladwell, 2005; Hammond, 1996).

Intuition involves heuristic reasoning, the rules of thumb that may be based on individual experience but that are also based on hard-wired neurological operations. In an evolutionary sense, humans have developed heuristics because there are events facing them that do not allow the time for careful reasoning and because people would be crippled by the need to think through every decision, every minute of every day. The use of intuition is economical, saving the expenditure of energy and time. It also allows people to do several things at once if each task is simple. Kahneman (2011) and Ariely (2008) point out the useful work of this kind of rapid observation and thinking when it is also accompanied by careful, analytic, and critical thinking to correct for error.

The intuitions that are so helpful in some areas can also be the source of irrational decisions. These decisions are evident in studies of people evaluating risk, thinking while distracted by another task, judging the honesty or goodness of people of different racial groups, or evaluating "value" in decisions about purchases, among other decisions studied. Daniel Kahneman won the Nobel Prize in Economics by his lifetime's research into the irrationality of economic decision making, and others have recently looked at this "predictable irrationality," to use Ariely's term (Ariely, 2008, 2009; Kahneman, 2011).

One of the really interesting things about intuition is that once someone has a "hit" on something, that person tends to hang onto that intuitive thought with a death grip (Kahneman, 2011). The good news is that if the intuition is right, the person will be absolutely sure that he is right, and he will stand up for his intuitive thought with conviction. When the intuitive thought is wrong, that is, when his "gut" feeling is wrong, he will hang onto that erroneous thought or decision with the same kind of fervor. A person will stand up to challenges to that kind of thinking with the same kind of confidence that they do if the intuition were right. People often tend to block any new information coming in that would shake their original intuition, which results in them being very sure that they are right even though they are wrong. There are other reasons for resisting change in one's opinions, and those will be discussed below.

Clinical judgment is the unarticulated decision making used daily (and often effectively) by therapists and by mental health interviewers, and it may represent a more sophisticated level of intuition, but it remains vulnerable to the same flaws as ordinary intuitive thinking.

Analytical thinking is called "System 2 thinking" or "slow thinking" by Kahneman. This book will use the more widespread term analytical thinking to describe the step-by-step process by which facts are investigated and various hypotheses are considered before a decision is made. It is the only cognitive process that "can follow rules, compare objects on several attributes, and make deliberate choices between options" (Kahneman, 2011, p. 36). This is the thinking that is the intended basis for all decisions in law and the necessary mode of cognitive operations for the careful work of forensic mental health professionals. It is associated with the feelings of concentration, choice, and agency.

Analytical thinking exerts a high cost in terms of energy expended. Analytical decision making is dependent on the thinker's state (rest, glucose levels, time pressure, stress) and on the thinker's awareness of his or her own emotional reactions. People—all people—will tend to use the easier, less effortful thinking of intuition unless they push themselves to use analytical thinking. When people are preoccupied, stressed, tired, or hungry (literally, when the brain is depleted of glucose), their ability to operate in the mode of analytical thinking is compromised. These findings about the energy costs of analytical thinking have important implications for the work of parenting plan evaluators and will be discussed more in later chapters.

Kahneman (2011) has written about this active rather than passive approach to decision making and its costs: "Sustaining doubt is harder work than sliding into certainty" (p. 114). It is the purpose of this book to help evaluators to keep from "sliding into certainty" prematurely.

In looking on Google for "expert systems," one of the authors found a website offering advice to attorneys who must counter an expert's testimony in court (Nmlawyer, 2012). They used information from Kahneman and suggested that the experts "are vulnerable to the same reasoning pitfalls that affect us all: biased thinking that finalizes judgments too quickly" (Nmlawyer, 2012). They go on to describe ways to question the expert intensively about the active process of considering alternative explanations of their data until they arrive at the best explanation, rather than the simple acknowledgement that there are alternative explanations. The reference is made here to demonstrate that these ideas are not obscure and are not without direct practical use in the work of child custody evaluators. In fact, the authors want all evaluators to approach all evaluations as though they were being reviewed and critiqued or cross-examined. Evaluators set themselves up to be critiqued if they are not following a systematic methodology and transparently presenting it. Looking at one's own work as though it were a critique can be a valuable part of the evaluation process.

For all of the advantages of analytical thinking—with its intense, focused attention—there are also disadvantages: It can make people blind to things that would ordinarily be very obvious. This "attentional blindness" is a common factor in midair crashes of airplanes, whose pilots are concentrating intensely on instruments, a crisis, or something else other than the immediate surroundings. One of the most striking demonstrations of attentional blindness can be seen in the Invisible Gorilla experiment by Chabris and Simons (2010). In their classic experiment, subjects view a short film showing two groups of people in white or black t-shirts, passing a basketball quickly among themselves. The viewer is instructed to count the number of passes by people in white t-shirts, ignoring the people in black t-shirts. During the film, a person in a gorilla suit walks across the court, thumps his chest, and walks off. The gorilla is in view for 9 seconds. About half of the thousands of people who have seen the video with those instructions do not notice anything unusual. No one who views the video without the attention-focusing instructions fails to see the gorilla. The analogous attentional blindness can be seen in PPEs that focus on one factor as determinative in a family, say the attachment relationships or the interparental conflict, and ignore a significant fact such as serious substance abuse or a history of domestic violence.

A slightly different kind of attentional blindness can occur when one holds the belief that a particular psychological theory trumps other theories or information. For example, an evaluator may see "attachment" as the central factor in every family to the exclusion of other factors that affect parenting and the safety of children—factors like domestic violence. It is the purpose of this book to help evaluators avoid attentional blindness by organizing the information they gather in such a way that all factors remain visible and available for analysis.

One conclusion of the many researchers in the area of cognitive errors is that these errors are universal; they are based in brain functions that have evolved over millions of years because they are effective in day-to-day life. Another conclusion from the research literature is that intelligence provides little or no protection against the pull toward the easy and automatic responses based on System 1 (intuitive thinking) heuristics. In fact, Kahneman and many others (Lehrer, 2012; West, Meserve, & Stanovich, 2012) have shown that people with higher intelligence and cognitive sophistication, at least as measured by SAT scores, are more prone to make these common errors than the rest of the population. One explanation for that finding may be that highly intelligent and cognitively sophisticated people are overconfident in their own intellectual prowess (Bell & Mellor, 2009).

The tendency to avoid the hard work of logical, analytic thinking is demonstrated in research on psychological clinical practice, where the majority of clinicians do not use empirical evidence to inform their decisions, despite extensive research showing the greater accuracy of statistical, actuarial approaches (where appropriate methods exist; Bell & Mellor, 2009). The tendency is demonstrated in research on medical practice as well, where a large minority of practicing physicians do not follow practice guidelines that have been established as superior for decades (Gawande, 2011).

In a current article, D. A. Martindale addresses this difficulty quite clearly:

> The repetitive, successful use of a particular method for tackling tasks significantly increases the likelihood that the previously successful method will be employed in approaching the next task. . . . Education, especially in specialized areas, channels our thought processes. We learn to eliminate from consideration problem solving techniques that, in the past, have not borne fruit. In other words, our problem-solving successes are attributable, in large part, to the fact that education and experience teach us how to differentiate the important from the unimportant. We learn to think within the confines of a cognitive box. As a result, strategies that have produced success in the past are likely to lead to failure when that which, in the past, was unimportant, turns out, in today's context, to be quite important. (D.A. Martindale, 2013)

The resistance to changing one's established ideas and habits to new ones that are proven superior is often described as the Semmelweis Reflex, based on a dramatic historic story (K. C. Carter & B. Carter, 1994; Semmelweis, 1860/1999). Dr. Ignatz Semmelweis was a Hungarian obstetrician in Vienna in the mid-1800s, a time when many women died of childbed fever in the hospital. The mortality rate was significantly higher in the wards where the women were attended by physicians (1 in 10) than in the wards with midwives (1 in 50). Semmelweis connected the deaths to infections from cadaver autopsies done by the physicians doing research at that prominent hospital and insisted that staff wash their hands with chlorine before assisting at births. No one understood germs at the time, and no one had considered hand washing to be necessary or effective; Semmelweis was opposed and ridiculed, despite the fact that mortality was lowered in those instances in which hospital staff washed their hands. The Semmelweis Reflex now refers to the tendency to rely upon methods that have appeared to be successful in the past and the resistance to and resentment of suggestions that one's cherished methods or procedures are wrong. One example of a way that the Semmelweis Reflex might show itself in the context of child custody would be well-trained and experienced mental health professionals using open-ended interviewing with active listening, a technique that is appropriate and effective in many therapeutic situations but one that is inappropriate and can be leading in forensic interviewing.

The use of heuristics, of shortcuts of many kinds, and the established difficulty of thinking in logical and complex ways all lead parenting plan evaluators (like everyone else) to be sloppy in their thinking, to not notice that they have formed preliminary opinions and then operated out of confirmatory bias thereafter, to have "anchored" their thinking in a beloved (or closely held) theory or a most recent case, or to have made many other possible cognitive errors that will be described.

In making everyday judgements, people take mental shortcuts. If they were perfectly rational, they would carefully consider all of the relevant evidence before reaching a conclusion. In daily life, a person would be crippled by the effort to consider all relevant evidence before making simple and unimportant decisions. PPEs, of course, are not simple and unimportant decisions. They involve complex decisions, which are extremely important for children and families. Errors must be prevented to whatever extent is possible. A list of common biases leading to errors or biases can be found below in Table 1.2.

Knowing the common errors is a start toward avoiding them, but awareness of the pitfalls is no solution in itself. In the domains of airline safety and minimizing medical errors, a great deal of attention has been focused on the problems of preventable errors. In fact, there was evidence published over a decade ago that almost 100,000 people per year are killed by preventable medical errors in the United States (Institute of Medicine, 1999; Landrigan et al., 2010). There is substantial evidence from medicine and other fields that the best hope to prevent these errors lies in tools such as checklists, rules, and decision trees—tools that remind, or force, the practitioner to be organized and to think clearly. Airplane pilots use preflight checklists, as do technicians involved in NASA space flights. Dr. Atul Gawande is a leading proponent of making the use of checklists universal in hospital practice in general and in surgery in particular. Interestingly, Dr. Gawande told an interviewer that he decided to use a surgery checklist himself just as an example to his junior staff and found two errors in his own presurgical procedures. The authors believe that such tools should be used in forensic evaluations in general and in PPEs in particular, and they will be presented in Chapter 2 and later chapters.

Specific Errors and Biases

There are a series of errors common to PPEs. Those errors are summarized in Table 1.2 and some will be discussed here in more detail.

Table 1.2 Types of Biases

Selective evidence/Confirmation bias: People tend to gather facts that support certain conclusions but disregard other facts that support different conclusions (D. A. Martindale, 2004).

Premature termination of evidence: People tend to accept the first alternative that looks like it might work. Conflicting evidence often is not discounted but apparently just ignored (Munro, 2008).

Wishful thinking or optimism bias: People tend to want to see things in a positive light, and this can distort their perception and thinking. Evaluators tend to provide recommendations as if the parties will understand their feedback and follow their exhortations to be better parents and then live happily ever after.

Choice-supportive bias: People distort their memories of chosen and rejected options to make the chosen options seem more attractive or even inevitable.

Recency bias: People tend to place more attention on more recent information and either ignore or forget more distant information (Plous, 1993).

Repetition bias: People have a willingness to believe what they have been told most often and by the greatest number of different sources.

Dichotomous thinking: People get stuck in validating specific claims, pro or con, rather than looking at broader, big picture issues.

Source bias: People reject something if they have a bias against the person, organization, or group to which the person belongs: People are inclined to accept a statement by someone we like.

Incremental decision making and escalating commitment: People look at a decision as a small step in a process, and this tends to perpetuate a series of similar decisions.

Illusion of control: People tend to underestimate future uncertainty because they tend to believe they have more control over events than they really do.

Research bias: People assume that something is true because "the research" says it is true. Research studies vary in their reliability and validity, and the research per se rarely speaks with one voice. The opposite of this is true as well, that is, for some the research bias is that uniformly, they believe that the research has nothing to offer the court, attorneys, or families in regards to child custody.

One of the most common and best-known sources of error is confirmatory bias. This refers to the disposition of the evaluator to seek out evidence in the case that confirms a previously held opinion. It could be a prior theoretical opinion, such as the proper access schedules for very young children, or it could be a personal opinion, such as a favorable first impression of one of the parents, but in either case, it is an opinion that is not examined in light of the specific facts of the case but instead a prior opinion that guides the search for evidence to support it (D. A. Martindale, 2005).

Another source of error is related but somewhat different: the premature closure of evidence seeking. This refers to the process by which the evaluator accepts the first plausible explanation for the phenomenon observed and stops the process without considering other, alternative explanations. In this case, the evaluator may have no original reason to prefer one hypothesis to another but accepts the first and ignores evidence that would contradict it (Munro, 2008).

"Anchoring" is widely researched in cognition studies, because it is almost never evident to the decision maker and it exerts a powerful effect. It is often discussed in terms of economic decisions. For example, seeing a price tag on a sweater with a prior price of $100 leads the buyer to purchase an item at $40, seeing it as a bargain, when the same purchaser would not have bought the sweater if it were simply priced at $40. The "anchor" of $100 leads the person to compare the current price and to see it as a bargain. Anchoring is at work when a driver continues at too high a speed when he exits a freeway and fails to adjust his speed for the new, slower road. Kahneman described a number of studies demonstrating that moving away from the anchor requires active effort. Anchoring can also describe a "priming effect" in which the anchor serves as a suggestion that then "selectively evokes compatible evidence" (Kahneman, 2011, p. 122). Anchoring is common in child custody disputes as well. If a case is presented by an attorney as a "domestic violence" case or an "alienation" case, those terms become anchors against which the data is compared and evidence is selected, unless there is awareness and the hard work of analytic thinking to fight against it.

The authors have often seen the optimism bias in child custody evaluations. This refers to the wishful thinking that things will turn out all right. Evidence of risk or deficiency may be discounted or ignored in favor of providing recommendations as if the parties will change, accept feedback, and follow the exhortations to be better people and better parents.

There is a related source of bias, that of disaster neglect, in which the evaluator does not consider the worst-case scenario but ignores evidence that there may be more pernicious behavior in the future than the evaluator has counted on. This is particularly dangerous, for example, when there is significant and documented domestic violence but the evaluator does not consider the possibility of escalating or even lethal violence.

The last source of error to be discussed in this chapter is the "availability heuristic." Again it is widely discussed in the cognition literature, but there is a particularly clear discussion in Kahneman (2011). The availability heuristic describes the fact that a person's judgment of the frequency or likelihood of an event is based on the ease with which instances of the event come to the person's mind—literally how available the memory is to him. This phenomenon is sometimes referred to as saliency because the person's judgment about the event's likelihood is influenced by immediate reminders of the event. For example, one can think about the ways that people overestimate the dangers of flying immediately after a plane crash that was in the news. The more recent, the more vivid, the more personal the experience, the more likely there is to be a bias toward believing the event to be highly likely. This source of error is also prevalent in child custody evaluations. For example, the evaluator's judgment of the likelihood of sexual abuse in a particular case is determined to some extent by that person's previous personal experience with sexual abuse or by seeing sexual abuse in his or her cases or in recent news.

Parenting Plan Evaluator's Cognitive Errors Checklist

The authors have developed a checklist for the evaluator to examine his or her work for a variety of cognitive errors and sources of bias (Parenting Plan Evaluator's Cognitive Error Checklist) and a list of the flaws in thinking that may occur in PPEs (Parenting Plan Evaluations Flaws). Both are found in the Appendices section in this book (Appendix H and Appendix I).

Given the human errors that parenting plan evaluators, like all human beings, are subject to, there is a call in the field of PPEs for a new approach to this work, a change in perspective of sorts. The decision tree, matrices, and checklists provided in this chapter and others to follow are designed to help the field move forward to better serve families.

Summary

- Human cognition is subject to errors based on reliance on quick, intuitive thinking and overly focused analytical thinking.
- There are many sources of error that can lead PPEs to be dangerously flawed.
- There can be errors in the procedures used in the evaluations or in the use of social science research or in the thinking that is used to analyze the data that was gathered or all three.
- This book proposes a systematic approach to conducting and organizing and analyzing PPEs.
- The goal of the book is to minimize preventable errors, to make it possible for evaluators to keep in mind the many facts and factors in a case, and to develop transparent methods for the analysis and synthesis of inferences and the generation of opinions.

Annotated Bibliography

Ackerman, M. J. (2006). *Clinician's Guide to Child Custody Evaluations (3rd ed.).* Hoboken, NJ: John Wiley & Sons.

This book provides a step-by-step overview of PPEs from beginning to end. The author grounds this process by including new evaluation and testing findings and new ethical guidelines from the American Psychological Association (APA). This book also features coverage of important legal decisions affecting PPEs. Each chapter ends with critical issues for the practitioner to consider. The accessible reference format provides a quick review of relevant discussions in the text.

Erard, R. E., & Pickar, D. B. (2008). Countertransference bias: Self-examination, not cross-examination. *Journal of Child Custody: Research, Issues, and Practices, 4*(3/4), 101-109.

The authors clarify the distinction between self-examination for countertransference bias as a heuristic for improving the sensitivity and objectivity of expert testimony and its use as substantive evidence. They argue that countertransference bias is a highly personal, emotionally charged kind of bias, unlike the cognitive biases more frequently discussed in the child custody literature. They conclude that recognition of the insidious emotional influences that threaten our objectivity in working with families in high-conflict divorce is an important ethical responsibility.

Fridhandler, B. (2008). Science and child custody evaluations: What qualifies as "scientific"? *Journal of Child Custody: Research, Issues, and Practices, 5*(3/4), 256-275.

This article provides a review of the use of social science within PPEs and supports those in the literature who advocate for the use of disciplined clinical judgment to integrate case observation, empirical research, and clinical experience to provide the courts with responsible answers to the questions they pose.

Martindale, D. A. (2007). Setting standards for custody evaluators. *Journal of Psychiatry & Law, 35*(2), 173-199.

In this article, the author reviews the controversy concerning the qualifications and methods employed by parenting plan evaluators. The author proposes that legislatures and court systems develop standards to be used in regulating the professional preparation and conduct of those who perform PPEs.

Martindale, D. A., & Gould, J. W. (2008). Countertransference and zebras: Forensic obfuscation. *Journal of Child Custody: Research, Issues, and Practices, 4*(3/4), 69-75.

The authors comment on the use of countertransference within PPEs and suggest that attaching new labels to familiar dynamics fails to add additional knowledge to our understanding of interpersonal dynamics. The authors opine that biases are only relevant when they are manifested in identifiable behavior. These behaviors include the application by the evaluator of different standards in examining and commenting on the actions of the two parents, the use of insulting terminology in describing the nonfavored parent, the use of glowing terminology in describing the favored parent, assignment of minimal importance to possible parenting deficiencies in the favored parent, the assignment of much importance to reported flaws in the nonfavored parent, an apparent unquestioning acceptance of the favored parent's perspective, and an apparent rejection of the nonfavored parent's perspective.

Pickar, D. B. (2008). Countertransference bias in the child custody evaluator. *Journal of Child Custody: Research, Issues, and Practices, 4*(3/4), 45-67.

The author focuses on the concerns about bias, which can arise in PPEs. The types of biases addressed are those that primarily stem from cognitive psychology, as well as social and cultural sources of bias. The author also focuses on biases that can stem from evaluator countertransference, which if unrecognized can potentially lead to biased and nonobjective recommendations. The author suggests that while one must strive to be objective and impartial, parenting plan evaluators are frequently working with highly charged emotional issues, which may interact with their own personal issues or past experiences. This article examines the types of countertransference phenomena, which may arise in the child custody evaluation, and it presents tips for identifying and managing such reactions.

Robb, A. (2006). Strategies to address clinical bias in the child custody evaluation process. *Journal of Child Custody: Research, Issues, and Practices, 3*(2), 45-69.

The author reviews studies that suggest that mental health professionals are not immune from unintentional bias in judgments, including those in forensic situations. The author suggests that parenting plan evaluators should be aware of the pitfalls that exist in clinical decision making as well as strategies to address them. This article connects existing insights from therapeutic and forensic literature to the field of custody evaluations. An overview of clinical bias in custody evaluation is offered to familiarize practitioners with the range of possible problems. Examples, such as biases inherent in the scientific process and in the clinical relationship, are followed with specific recommendations regarding how to address issues of clinical bias during evaluation. Insights are offered for judges and attorneys to improve the quality of reports they receive.

Saini, M. A. (2008). Evidence base of custody and access evaluations. *Brief Treatment and Crisis Intervention, 8*(1), 111-129.

This evidence-based review systematically draws on studies of custody evaluations to determine the current state of scientific knowledge. Multiple databases of peer-reviewed and unpublished literature were searched to critically review the existing evidence. Data from cross-sectional designs, content analysis methods, and outcome-based studies represent aggregate data of over 1,945 mental health professionals, 417 lawyers and judges, and 568 children and families involved in custody evaluations. Outcome-based studies reflect the dual focus of evaluations to provide the courts with the best evidence and to provide families with opportunities to step out of the litigation process. Data synthesis within the evidence-based approach provides the opportunity to evaluate the current empirical evidence, identify gaps, and highlight areas for further review and for future research work.

Waller, E. M., & Daniel, A. E. (2004). Purpose and utility of child custody evaluations: From the perspective of judges. *Journal of Psychiatry & Law, 32*(1), 5-27.

This study examines the perspective of judges regarding PPEs by mental health professionals. Ninety-seven judges completed an anonymous survey regarding the legal standards and personal biases influencing judicial custody decision making and the expectations of the PPE. Findings indicate that judges are most likely to order custody evaluations for allegations regarding sexual or physical abuse or parental unfitness. Judges reported that they expect a comprehensive procedure and find utility in an inclusive report. Survey findings suggest that PPEs play a significant role in judicial decision making; however, judges are hesitant to have mental health professionals testify as to the ultimate custody question.

Waller, E. M., & Daniel, A. E. (2005). Purpose and utility of child custody evaluations: The attorney's perspective. *Journal of the American Academy of Psychiatry and the Law, 33*(2), 199-207.

This study attempts to fill a gap in the literature by assessing the perspectives of attorneys regarding PPEs. Fifty-nine attorneys completed a survey designed to ascertain their opinions about their expectations regarding these evaluations. Findings indicate that attorneys are most likely to seek evaluations in the context of allegations regarding physical abuse, sexual abuse, or parental fitness. In addition, attorneys reported that they expect a very comprehensive evaluation procedure and find utility in an inclusive report.

Chapter 2

Decision Tree for Working With Parenting Plan Complexity

"The art of simplicity is a puzzle of complexity."
Douglas Horton

Creating a PPE is a difficult task, perhaps one of the most challenging of all evaluations. Some seasoned clinicians have jokingly said, "Give me a good murder any day as opposed to a family in the midst of a custody battle." If you couple the difficulty of this kind of evaluation with the information about human error presented in the first chapter, it is no wonder that malpractice carriers and licensing boards have found that amongst the highest risk areas in which to practice is child custody work. These are even more reasons that the parenting plan evaluator needs a systematic method of approaching the task.

In addition, parenting plan evaluators and judges are human. PPEs can be flawed. There are, though, solutions—solutions to minimize the errors and biases through the use of decision trees and checklists—all resulting in transparency that is called for in the PPE process.

People often want simple solutions, and may even need simple solutions, in terms of the parenting plans that reasonably can be implemented. The fact of the matter is that to come up with simple solutions that can be implemented readily, evaluators must understand the complex factors that are at the roots of the problems in the family. Rather than isolate discrete causes of strained family relationships, parenting plan evaluators need to consider new and innovative ways to embrace the full complexity of these problems. To do that, parenting plan evaluators need a more comprehensive and systematic method for considering all possible influences leading to parent--child problems—a method that can accommodate the interactional influences among various factors that both impede and facilitate healthy relationships between children and parents after separation and divorce.

A Decision Tree for Understanding the Complexity of a Parenting Plan Evaluation

One way to embrace complexity is to have a mental picture of the process, in this case, the process of a PPE—a decision tree of sorts. The purpose of the evaluation decision tree is to make transparent for the parents, their counsel, the court, and potential reviewers of the evaluation the process from beginning to the end. Such a decision tree follows in this chapter in two forms: the first is an aerial overview of the process, and the second is one that results from zooming in on the details of the PPE process.

The aerial view, a brief schematic diagram of the course of the evaluation found in Figure 2.1, can serve as a useful prop for the evaluator's description of the process to the parents in the first meeting, when questions about the evaluation process must be answered. The evaluator will actually work from the more detailed PPE decision tree that is described in Figure 2.2.

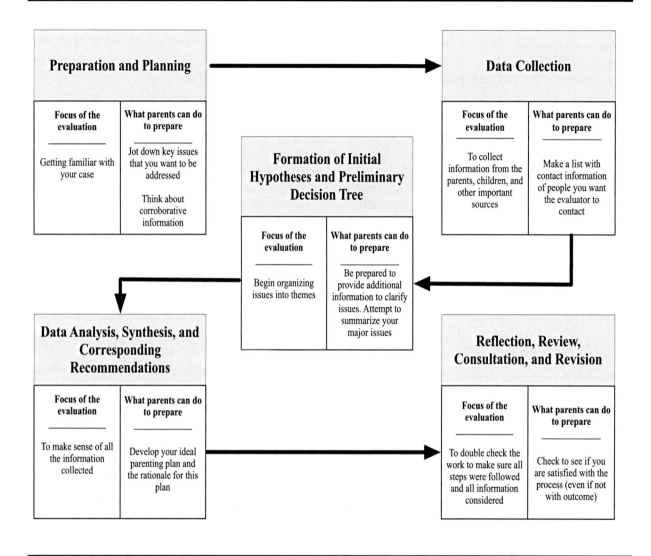

Figure 2.1 An Aerial View of a Decision Tree for Parenting Plan Evaluations

A different visual tool to describe this same process is found next in the form of a more detailed decision tree of the evaluation process. This tool provides on one page a roadmap for the systematic approach for PPEs that is described in this book. The evaluator works through the steps shown in Figure 2.2 as will be described below. There is another copy of this road map in Appendix C for ease of use by the reader in his or her own practice.

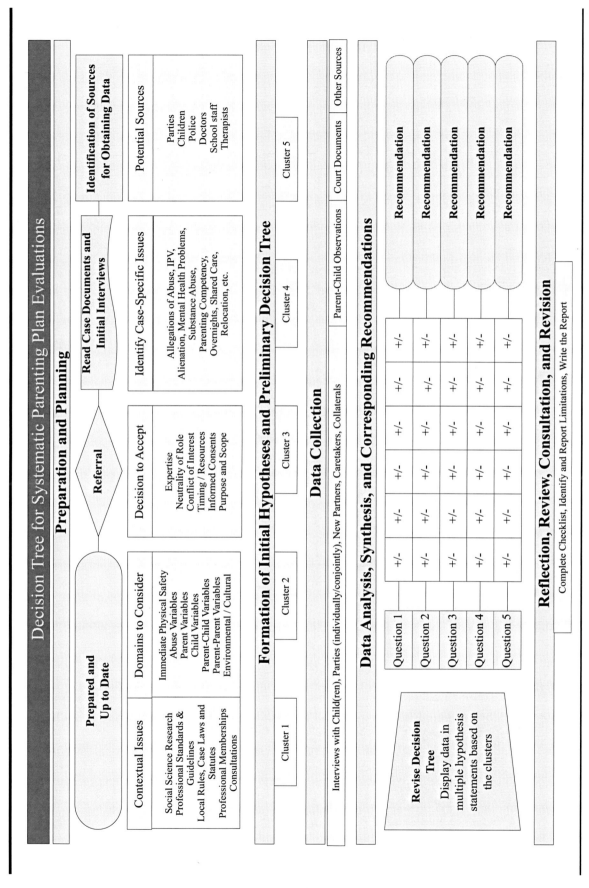

Figure 2.2 Parenting Plan Evaluation Decision Tree

Preparation and Planning

For any given parent, it may seem that the evaluation begins when he or she first meets with the evaluator, though in reality the first part of any evaluation occurs before the family walks in the evaluator's door to begin the first interview. The evaluator must have years of forensic experience, have many years of practice, and in most jurisdictions, be required to be supervised before he or she takes on the first evaluation. See Table 2.1 for necessary evaluator preparation.

Table 2.1 Preparation to be a Parenting Plan Evaluator: A Process Not a Goal

---

- Good basic training and licensed as mental health professional at least 2 years, preferably longer.

- Specific training in the assessment of common psycholegal questions that arise in PPEs. Association of Family and Conciliation Courts (AFCC) Model Standards specify the areas in which the parenting plan evaluator must have advanced training (www.afccnet.org/resources/PracticeGuidelinesandStandards). These also may be set forth in statutes or rules of court in many states. California, for example, has rule of court 5.225 that lists the areas of advanced training required (www.courts.ca.gov/cms/rules/index.cfm?title-five&linkid-rul5.225).

- Ongoing continuing education about issues relevant to forensic evaluation: state statues and case law, forensic techniques, standards and guidelines, special issues such as domestic violence, child abuse, alienation, and relocation.

- Attendance at professional conferences such as AFCC, APA, or the American Board of Forensic Psychology (ABPP), and at continuing education workshops.

- Development of a library of books with current research summaries and current information about, for example, family dynamics, parenting, and child development. An example is the 2012 Oxford University Press book, *Parenting Plan Evaluations: Applied Research for Family Courts* (Kuehnle & Drozd, 2012).

- Subscription to family law publications relevant to custody questions, for example, *Family Court Review*, *Journal of Child Custody*, or *Family Law Quarterly*.

- Formation of peer consultation groups to review current research and to review the forensic work you do.

- Joining listservs to keep up with current thinking.

- Serious thought about one's own long-held opinions about childhood and children, about parent-child relationships, and about people from other cultures, religions, and ethnicities. Conduct an investigation of the social science research on those questions if not done recently.

- Serious thought about one's own time limitations, financial concerns, and what categories of cases or problems the evaluator will be willing to evaluate. Evaluators must be ready to say honestly how quickly they can complete a particular evaluation.

When the evaluator receives the appointment by the court or a stipulation from the attorneys, the evaluator and the parents involved in the custody dispute have similar tasks: to make sure that the issues to assess in the course of the PPE are thoroughly delineated and described, and the decision on all sides for the evaluator to take the case is appropriate. In Table 2.2 we have made a list of case-specific preparatory and initial tasks that must be completed as the evaluation gets started.

Case-specific issues may include allegations of abuse, intimate partner violence (IPV), alienation, mental health problems, substance abuse, parenting competency, overnights, shared care, relocation, and the like. Potential sources of data may include the children, parties, significant others, police, child protective services, doctors, dentists, school staff, coaches, and therapists as well as written documents and records.

There are three sources of questions in PPEs: (a) questions related to the statutory factors used for best-interests-of-the-child determinations; (b) questions related to factors identified in the relevant research as central or crucial to a best-interests-of-the-child determination; and (c) questions of fact related to the specific

---

Table 2.2   Preparation for a Specific Case

- Check for conflicts of interest such as prior relationships with parties or attorneys, or prior knowledge of or information about the case.

- Check for one's ability to be neutral and for the relevant expertise for the issues in the case.

- Decide if the time constraints are realistic for completion.

- Confirm that the referral questions are clear and specific.

- Get initial starting paperwork completed:

  o   Informed consent and agreement discussed, questions answered, signed.
  o   Court order for evaluation, naming the specific evaluator and the questions to be addressed, signed and filed.
  o   Initial retainer paid.
  o   List of collaterals to be contacted.
  o   Documents requested from each attorney, with copies to the other side.

- Look at case-specific issues such as domestic violence, child abuse, mental health or substance abuse problems. Identify:

  o   research to be consulted.
  o   tools to use in data collection.
  o   additional sources of information to seek.

- Confirm that all issues to be investigated in the evaluation are thoroughly covered in the court order.

---

dynamics, facts, and issues in this particular custody dispute. It is critical that the court order includes points that cover the information sought from all three of these sources.

Filling Up the Research Tank

Clearly a critical part of the evaluator's preparation and planning is for him or her to become knowledgeable about current research concerning PPEs—to "fill up the research tank"—to become familiar with the social science research relevant to this work and with the range of issues that are common across many families. The authors have provided a detailed chapter in Appendix A with information about ways to find, interpret, and use appropriate research articles and ways to report results from them responsibly.

Accepting the Case

Once the evaluator has received the referral, he or she needs to decide whether to accept the case. That decision must be based on a variety of factors that are listed in Table 2.2 along with other factors that are part of preparation.

Data Planning

Data planning involves becoming familiar with the case and learning about the specific issues of the case based on the parties' positions, the identification of issues listed in the court order, what the lawyers think the pertinent issues are for the case, and speaking with the parties about what they want from the PPE and the rationale for their positions. Based on this preliminary overview of the case, the parenting plan evaluator can begin to map out the issues and factors that may be part of the overall investigation.

Forensic procedures for the collection of data and the identification of sources of information are well described in many basic books about PPEs, including Stahl (2010), Gould (2006), and Gould and D. A. Martindale (2007), and the new evaluator should review those before going further in the evaluation process if unfamiliar with them. Planning the methods and instruments to use will involve knowledge of the research on each method and the reasoned choice of which method(s) to use.

The responsible evaluator will consider the empirical literature to ensure that the methods and procedures chosen are based on sound scientific evidence. For example, in making the decision of whether to conduct the observation visit at the office or at the parents' home, it would be important to consult the research literature to determine if the location has any impact on the biases that can arise in the evaluator or if the location creates systematic changes in the child's behavior that could skew the results of the observations. The evaluator could also check whether there are any known strategies to control for confirmatory bias in parent-child observations.

Key questions to ask at this stage include:

- What does the research say about various methods for conducting the evaluation?
- What can be learned from common practices in the field (professional views) regarding the various styles and procedures for data collection?
- Are some methods better than others for collecting reliable and valid information?
- Are there methods that do not provide the kinds of reliable and valid information that the evaluator is looking to collect?
- Is there a manual describing the correct methods of administering and scoring a test or method?

One consideration for the evaluator is whether or not to use psychological testing in the evaluation. Much has been written about the information to be gained from appropriate testing and the risks of the inappropriate use of testing. There are experts who state that no psychological test should be used in a forensic context (Grove et al., 2002; Lilienfeld, Lynn, & Lohr, 2003). There are other experts who describe the appropriate uses of psychological tests (Erard, 2012; Flens, 2005; Meyer & Archer, 2001). If the evaluator is well trained and experienced and has kept up with the research in the field of assessment as it pertains to child custody issues, and the parent's education and cultural background makes a psychological assessment appropriate, he or she may want to use testing to help generate hypotheses and to test other hypotheses generated from other sources. The *Journal of Child Custody* published a special issue and later a book on testing within child custody evaluations (Flens, 2005; Flens & Drozd, 2005). The APA journals *Assessment and Psychological Bulletin* and the *Journal of Personality Assessment* published by the Society for Personality Assessment are sources for current research about the uses of and best practice in psychological testing.

The major psychological tests that have sufficient reliability and validity to be used forensically were developed to diagnose mental and emotional illnesses for clinical populations. Even when there is a direct question about a parent's mental functioning, there are differences in the context and meaning of the assessment that make it difficult to compare custody litigants' scores with either the nonpatient normative samples or the clinical samples. In some cases, there are "custody norms" available, in the sense that researchers have provided summary tables of scores from people who were tested as they were engaged in custody litigation, but there are no studies that demonstrate the meaning of the scores in the custody context (Minnesota Multiphasic Personality Inventory–2 [MMPI–2] from Bathurst, A. W. Gottfreid, & A. E. Gottfreid, 1997, and Otto, 2002; Rorschach from Singer et al., 2006). At a minimum, good psychological testing can provide information about the person's thinking and problem solving, and about their characteristic ways of thinking about and presenting themself.

Another example of an area of practice in which there is research and a research-based procedural manual is the interview protocol for investigating child sexual abuse. This is the interview protocol developed by Michael Lamb and colleagues at the National Institute of Child Health and Human Development (2000; Lamb et al., 2009; Lamb et al., 2007). Again, the evaluator can request that interviewing is done by someone trained and experienced in such work, or he can do the interview himself if he is qualified to do so. But it is never acceptable to use an unproven method when a method is available that has a body of research behind it.

Not only must the evaluator be concerned about data to collect during the course of the evaluation, but he also must be concerned about data not to collect. It is best not to collect data that is repetitive information. Further, it also is not wise to collect data where the benefit of the acquisition does not outweigh the level of intrusiveness of the collection process. And finally, it is unnecessary to put information in the report that is not relevant to the questions before the court. For example, the fact that the 40-year-old mother in a PPE had an abortion when she was age 19 should not be included in the report unless it is relevant to the current custody battle. That is, having had an abortion over 20 years ago may be more prejudicial than probative.

A final aspect to consider in data collection is the degree to which the evaluation is child-focused versus allegation-focused. The authors are of the opinion that whereas allegations of abuse, for example, are important to explore, the main focus of the evaluation should not be the he said-she said and repeated finger pointing in which one parent and the other engage (Kelly & Johnston, 2001). Instead, the focus is best on the child and thus the effect that any of the actions of the parents have on their child—the child's strengths, resiliency factors, the vulnerabilities, and aggravating and mitigating factors in the family environment. In the end the data collection is about the child (Moran & Weinstock, 2011).

Using the sources identified in the referral and those sources common to most evaluations, while remaining open to new sources that may be identified during the evaluation, the evaluator will collect data. The data collected is organized into themes about which the parents are encouraged to provide all direct information they have, in order for the evaluator to get the clearest picture of their family possible. Then the hypotheses are articulated and a preliminary decision tree is created.

Preliminary Hypotheses and Decision Trees

One way to look at PPEs is that they are risk assessments in terms of the risks and benefits of different parenting plans for the family. There are two major tools to instruct decisions about risk. One is a decision tree; the other is data aggregation or actuarial method. Actuarial methods are very helpful when hard numbers can be assigned to risks. One sees these tools used, for example, to guide decision making about cancer treatment, where the risks of cancer recurrence are known based on established parameters of various tumors, and numbers can be assigned to compare risks and benefits of different treatments.

There are no data in the social science research that are sufficient to predict the outcomes related to child adjustment postseparation in a numerical way, as would be needed for actuarial methods of prediction. It should be the aspiration of everyone working in the field to contribute to developing the body of valid research that would allow for actuarial analysis of risk, but it is not present now. The best approach for now in terms of a risk analysis is a decision tree approach, which allows the decision maker to organize the factors and assign weights based on his or her training and experience.

The evaluator creates active hypotheses, that is, proposed explanations as a starting point for further investigation that will be tested by the facts that are gathered; then those hypotheses are organized into decision trees. The decision trees give the evaluator a picture of the many possible explanations for the issues that are present in the family. They allow the evaluator to hold in his or her mind all possible explanations for each particular issue that is present in the family. It allows the evaluator to zoom in on one issue—alone—and/or in interaction with other issues.

The purpose of the evaluation decision tree is to bring forward every potential explanation of parenting and parent-child relationship strengths and weaknesses and to develop every tenable hypothesis respecting the history and causes of the issues that are presently facing the given family. A decision tree is a way of systematizing the evidence, a way to organize different bits of information—to keep track of all and to avoid getting caught up in some while losing sight of others (Drozd & Olesen, 2004). A written decision tree allows the court, attorneys, and parents to understand the thinking of the evaluator. In the Appendices of this book there are some sample decision trees on various topics.

The preliminary decision tree will change as new information comes, leading the evaluator to consider other ways to think about and organize the data. The decision tree aids the evaluator in writing a coherent, comprehensive report because the information is already organized into logical units. Most importantly, a decision tree allows every hypothesis that may be applicable to the case under investigation to be considered during the analysis and conclusion-building stages. By providing a mechanism to explore all potential hypotheses, the decision tree process controls against the premature and unduly narrow selection of a single hypothesis, until such time as all have been considered. In this way, the decision tree process works to create a method to neutralize biases (selection bias, premature closure, etc.) (Dutton, 2006a, 2006b; Johnson, 2006a, 2006b).

The factors in a decision tree are not presented as "yes/no answers" to a set of questions but rather as clusters of related issues that should be considered when weighing multiple data points as part of the data collection process. It can be useful in examining many issues in divorce and custody. Within this early phase of the preliminary evaluation decision tree process, the evaluator can use social science evidence to inform him- or herself about the correlation/association among factors in the research to begin mapping out these associations in the specific case. Key questions to ask at this stage include:

- Are any of the factors presented so far in this case determinative?
- What are the relationships that have been found in the research regarding the presenting issues?
- How have these issues previously been clustered in the literature (e.g., alienation, estrangement, hybrid)?
- What associations are shown in the research literature both within and among the clusters of factors?
- Are there factors that have more weight in considering the relationship among these factors (e.g., is safety a stronger factor than well-being?)?
- How might the factors interact both positively and negatively?
- What factors might serve as buffers, protecting the children's well-being?
- Are there other confounding variables not included in the referral questions?

How to Form Hypotheses and Make a Decision Tree

The decision tree can be thought of as a page of multiple hypotheses made visible. A hypothesis is a "tentative explanation" for what is observed (Campbell, 1993). Humans are hypothesis-building creatures, and they create hypotheses whenever they get information. In the case of a PPE, the authors strongly suggest evaluators make the hypotheses conscious and explicit and that to the degree possible the hypotheses be based upon operationalizable and measurable questions that fit the psycholegal questions that the court must answer. A well-written clinical/forensic question is vital because it forms the foundation upon which hypotheses are built. Refined clinical/forensic questions are framed as declarative statements that become the hypotheses. A hypothesis is a formal statement of the proposed relationship(s) between two or more variables in a specified population that suggests an answer to the evaluation question.

To give some background, one can create/have one of many kinds of hypotheses:

- *an explanatory hypothesis (cause and effect)*: With this kind of hypothesis, the evaluator examines how an action or event changes another future object, an action, or an event. Two examples follow: (a) When this child is exposed to the cats in his father's home, he always suffers a serious asthma attack directly caused by his allergy to cats and the exposure to them. (b) A child resists contact with his father because his father has been physically abusive. Or
- *an associative hypothesis (co-occurrence)*: With this kind of hypothesis, the evaluator examines how certain events co-occur. Again, two examples follow: (a) The child is frequently sick during the mother 's parenting time. (Note there is no attempt at a causal statement). (b) The child has been physically injured when left alone in her father's care. (Note there is no attempt at a causal statement.) Or

- *a predictive hypothesis*: With this kind of hypothesis, the evaluator is making a statement of what can be expected in the future based upon current information. Two examples of predictive hypotheses follow: (a) If mother, who has been diagnosed with a problem with alcohol, drinks, her relationship with her children will be affected. (b) If the child lives primarily with the mother, his relationship with the father will weaken substantially.

Hypotheses should clearly identify the variables about the family being assessed that are under consideration. The interaction between the variables should be described. In most PPEs, there will be many hypotheses that describe issues unique to the given family as well as the predicted interactions between many of the variables found in the decision tree.

The human cognitive tendency is to select a single cause for an event (A causes B). When evaluators do that, they can too quickly lose sight of A being only one of many factors to consider. A single working hypothesis may lead evaluators to neglect other equally important hypotheses, and thus their work lacks thoroughness. It may also lack accuracy if the neglected hypotheses were the most important or the true causal direction was the opposite of what they think it is. There is an extended discussion of causal reasoning and errors in Appendix A. The utilization of multiple hypotheses helps the evaluator move away from simple causal explanations by considering multiple variables at the same time. Even the most apparently trivial factors are brought in to the model to be considered, thus "leaving no stone unturned," and the decision maker is reminded of the folly of simple cause-and-effect conclusions.

The development of clear, operational criteria in the formation of each hypothesis helps the evaluator to sharpen his or her appraisal skills. By writing down each potential hypothesis, the evaluator ensures that each working hypothesis provides one piece of the puzzle to consider when assessing the evidence in the case. This method provides a transparent process because each hypothesis is documented and considered and assessed for its weight and validity. Using this clear and transparent process provides the paper trail of your thought process and decision-making points so that these can be revisited, reworked, and revised as new information is collected during the PPE process. Once hypotheses are formed, they naturally fall into clusters, which can in turn be arranged into a decision tree.

A decision tree, as it is meant here, is a drawing or a chart that is drawn by the evaluator as he brainstorms the factors and issues that need to be considered in a particular evaluation. Some issues will be in every evaluation (e.g., issues of safety and abuse or of parenting capacity). Some issues will only be raised in particular evaluations such as whether a child should move with one parent or whether a parent's time should be restricted and/or supervised because of specific dangers such as substance abuse.

At the top of the paper is written the central question of the PPE. "Should Johnny move to Chicago with his mother?" is an example of such a question. It may be a more complex question, such as "Should this child's time with either parent be limited by the court?" or "Why is the child resisting contact with one parent?"

Next, the evaluator brainstorms the possible factors that will enter into a decision about the question or questions. When they are written as factors, the evaluator can look at how they can be viewed in clusters. As a rule, there will almost always be factors and clusters involving abuse/safety, parent variables, child variables, parent-child relationships, parent-parent relationships, and extended family relationship variables. The list should include the specific issues within each cluster. For example, child variables can include age, special needs, developmental history, wishes, symptoms/mental health, academic history, and others that are necessary for the particular family. When they are written down, they are less likely to be ignored or forgotten as the complex and voluminous data pile up. A sample non-case-specific decision tree about "Why Children Resist Contact With or Reject a Parent" can be found in Figure 2.3. Sometimes the evaluator will write down the items in the decision tree as statements as is the case in the "Why Children Resist Contact With or Reject a Parent" decision tree, and other times the statements are written in the form of hypotheses, as will be shown in a case-specific example to follow in Chapter 3.

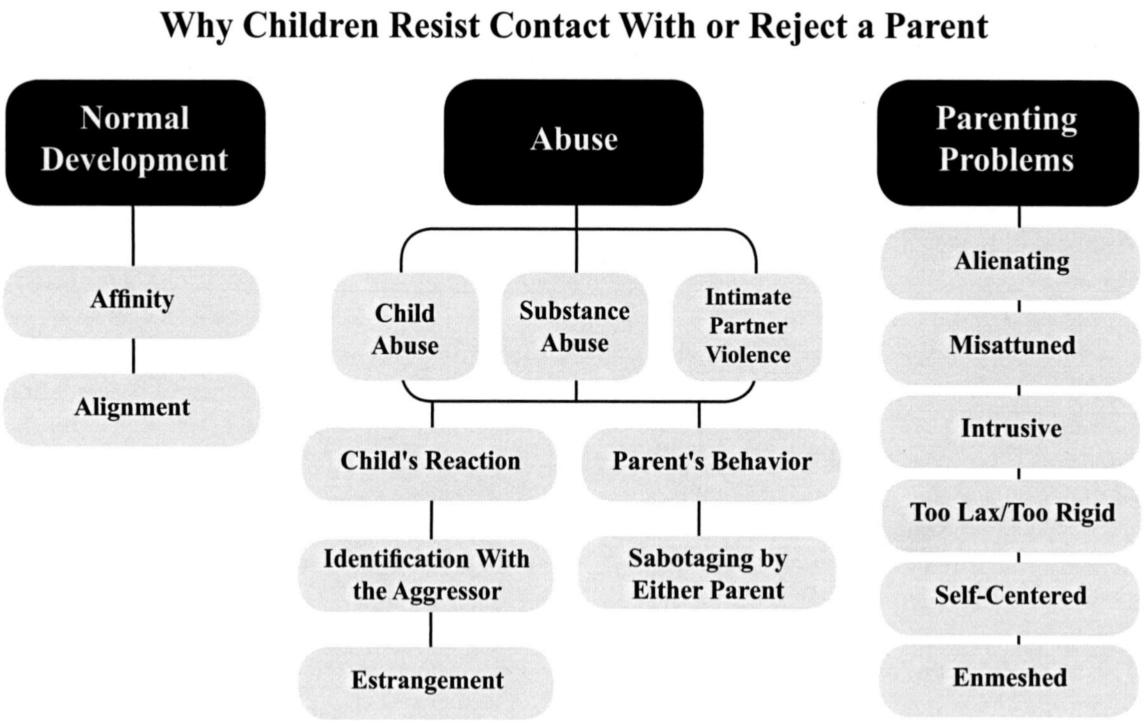

Why Children Resist Contact With or Reject a Parent

Normal Development

Affinity

Alignment

Abuse

Child Abuse | Substance Abuse | Intimate Partner Violence

Child's Reaction | Parent's Behavior

Identification With the Aggressor | Sabotaging by Either Parent

Estrangement

Parenting Problems

Alienating

Misattuned

Intrusive

Too Lax/Too Rigid

Self-Centered

Enmeshed

Figure 2.3 Sample Decision Tree

Data Collection

Whereas some data are collected before the initial hypotheses are formed and the decision tree created, once the issues have been identified and clustered, the next step of the process is to continue the data collection from relevant sources. A chart with the possible sources of data follows as Table 2.3.

Table 2.3 Data Sources for Different Factors

Points to Explore	Where to Get More Data
Safety Issues	
Domestic violence	Interview parents
	Interview children
	Review records from:
	Police
	Medical providers
	Witnesses
	Witnesses
	Psychological testing
Child abuse	Interview parents
	Interview children
	Teachers, doctors, witnesses
	Neighbors
	Child Protective Services

Table 2.3 Data Sources for Different Factors *(continued)*

Points to Explore	Where to Get More Data
Safety Issues *(continued)*	
Substance abuse	Interview parents
	Interview children
	Teachers, doctors, witnesses
	Neighbors
	Drug and/or alcohol testing
	Review pharmacy records
	Psychological testing
	Child Protective Services
Child Variables	
Children's wishes	Interview children, if old enough
	Interview therapist, if any
Age, gender, and temperament	Interview parents
	Interview teachers
	Child behavior checklists
	Observations in home, office
Health and well-being	Medical records
	Day care records
	School records
	Psychological tersting
Attachment/separation of two younger children	Observe with parents
	Interview teachers
	Interview day care providers
Parent Variables	
Personal/family history	Interview parents
	Interview other family
Cognitive/emotional functioning	Interview parents
	Psychological testing
Parenting capacity	Observe each parent with all children
	Interview re: Knowledge of child development behaviors at relevant ages
Risk and protective factors	History interviews with parents
Recent losses/betrayals	Interview collaterals, including therapists
Social support	
Current/historic	
Employment	
Parents' availability and wishes	Interview parents
Parent-Child Variables	
Relationship quality	Observe parent-child dyads
	Observe parents with children
	Collateral interviews
Discipline	Interview parents
	Interview children, if old enough
	Observe parents/children
	Collateral interviews

Table 2.3   Data Sources for Different Factors *(continued)*

<u>Points to Explore</u>	<u>Where to Get More Data</u>
Parent-Child Variables (continued)	
Parent-focused vs. child-focused	Psychological testing (narcissism) Observe parents with children Interview children
Boundary Problems Enmeshment Parentification Intrusiveness Inclusion of the child in the conflict	Interview parents Observe parent-child interactions School or therapy records Interview children, parents
Parent-Parent Variables	
Ability, willingness to cooperate and communicate	Interview parents Observe parents together Review history of communication, emails,
Level of conflict	Review emails, court filings Interview parents Interview children
Gatekeeping	Interview with parents Interview collateral witnesses Review history of communication
Relationship quality	Interview parents Interview children, if old enough
Environmental Variables	
Support systems for parents Support systems for children	Interview parents Interview parents, children Interview coaches, teachers

Ordinarily the collection of the data, after all of the planning and the clarifying, is a fairly straightforward task. After the data is collected, as we do in our case example in Chapter 3, we propose that the data be entered into a grid system, the Parenting Plan Evaluation Matrix, presented in Chapter 5, in which the information is tied to its source and its meaning and cross checked against other information. In Chapter 5, we present a demonstration of how to use this matrix, using the case example. A blank version of the matrix for the use of the reader in his or her practice is included in Appendix D.

Analysis and Synthesis

As the data collection continues and nears completion, the data is analyzed, that is, each piece of information in the decision tree is held up to the light and looked at from all different angles. The issues and themes that have emerged are looked at, not only in isolation, but also in the ways they interact with one another. The decision trees that develop evolve as the data is further analyzed, and eventually the clusters of data are synthesized into comprehensive opinions and then into parenting plan recommendations.

The analysis and synthesis of data can be the most challenging part of the work for evaluators as they attempt to make sense of an enormous amount of information. Considering the multivariate contribution of several factors is challenging and requires careful and systematic understanding of the potential impact of each factor included in the model. Empirical evidence can help to inform the evaluator about the kinds of relationships and interactional effects that have been found in the literature. This can help guide the weight given to the various factors that are included in the hypotheses to be tested. Key research questions at this stage include:

- What does the research say about the interactions among the factors being considered?
- Do some factors carry more weight than others?
- What are the long-term consequences of these factors, both individually and as a group of inter-related factors?
- What are the protective buffers that have been identified that can help mitigate the negative results of the long-term consequences?

Similar to the fact that data collection is about the child so should be the analysis and ultimately the synthesis of the data. This can be manifested in the simple difference in how the data is reported. For example, take what Justice Neely reported: "The loss of children is a terrifying specter to concerned and loving parents; however, it is particularly terrifying to the primary parent, who, by virtue of the caretaking function, was the closest to the child before the divorce" (*Garska v. McCoy*, 1981, at 360). In the foregoing statement, the emphasis has been placed not on the loss to children of primary caretakers, but on the "terrifying specter" that must be faced by the affected adults. In this example, the greater emphasis has been placed on the needs of the parents than on the needs of the children. Clearly the most useful evaluations for families, their counsel, and the courts are those that place the emphasis on the needs of the children.

Recommendations for a Parenting Plan

Recommendations regarding the parenting plan for the children are the ultimate product of the decision tree approach, including the data collection, the multiple hypotheses, and the analysis and synthesis of the data. These recommendations should consider all of the issues and the interaction of the factors already considered in the preceding steps. It is also important to consider the practical aspects of parenting plans, which include the resources in time and money available to the parents, distance between homes, and developmental status of children (Pruett, Arthur, & Ebling, 2007). Additional considerations include whether changes in risk factors and/or protective buffers can help to transition the parenting plan over time, and the effectiveness of potential interventions to help change/reduce/ameliorate risk factors. Key questions at this stage include:

- Are there parenting plan arrangements (e.g., sole custody vs. shared care) that generally work better for children similar to these children and this family?
- Which factors (such as age, temperament, etc.) seem to be related to whether particular parenting plan arrangements work for children?
- Which factors contribute to the parents' ability to make joint decisions?
- If a child/parent is amenable to receiving counseling, what evidence is there that would suggest that counseling would actually make a difference on the specified outcomes identified within the evaluation?

Review, Consult, Revise

To ensure that the evaluation and its findings and recommendations are sound, it is critical for evaluators to consistently follow the steps suggested by best practices, guidelines, and standards. At this stage, it is important to go back and consider the process and whether all steps were carried out to the fullest to generate and support the discussion and recommendations made within the report. Key questions include:

- Has the data that has been collected and presented been kept separate from the analysis and recommendations?

- Have the process and procedures been transparent?
- Are there standards that have been followed in the report?
- Are there ways to better vet for bias and missed information?
- Do the recommendations logically follow the data reported and the analysis conducted?

Decision tree analysis provides a framework for thinking about interventions at various entry points and in various systems. The goal is to provide best practices rather than a rigid set of activities that the evaluator must perform. In other words, this book provides key ingredients for understanding complex issues within PPEs rather than a recipe for sorting and weighing specific competing allegations and data sources.

Strengths and Limitations of the
Parenting Plan Evaluation Decision Tree

In Chapter 1, the myriad of procedural and process errors that can emerge in PPEs, including a plethora of cognitive errors, were discussed. A call for a systematic process, one that is transparent from Day One, was made. In this chapter, a decision tree for PPEs was set forth. A key component of the proposed process involves the use of multiple hypotheses and decision trees. When the multiple hypotheses or decision tree method is adopted as a habit for data analysis, the method itself provides the evaluator with the habit of thinking in parallel and complex ways. It helps the evaluator move away from simple, linear thinking. It allows for the consideration of multiple standpoints and views of a subject. The multiple hypotheses or decision tree method allows the evaluator to increase his or her capability for viewing complex issues systematically and transparently.

The wisdom of the decision tree approach is that it allows the evaluator to have in view, on one piece of paper, a picture of the whole case including the possible variables that may be interacting with one another and resulting in the dilemmas faced by the family being assessed. The decision tree approach facilitates the evaluator having a clear perspective of the multiple layers of data that may feel overwhelming for the family and the court. The decision tree approach allows for the switch in perspective that is needed in PPEs, a switch from the kind of forced choice all-or-nothing, it-is-abuse-or-alienation thinking to one that embraces many perspectives simultaneously. And finally, the decision tree approach facilitates the paradigm shift that these authors believe is called for in the field as well as for the benefit of the individual family in a given PPE.

The authors do not propose giving specific weights to various factors that may influence parent-child relationships because there is no evidence that there is predictive value in organizing the data in any specifically weighted way. Beautiful charts should not be used to imply a greater scientific rigor than they actually have. The decision tree process will not prevent the evaluator from ever being wrong in an assessment of some kind in a particular case. It will make the evaluator's process transparent so that errors may be seen by the attorneys or the courts. It may help the evaluator to see some errors, but it will not cause evaluators to achieve perfection in their evaluations.

Evaluators will learn to lay out scientific research and practice wisdom along with the perspectives and preferences of the family members so that multiple viewpoints can be organized and presented in the report. Prioritizing and weighing factors remain in the province of the evaluator's thinking and expertise, and it is proposed that the evaluator work to make that thinking as systematic and transparent as possible. In the future, eventually, there should be actuarial analysis tools to more easily make decisions among competing factors, but that is not the state of the field in child custody evaluation. For now, this approach is one that is likely to offset cognitive errors and to improve transparency and decision making.

Summary

- A structured format is proposed for conducting PPEs that starts with preparation, both in learning the relevant research and standards (research planning) and in considering the parameters of the cases parenting plan evaluators are asked to evaluate (data planning).
- Data collection was outlined, with suggestions and descriptions of the decision tree process and discussion of choosing and implementing the most reliable and effective tools for information gathering.
- For the Analysis and Synthesis stage in the evaluation, the chapter presented the decision tree process and the generation of multiple hypotheses.
- The last stage presented was a discussion of the necessity to review and revise one's work and consult with colleagues to minimize the risk of systematic bias.
- Lastly in this chapter, the authors described the strengths and limitations of the decision tree process.

Annotated Bibliography

Bow, J. N., & Boxer, P. (2003). Assessing allegations of domestic violence in child custody evaluations. *Journal of Interpersonal Violence 18*(12), 1394-1410.

In determining the factors to consider within a PPE, the authors point to the need to assess and screen for violence. The authors point out that there has been criticism of evaluators' training, practices, and procedures to date in assessing for violence. Based on a national survey of 115 parenting plan evaluators, findings revealed adequate training, multiple sources of data collection, and practices/procedures that closely adhere to child custody guidelines. However, robust, specialized domestic violence instruments, tests, and questionnaires were underutilized. Respondents indicated that findings supporting domestic violence allegations had a substantial impact on their subsequent recommendations. Results are discussed in terms of the importance of assessing domestic violence when conducting custody evaluations and in terms of the need for developing practice standards in this domain.

Kuehnle, K. F., & Drozd, L. M. (Eds.). (2012). *Parenting Plan Evaluations: Applied Research for the Family Court.* **New York, NY: Oxford University Press.**

This book addresses gaps in the literature by presenting an organized and in-depth analysis of the current research and offering specific recommendations for applying these findings to the evaluation process. Written by experts in the child custody arena, chapters cover issues such as attachment and overnight timesharing with very young children, dynamics between divorced parents and children's potential for resiliency, coparenting children with chronic medical conditions and developmental disorders, domestic violence during separation and divorce, gay and lesbian coparents, and relocation, among others. The scientific information provided in these chapters assists forensic mental health professionals to proffer empirically based opinions, conclusions, and recommendations.

Drozd, L. M., & Olesen, N. W. (2004). Is it abuse, alienation, and/or estrangement? A decision tree. *Journal of Child Custody, 1*(3), 65-106.

This article advances the discussion of alienation by distinguishing alienation from abuse and by presenting a hybrid model that takes into account situations when both abuse and alienation are present within the family dynamics. By using a decision tree, the authors present a comprehensive approach for considering the complexity of strained parent-child interactions postseparation and postdivorce.

Fidler, B., Bala, N., & Saini, M. (2012). *Children Who Resist Postseparation Parental Contact: A Differential Approach for Legal and Mental Health Professionals.* **New York, NY: Oxford University Press.**

This book is a critical and empirically based review of parental alienation and resistance to contact with a parent after separation and divorce. This book summarizes the historical development of the concept of alienation and discusses the causes, dynamics, and differentiation of various types of parent-child contact problems. The book reviews the social science literature with respect to prevalence, risk factors, indicators, assessment, and measurement. Children's rights and the role of their wishes and preferences in legal proceedings, and the short- and long-term impacts of alienation, are also discussed. The book considers possible educational, clinical, judicial, and legal interventions and remedies and concludes with recommendations for practice, research, and policy.

Jaffe, P. G., Johnston, J. R., Crooks, C. V., & Bala, N. (2008). Custody disputes involving allegations of domestic violence: Toward a differentiated approach to parenting plans. *Family Court Review,* *46*(3), 500-522.

This article provides an overview of the relevance of domestic violence in custody and access disputes, then provides a framework for differential assessment and interventions that are based on a thorough and comprehensive understanding of the dynamics of violence in a particular family relationships.

Chapter 3

Paradigm Shift: Embracing Complexity In a Real Case

Now that the authors have provided a general overview of the Parenting Plan Evaluation Decision Tree, this book now introduces an example of a case and of the process of embracing and organizing the complex data inherent in this and in most evaluation cases. The reader will look at the case through the lens of a decision tree—through the process described in the previous chapter. The goal here is to demonstrate how to create and use a decision tree to keep the evaluator from engaging in bias and error and to keep the data manageable and able to be easily seen.

For the purpose of explaining the process of the Parenting Plan Evaluation Decision Tree, here is the hypothetical case of Maria and Timothy, who are currently involved in the courts with a dispute about the custody of and access to their three children, Peter (age 12), Rita (age 7), and Sarah (age 2).* Information about the case will continue to be provided as the process is discussed so that the reader can see how the tools work as new information is made available. But before consideration of the issues of the case, there is a preparation and planning phase for this case to go through first.

Preparation and Planning

Be Prepared and Up To Date

As highlighted in Chapter 2, an evaluator needs to begin thinking about the contextual issues prior to embarking on the evaluation. This preparation and planning ahead pays off when the phone rings and it looks like a potential child custody case is about to come the evaluator's way. One or more of the attorneys on the case (or possibly even the court) is on the line: "Dr. X, I have a tough case that needs a custody evaluation. Can you do a custody evaluation?" Immediately, without going one step further, a conflict check is necessary. Does the evaluator know the parties? Has he or she served as a therapist for any member of the family? Has he or she worked extensively with one of the attorneys? Is one of the attorneys a good friend of the evaluator? Can he or she remain neutral? Does he have the time to do what he is being asked to do? Is he or she available for the court date in case the evaluator is needed to testify? How quickly could the evaluation be completed with a report to the court and counsel? What retainer is required? Best practice is for the evaluator to arrange a joint telephone call with the attorneys to have a preliminary discussion about the case in order to make a decision as to whether he or she is qualified and specifically knowledgeable to conduct a PPE or child custody evaluation, given the issues in this case. These conference calls become more difficult and more important when one or both of the parents is self-represented. Some evaluators make these communications by email only so that there is a record of everything said and of every understanding reached.

---

*All characters in this case example are fictitious. Any resemblance to real persons, living or dead, is purely coincidental.

Identification of the Sources for Obtaining Data

The evaluator asks himself, "What factors are potentially relevant and about which potentially relevant factors do I need to know more? Where will I look for information about those factors? What documents will I need to get? To which collateral witnesses will I need to speak?"

In the previous chapter, Table 2.3 sets forth the possible sources of data for different factors in cases. The reader is urged to use that table as a guide to begin to seek data from a multitude of sources. Some of the data should be sought immediately. For example, in the case of Timothy, Maria, and their family, as will be evident later, it is probable that child abuse or police reports have been filed. Those reports often take some time to obtain. Thus, they should be requested immediately upon the appointment order being filed, the retainer agreement being signed, and the retainer being paid. It is critical to begin requesting the information quickly, at the start of the evaluation, so that there are no delays in the process. Delays can occur with agencies that are slow to respond and when collateral sources need a court order before they can release information. In addition, the information that the evaluator gathers in these steps will probably help guide further inquiries.

All of this material (that which is acquired by the evaluator as expertise before this referral comes in, and that which was acquired during the initial preparation and planning portions of the evaluation process and during the first round of informational gathering) will be organized into a decision tree. The preparation of that grid or decision tree follows in a limited way for the case of the family of Timothy, Maria, and their three children. This is a limited excerpt, of course, of what would be longer and more detailed and comprehensive if it were an actual family undergoing an evaluation.

Initial Data: The Case of Maria, Timothy, and Children

In a joint phone conference with the attorneys, this is the information provided:

> Maria and Timothy were married for 15 years. They have three children: Peter (age 12), Rita (age 7), and Sarah (age 2). Both parents work outside the home. Timothy left his employment 5 years ago at which point he took care of the children on a daily basis, but recently he has returned to work full time. The couple separated in March of this year. Maria stayed in the home at first, but when Timothy would not leave the home, she moved out without the children. Eventually Maria and Timothy each rented apartments. At this time, 7-year-old Rita and 2-year-old Sarah live primarily with Marie, while 12-year-old Peter lives primarily with his father.
>
> Maria accuses Timothy of being physically and emotionally abusive of her. She also accuses him of being abusive with their oldest child. She says Timothy drinks heavily on a daily basis and becomes aggressive when he is drunk. She says that the children are scared of their father, and she reports that Timothy has been pretty rough with 12-year-old Peter and that he has used poor judgment with the children. Maria also reports that Timothy has intentionally interfered with her relationship with their son, Peter, and that overall he has put the children in the middle of the conflict between Timothy and her.
>
> Seven-year-old Rita sees her father daily, though she does not spend the night at her father's, and 2-year-old Sarah sees her father during the day on weekdays only. At transitions, Sarah clings to her mother. Timothy accuses Maria of interfering with his relationship with their 7- and 2-year-old daughters. He also alleges that Maria blocks his access to their younger two children and is physically and emotionally abusive with Peter. Timothy denies the alleged abuse and states that Maria is making up the abuse to gain an advantage in litigation.
>
> Timothy also reports concerns about Maria's use of prescription Ritalin, stating that he feels that she began taking the substance to keep up her performance at work. He reports that

when she nears the end of her prescription, she becomes particularly moody, irritable, and "snappy" towards the family. Timothy says that he overheard Maria contact her pharmacy 11 times in one night and reports that she was yelling and swearing because they would not refill her prescription without a doctor's note.

Both parents claim that they have done the primary care of the children. Maria seeks sole custody of the children. Timothy wants custody of the 12-year-old and weekend visitation with the other two.

Hypotheses and Decision Trees

As the evaluator listens to the issues about this family, he moves from the theoretical to the concrete. It is no longer simply a hypothetical question about whether he or she should take the case; he is in the process of learning the specifics about the real case.

There will be questions. What is the purpose of the evaluation? What is the scope of the evaluation? At what issues is the evaluator being asked to look? In this matter, fortunately, the scope and the purpose of the evaluation have been defined by the court as follows: to assist the court, counsel, and family in determining the best interests of the minor children (Peter, Rita, and Sarah) in regards to the issues delineated below and further to make recommendations in regard to what parenting plan and what custodial and timeshare arrangements are in the best interest of the parties' minor children. The issues or referral questions that were set forth by the attorneys are included in the first part of Table 3.1.

If the purpose and scope and/or the questions are not clear, the evaluator can and should take responsibility for creating the questions from the joint telephone call. Those questions may be written by one of the attorneys or by the evaluator in a letter to the attorneys and the court, with a request that they be made part of the stipulation or order for the PPE. Fortunately, the attorneys in this case have defined the purpose, scope, and referral questions in a manner that needs no further clarification.

Those issues set forth in the first part of Table 3.1 are ones that are typically found in child custody evaluations (and are found in this case as well)—ones about safety, ones having to do with the child's areas of strength and vulnerability, and ones having to do with the mother and the father, the interaction between the two parents and issues of how each of them parent and coparent. A deeper look into the issues in a specific case might result in additional questions coming to mind as are found in the later portions of Table 3.1. As one vets these questions, specific issues and themes will emerge. To see them more clearly, it is suggested that the evaluator list the issues and/or put them on sticky notes on a piece of paper, as is illustrated in Figure 3.1.

The individual issues will fall into clusters as illustrated in Figure 3.2. The clusters frequently center around themes having to do with safety, the child, and the parents. An initial and still general clustering of the issues will become the basis of the formation of hypotheses and ultimately the cluster of issues will become the foundation of a decision tree.

Formation of Hypotheses and a Preliminary Decision Tree

The next step is to form hypotheses, that is, hypothetical statements that can be tested as the data are collected, analyzed, and synthesized in the course of this evaluation. The reader can turn to a section in Chapter 2 as a guide in the process of designing these hypotheses. In this case, the authors are going to write some explanatory hypotheses as a demonstration of the process.

In writing the statements as hypotheses, one simply makes a statement in the direction that the accusation is made. For example, if a parent is accused of having a substance abuse problem that in turn affects his or her parenting, the statement would be, "Father abuses alcohol, which affects his parenting by putting his son, Johnny, at risk physically and emotionally while in his care." This is a compound hypothesis and may be written better in separate statements. For example, "Father abuses alcohol"; and "Father's alcohol

---

Table 3.1 Initial Referral Questions From Attorneys for the Case of Timothy, Maria, and Children

---

What is the optimal parenting plan for the safety and well-being of Peter, Rita and Sarah?

- What are each parent's strengths and weaknesses in terms of their parenting of their three children?
- To what degree, if any, has either parent engaged in any kind of abuse, whether that is IPV, substance abuse, and/or child abuse?
- And if any abuse has been or is present, what is the nature of the effects of the abuse on the children?
- What is the nature of each parent-child relationship as well as the nature of the parent-parent relationship?
- To what extent does each parent support and/or interfere with the children's relationships with the other parent?

Other Questions Related to the Individual Issues in the Case of Maria, Timothy, and Children

- Has Timothy perpetrated IPV?
- Is he abusing alcohol?
- Is Maria abusing prescription drugs?
- Have any of the children become estranged from either parent due to the abuse, if it occurred?
- Is either parent sabotaging the parenting relationship of the other?
- Has any child identified with an aggressive or abusive parent?
- Has there been some sort of problematic parenting going on in this family?
- Has a parent been so hypervigilant that the child feels acutely uncomfortable?
- Has Timothy or Maria been intrusive in the children's lives or too lax or too rigid in their discipline methods, resulting in the children not wanting to spend time in either parent's home?
- Has either parent been much more self- than child-centered such that the children tire of only doing things that the parent wants to do?
- Is any one of the children uncomfortable spending time with either parent because he or she is too enmeshed with the other parent and worried about how "poor mommy" or "poor daddy" has been doing while the children are away?

Another Layer of Questions to Vet the Interaction Between Issues in the Case of Maria, Timothy, and Children

- Are any of the factors that are included in the preliminary decision tree determinative?
- What are the relationships that have been found in the research regarding the presenting issues in this family?
- How have these issues previously been clustered in the literature (e.g., alienation, estrangement, hybrid)?
- What are the variations both within and among the clusters of factors?
- Are there factors that have more weight in considering the relationship among these factors (e.g., is safety a stronger factor than well-being?)?
- How might the factors interact both positively and negatively?
- What is the relevant literature on the issues in this evaluation?
- Are there other confounding variables that are not included in the referral questions?
- What factors might serve as buffers protecting the children's well-being?

---

abuse affects his parenting by putting his son at risk physically and emotionally." The evaluator makes a preliminary list of questions leading to hypotheses, which will be refined as he works (see Table 3.2).

Although it is simpler to make these hypothetical statements in one direction (either the absence or presence of the concern), it is important to note that there is another side of the hypothesis if there is insufficient evidence to accept the stated hypothesis. In other words, if the father does not have a problem with alcohol and if the child's safety is not a concern when he is with his father, it is important to consider the potential benefits to the child of having an ongoing relationship with that parent. Or the evaluator can consider a hypothesis that the mother is making false allegations to increase leverage for her position in the custody litigation or to weaken the father-child relationship. Whereas a given hypothesis is written in one direction, it is imperative that the evaluator proactively collect data to support each side or direction of the hypothesis—in this example, data to support that the father has a substance abuse problem, that the father does not have a substance abuse problem, that the father's substance abuse problem affects the child, and that the father's substance abuse problem does not affect the child. The hypotheses as defined by the authors for the hypothetical case follow in Table 3.3. For economy, they are only presented in one direction.

Figure 3.1 Brainstorming the Issues to Consider in the Case of Timothy, Maria, and Family

The next step in this process is to put everything together in a decision tree as was described in Chapter 2. A decision tree is simply a picture of the issues, clustered together into themes, written in the language of hypotheses about each issue in the case. In the following decision tree for this family, three major themes and the associated issues have been delineated. As the reader will note in the description of this case, initially in this chapter with more to follow in the next chapter, all themes and all issues in the case have not been put into the decision tree—at least not within this chapter. In practice, the evaluator will not write out completely each of the facts but simply a few words to remind him or her of the facts involved, and in that way the decision tree and later matrices can be small enough to be simple and useable.

For the case of Maria and Timothy and their family, the clusters form a decision tree as shown in Figure 3.3.

Table 3.2 The Final Step in Making Hypotheses

Topic of Concern	Question	Hypothesis
Safety		
IPV? Child abuse?	Are there allegations of either parent being emotionally, physically, or sexually abusive of the other parent?	
Neglect?	Have any one of the children been abused or neglected, and if so, by whom?	
Substance use?	Are there allegations of either parent misusing, abusing, or being dependent upon alcohol or drugs?	
Child		
Child's perspective?	Has any one of the children expressed his or her wishes about the parenting plan, and if so, are his or her wishes thought through and nuanced, showing the level of emotional maturity needed to have a reasoned preference?	
Ages & stages?	Do the ages and stages of the child and his or her development have any impact on the parenting plan?	
Adjustment and resiliency?	What has each child's adjustment and resiliency been?	
Relationship history?	Is the history and the nature of the parent-child relationship an important variable to consider?	
Parent		
Mental health?	Does the parent have any mental health issues?	
Personal history?	Is there any personal history of the parent's that is relevant in this case?	
Parent-child relationship?	What is the nature of the parent-child relationship with each parent-child dyad?	
Parent-parent relationship?	What is the nature of the parent-parent relationship in this case, and how does it affect coparenting (strengths and vulnerabilities)?	

Table 3.3 Hypotheses for the Case of Maria, Timothy, and Children

<u>Topic of Concern</u>	<u>Hypothesis Number</u>	<u>Hypothesis</u>
Safety		
IPV? Child abuse? Neglect? Substance use?	S-1	Timothy has problems with anger management and aggression, leading him to be verbally abusive and controlling with Peter and physically and verbally abusive with Maria.
	S-2	Timothy has a problem with alcohol abuse or dependence.
	S-3	Maria has a problem with prescription medication abuse or dependence.
Child		
Child's perspective? Ages & stages? Adjustment and resiliency? Relationship history?	C-1	The younger girls, Sarah and Rita, are reacting to separation from their mother as an attachment figure.
	C-2	The younger girls are afraid of their father.
Parent		
Mental health? Personal history? Parent-child relationship? Parent-parent relationship?	P-1	One or both parents is fabricating allegations for the litigation: Maria about IPV and Timothy about the abuse of Ritalin.
	P-2	Maria has mental health problems leading her to be verbally and physically abusive with Peter and to be enmeshed with Ruth and Sarah.
	P-3	Maria's depression is the result of her experience of domestic violence.
	P-4	One or both parents is engaged in restrictive gate keeping: Timothy with Peter and Maria with Rita and Sarah.

Figure 3.2 Clusters in the Case of Timothy, Maria, and Family

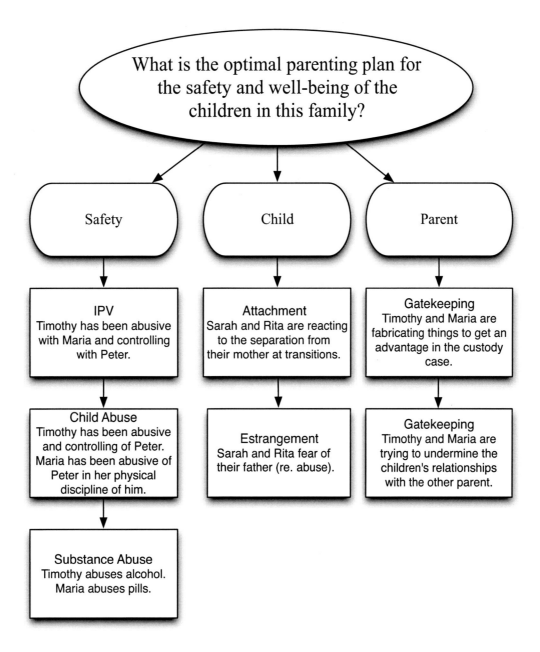

Figure 3.3 A Preliminary Decision Tree for the Case of Maria, Timothy, and the Children

Summary

- This chapter presented a step-by-step method for organizing the questions and preliminary hypotheses in a child custody evaluation.
- These steps include listing the court-ordered factors, additional questions raised by the preliminary data about the family, and the concerns and allegations.
- Those questions are then expanded and cross-checked for interactions, and a new list of questions is made by the child custody evaluator, who is actively involved in the process.
- The questions generated by the case are translated into formal hypotheses, which are then entered into a decision tree as a way to visualize the issues and clusters of issues.

Annotated Bibliography

Bow, J. N.,Gottlieb, M., Gould-Saltman, D. J., & Hendershot, L. (2011). Partners in the process: How attorneys prepare their clients for custody evaluations and litigation. *Family Court Review, 49*(4), 750-759.

The authors surveyed 113 family attorneys regarding what they did to prepare their clients for PPEs and litigation. The authors found that participants reported that they used professionally acceptable procedures, appropriately advocated for their clients, and dealt with complaints in a reasonable fashion. Referrals to mental health professionals in advance of a child custody evaluation were generally made to provide support rather than for evaluation or test preparation. Work product reviews by mental health consultants were infrequent, although such reviews were seen as highly useful by those who used them.

Connell, M. (2006). Notification of purpose in custody evaluation: Informing the parties and their counsel. *Professional Psychology: Research and Practice, 37*(5), 446-451.

The author considers the process of alerting parties to the purposes, procedures, and ramifications of the PPEs. The author suggests that full and complete notification of purpose can be accomplished only by a coordinated effort between the evaluator and the counsel. Because of the range of potential variations in the evaluator's approach, the author suggests that this notification may be individualized to reflect the evaluator's style and the case needs. Because of the abundance of information to be included and the importance of the inclusion of counsel in the process, the author further suggests that written notification, provided in advance of the examination, is useful. The basic elements of a notification are discussed, to be adapted to the parameters of the evaluator's practice.

Woodward Tolle, L., & O'Donohue, W. T. (2012). *Improving the Quality of Child Custody Evaluations: A Systematic Model*. New York, NY: Springer Science + Business Media.

The authors propose the Egregious/Promotive Factors Model as a reliable alternative to PPEs. The authors opine that the model is supported by rigorous assessment tools and is backed by the results of a pilot study of the model that was conducted among family court judges.

Chapter 4

Ongoing Data Collection

As the evaluator has made a preliminary decision tree, listing the factors and issues to be investigated, he or she has already planned what more information will be needed and how to get that information. Some data must be collected immediately upon having the appointment order, other applicable orders, and releases in hand. For example, child abuse reports and police reports often take specific orders to attain, and there can be significant delays in acquiring them. This can also be the case for medical records.

Standard Data Collection

Most evaluators have a standard set of instruments that they routinely use in child custody evaluations, plus a reserve of special instruments for particular cases and issues (e.g., trauma measures, or alcohol or drug use, misuse, abuse, or dependence questionnaires).

The standard set of instruments may include general data questionnaires, custody-specific questionnaires, and child behavior checklists that are appropriate for the ages of the children in the family. The authors have found it helpful to make a list of all of the instruments they use, which can be used in the final report as well as in the outline of the sources of data. The list can become a checklist on which the evaluator may note when each parent has been given the instrument and when they have returned it. The Appendices at the back of this book contain checklists and questionnaires that the authors have found useful.

Methods for Data Collection

The methods used in a PPE must be forensically defensible; that is, the methods need to meet minimum standards of reliability and validity, transparency, and acceptance in the field. All evaluators should be able to describe what they did and should be able to explain why they chose to do it that way. This holds true for the selected psychological tests, questionnaires, and structured interview protocols. It is recommended by many authorities that structured interview protocols are superior to free interview formats because they allow for an interview process that is likely to be more thorough and more balanced with both parents (M.J. Ackerman, 2010; Gould & D.A. Martindale, 2007). Of course, when using a structured interview, the evaluator needs to be an active participant, asking questions to follow up on the parent's answers and clarifying responses that are not clear. If an evaluator disagrees and interviews in a more open-ended manner, he or she should be prepared to explain the reasoning and the methodology used. An example of a nonstructured set of questions (to be presented to each parent) follows:

1. What do you want?
2. How are you stuck?
3. Tell me about the mess you are in. What keeps you stuck in the mess?
4. What do you think you need to do to make things better?

Recording of the Data

Before collecting the information, the evaluator should consider how to record the data. When testifying in court, or when one's work product is reviewed, failure to maintain a complete file record can be a difficult failure to explain. If there are handwritten notes, it is important that the date, time, and location of the interviews are identified as well as whether the interviews were completed in person or by telephone. The evaluator should produce legible notes that can be read by the court, counsel, parties, and/or an expert who is reviewing the file (American Psychological Association, 2011).

For computer note taking, it is important to save the interview notes without further altering or editing. When the evaluator saves the file on his or her computer, the computer will record the date and time of saving the file so any alterations to the file will change the date saved and thus be noted. It is perfectly acceptable to work from another copy, but forensic expectations are that the evaluator will preserve an original record of the interview or observation in an unaltered form. It is, therefore, unacceptable to have notes be morphed into the report without keeping a copy of the originals.

Although notes are used to help an evaluator recall the events, discussions, and observations, they do not necessarily need to be verbatim. However, two lines of notes for a 45-minute phone call is considered unacceptable as this will not help the evaluator recall the details when writing the report or when testifying months (or years) after the report is filed with the court. Nor can attorneys, families, or the court know what was asked or answered in such an undocumented interview.

Be wary of using minimally edited versions of the interview notes in the final report. Conversations wander from topic to topic, circling back to the original question and spinning off into asides. Reports that follow those conversational turns are difficult to read, chaotic, and disorganized. When the evaluator uses interview notes in this way, he fails to organize the data and frame the issues according to the meaning of the information. When the data is organized according to the decision tree, the integration and meaning of the information can be more clearly understood by the reader. One way to frame the interview would be to follow the main topics in the clusters as found in the preliminary decision tree. Sorting the data into decision trees should help to prevent an evaluator from taking this shortcut.

Observations of play and of parent-child interactions are difficult to record accurately by hand. In some situations, one may be able to audio- or video-record the observations, with permission and notification of the family. The evaluator should be sure that the initial contract discusses the video and audio recordings if they will be used, and be sure that it delineates proper storage and protection of them as records.

There is no consensus in the field on the amount of time to spend in gathering particular forms of information, whether it is time conducting interviews with the parents or time spent talking to collateral contacts. As outside parameters, the authors have seen cases in which the evaluator provided as much time as one of the parents wanted or felt he or she needed to cover every concern, even when that amounted to 8 hours or more for each parent. The authors also have seen cases in which each child was interviewed for 10 to 15 minutes. It is useful to talk openly with other parenting plan evaluators in the area to try to develop agreement about the parameters of time spent and to develop clear ways to inform the families and the attorneys about any limits that will be imposed on the number of documents, the number of collaterals, and the time spent in interviews.

Anchored in Research

Before beginning to collect data, it is also a good idea to identify in a preliminary way the research base needed for an appropriate analysis of this case. As the data comes in and the case develops, there may be new issues raised that require more research to be consulted. For example, if the evaluator learns about the presence of suspected attachment problems, he or she can begin to look at research on measures of attachment style, outcomes of attachment disorders, and so forth, depending on the questions that need to be answered. Or, if there is a question about alcohol abuse, the evaluator can read the most recent research on different types of tests to detect alcohol use, research on recovery and relapse, or research into various possible interventions that might be recommended. Such research can be concurrent with continuing data gathering and may lead to the collection of additional data based on the factors presented in the literature.

What is important here is not to look for research to support one particular perspective on the data but instead to find research that supports many different perspectives on the data to be gathered or on the data that is already gathered. A more open-minded approach such as the authors are suggesting may help offset bias in the research chosen.

Continuing Data Collection in the Case of Maria, Timothy, and Family

In Chapter Two, the authors provided possible sources for data for the myriad of factors that may come forth in an evaluation (see Table 2.3). As an example, parent interviews have the potential of producing data about a long list of issues. Other sources of information, such as medical records, may provide data about only one or two issues.

As the data comes in, the evaluator's knowledge of the family grows and the evaluator adds to the list of data needed for this specific case. In what follows there is a description of the additional information that has come to light about this hypothetical family after some initial interviews with the parents, collateral interviews, and additional document review.

> Maria is requesting sole custody of all three children because she has been the primary parent since the beginning. Timothy wants Peter to live with him full time and the younger two to be in his care much of the time as well. At transitions, Sarah clings to her mother. Maria has provided more detail about her allegations of IPV. She says that there have been several incidents of physical violence, such as kicking her, dragging her down the stairs by her hair, and choking her.
>
> Maria states that the children have been present for many of these incidents, and they have been exposed to domestic violence for many years. Maria says that she never reported these incidents to the police during the marriage because she wanted to make the marriage work and because she thought Timothy would change. A neighbor had heard fighting and called the police several times. Maria did not provide any information to the police. She says that during the past 7 years, she did talk to her psychiatrist about the abuse, and he has worked with her to help her gain the strength to disclose the abuse to the police, which she did on the day that she separated from the marriage.
>
> Maria reports that Timothy has a criminal record that includes two driving under the influence convictions from 2 years and 4 years ago, a conviction for public intoxication from last year, and a conviction for disturbing the peace from 3 years ago. She reports that she has always had concerns regarding the amount of beer Timothy consumes and reports that he drinks at least three to four beers daily, sometimes more. She reports that he began drinking after the birth of their first child, Peter. She reports that when he is drinking, he becomes easily agitated, yells, and becomes more physically aggressive. Maria states that the children appear to be fearful of their father when he is drinking.
>
> During the home visit of 90 minutes, Timothy drank four beers in the presence of the evaluator. Timothy strongly encouraged, even tried to pressure, the evaluator to join him to "just have one beer. No one will know." At the end of the visit, his speech was slightly slurred.
>
> Timothy states that he wants Peter to remain in his primary care given that he has been the parent who has done most of the hands-on parenting. He is okay with his daughters living with their mother, but he would like to have them stay overnight on the weekends.

He reports that the transitions of 2-year-old Sarah are difficult because Maria hangs onto Sarah and makes it impossible for the child to move to his care.

Maria says that Timothy has displayed a significant amount of anger and aggression towards their 12-year-old son, Peter, as well, usually due to Timothy's frustration with Peter's performance in competitive ski races and other competitive sports. She says that Timothy's anger towards Peter has often made the boy cry and rarely makes him feel adequate. She says that Peter has always sought his father's approval, but he rarely receives it when it comes to competitive sports because Timothy has always pushed Peter too hard to succeed. Maria further reports that Peter requested to take music lessons, which Maria supported given her upbringing in a musical home and given the interest that Peter displayed, but Timothy refused to allow it and referred to his son as a "sissy" for wanting to engage in music lessons. Timothy denies that Peter ever wanted to participate in music lessons and states that this was something that Maria wanted, and Peter "would never be interested in something like music lessons."

Maria says that Timothy has routinely exercised poor judgment in caring for the children. She says that Timothy rarely provides the children with fruits and vegetables; he usually provides them with microwaved food, and he gives them macaroni and cheese too often for dinner. Maria also reports that Timothy encouraged Peter to play video games that she felt were not very age inappropriate, including "Grand Theft Auto" and "Call of Duty."

Timothy states that he also is actively involved in the children's extracurricular activities. He says that he also brings the children to their dentist appointments and that he is involved in the children's school activities, including helping them with their homework. Timothy denies using poor judgment in caring for the children.

Timothy denies that he was ever abusive towards Maria. He says that she has no evidence of the allegations and that she has fabricated these allegations to gain a tactical advantage in the current custody and access dispute. Timothy counteralleges that Maria has suffered from chronic depression in the last number of years, and she has been under the routine care of a psychiatrist and prescribed antidepressants. He says that her depressive state negatively affects her behavior and attitudes towards him and the children. Maria says that Rita visits with Timothy on a daily basis and during weekend access visits, as per the schedule. She says that Rita typically cries when she spends too much time with her father, and he usually ends up dropping Rita off to her early due to her crying and missing her mother. This situation occurs especially on weekends when, per Maria, "She's away from her mommy too long for a 7-year-old." Maria says that Sarah visits with her father during the day on days during the week, but she does not see him on weekends. Sarah has not had an overnight with her father.

Timothy says that Peter often refuses to visit with his mother because the visits do not go well. He says that Maria sabotages her own time with Peter because she verbally and physically abuses him. He says that it is Maria's responsibility to build a better relationship with her son. He says that he does not need to alienate Peter from his mother because she is alienating herself with her aggressive and abusive behaviors including hitting him, dragging him up the stairs, and throwing him around while trying to bring him to his room. He says that when Peter is at Maria's home, he frequently receives telephone calls from Peter requesting to be picked up because of Maria's abusive behaviors.

Peter discloses that his mother was hitting him, sometimes on the face. He says that his mother was hitting him every time he visited with her because she got frustrated about his homework. He says that he sometimes refused to visit with his mother because she was hitting him too much, and he no longer wanted to get hurt by her. He says that the last time his mother hit him was 2 months ago. He says that during this incident, his mom became angry with him for calling his father to help him with his homework. He says that his mother hit him approximately 10 times on the buttocks. Peter says that he then refused to see his mother. He says that his father supported him in his decision and told him that he did not have to go to his mom's home if he did not want to. Peter says that his father told him that someone would be coming to his school to interview him, and he should tell that person that his mother hit him.

Timothy says that he is agreeable for Rita and Sarah to reside with Maria, but he wants to have both weekday visits and overnight weekend access with them, in keeping with their ages and preferences. He would also like all three children enrolled in sports practices and teams, and he would like to participate in their practices and games. Timothy reports that all three children enjoy spending time with him and that sometimes transitions with Sarah are tough "because Maria holds onto Sarah and whispers something in her ear that I can't hear." He denies returning any of the children early to their mother's.

Timothy states that he encourages Peter to speak to Maria every day and to visit with her as per the schedule. He says that Peter often refuses to visit with his mother because the visits do not go well. Further, he alleges that it is Maria who has interfered with his access to the children. And finally Timothy states that Maria's parents are abusive with the girls.

Collateral contacts have provided additional information. Paternal grandfather, Nicholas, says that he did not witness violence between these parents but that Maria "yelled a lot" at Timothy and the children. He says that he has never been violent with his own wife. When asked, he did not report any knowledge of Timothy having a criminal background.

Maternal grandfather, Gordon, says that he has been aware of the conflict between the parents "for a number of years." He describes Timothy as "very aggressive and violent," often screaming at Maria and the children. Gordon says that he once confronted Peter about not visiting them for more than 2 months and for being aggressive with Maria. He says that Peter became aggressive toward him and the grandmother and then called Timothy to pick him up. Gordon says that he and his wife often cared for the children when Maria was working, even though Timothy was at home, because Timothy refused to take care of them.

Gordon says that he called the police 1 year ago because Timothy came to his house with an aggressive demeanor and demanded to get into their home. Gordon says that he went to court to file a restraining order but did not pursue the matter because Timothy brought Peter to court to defend him and to accuse his grandfather of being the one who was abusive of him and his two sisters. Further, Gordon reports that the next day, 7-year-old Rita asked him why he wanted to put her daddy in jail. Gordon says that he had "gently kicked" the children in play, and he did not consider this behavior abusive. He says that it is a joke he has always done with his grandchildren and that nobody ever cried or was upset by it.

Pam is the day care provider who cared for Rita for 6 weeks last year. She describes her as a "happy and sweet" girl who was always well dressed. She says that Rita spoke positively about time spent with her father, mother, brother, and baby sister.

Dr. Connoly is Maria's psychiatrist, who has been seeing her once a week for more than 10 years, with a 2-year break between 2005 and 2007. Maria's presenting problems were related to life choices such as career planning and whether to return to school. He says that he diagnosed her with a mild Dysthymic Disorder because she had some depressive symptoms and was prescribed antidepressants, but primarily he saw her concerns as "specific to life issues and stresses." Dr. Connoly says that several years ago, he prescribed Ritalin for Maria as a trial to investigate the presence of Attention-Deficit/Hyperactivity Disorder, but Maria discontinued the medication after a few months because she felt that it did not help her. According to Dr. Connoly, Maria reported serious abuse by Timothy, including severe verbal abuse in front of the children. He reports that Maria briefly left the marriage 10 years ago, with her son, after a domestic violence incident in which Timothy hit her on the head. He says that Maria told him that Timothy was supposed to attend anger management after this incident, but he did not follow through with the treatment.

Dr. Connoly says that Timothy came to one session that was intended to be for marriage counseling, but he was hostile throughout the session, refused to talk about any personal issues, and used the time to berate the field of psychiatry. Timothy reportedly called Dr. Connoly after Maria separated from the marriage, describing his wife as "acting irrational and aggressive," which he attributed to the medication prescribed by Dr. Connoly. The psychiatrist states that Maria is aware that the stress has affected her parenting and her patience, and she has been "working on not yelling at the children" and establishing more structured routines for them. He says that he has no concerns about her ability to parent the children appropriately and that she is "basically a really good mother."

Dr. Swanson has been the children's pediatrician from birth. He says that Peter was healthy overall but had had behavioral and anxiety issues that necessitated a referral for supportive therapy. Dr. Swanson says that Rita had trouble growing and putting on weight as a baby, and she was treated in a hospital for what he called dietary choice problems. According to Dr. Swanson, Rita rebounded and is now healthy with no significant problems. He says that Maria was the parent who most often brought the children to the appointments. He described her as "perky and happy" and compliant with all medical advice.

Dr. Becan is a staff psychiatrist at the children's hospital and is the psychiatrist who assessed Peter for anxiety, based on a referral from Dr. Swanson. Peter was described at that time as having had problems with anxiety from the age of 3, having complained of nightmares of snakes, fears of dinosaurs, and fears that the bathroom door would be locked. Both parents described high levels of conflict in the home, with Maria "yelling at the children and her husband" on most days, a pattern that had begun when Peter was around 2 years old. Peter said, when asked, that he wanted his mother to "stop yelling," his father to "stop saying bad words," and his sister, Rita, to be "less annoying." Dr. Becan says that Peter met the criteria for Generalized Anxiety Disorder as well as Oppositional Defiant Disorder, due to his pattern of losing his temper and being highly argumentative. On the other hand, he was described as a sensitive child with a poor ability to modulate his mood. He was referred to a 12-week cognitive behavioral therapy program.

Marika is the principal at St. John Catholic School where Rita is in kindergarten and Peter is in fifth grade. She describes Rita as a cheerful and enthusiastic student who follows rules and plays well with the other children. She meets all expectations for the kindergarten. Marika says that Peter has an individual education plan with in-class accommodations and individual educational assistance. His homework is usually complete, and he gets along well with teachers and peers. Peter is doing well academically, but he needs the program accommodations and medications, extended time for tests, and clarification with individual assistance to be able to keep up with his work. There was an altercation in February of this year in which Peter punched another student who admitted he had punched and kicked Peter first. Marika says that Timothy was defensive of his son, saying that Peter "only reacted because the other boy bit him, breaking the skin." Peter denied that he had been bitten, and the principal describes there being a discrepancy between Peter and Timothy's versions of what happened, with Timothy's version being that the fight was entirely the other child's fault.

Maria was found to have no criminal charges in her history. Timothy had four convictions: two for driving under the influence, one for public drunkenness, and one for disturbing the peace. He was asked about them and said that they were all misunderstandings, and he refused to elaborate on the circumstances that preceded the convictions. There were several instances of contact with this family by the police, but charges were not filed until the end of the marriage.

Child Protective Services (CPS) social worker, Mr. Brown, says that Maria made the initial complaint that Timothy was exposing the children to interparental conflict and that he was driving dangerously in the car because he was angry that Peter refused to put on his seat belt. Timothy alleged that Maria was mentally unstable and that she was initiating the conflict and involving the children in the disputes. Mr. Brown says that CPS verified the presence of adult conflict and the presence of moderate levels of harm by both parents towards the children, based on the conflict. They took the family into protection services "to monitor and support the family during the parental separation."

A few months later, Timothy called CPS to report that Maria had physically hit Peter, which Maria acknowledged. The social worker cautioned her about the use of physical discipline. A few days later, Timothy called to report that the maternal grandfather bit Rita on the wrist, leaving tooth marks. The agency cautioned Maria to ensure that her father does not ever bite the children, even in play. A few days after that report, Maria called CPS and reported that Timothy slept naked in the bed with Rita. In addition, she said that Timothy left Rita in the home alone and unsupervised. Mr. Brown observed the children with both parents and states that none of the children appeared afraid of either parent, and both parents were appropriate in their parenting. He says that Maria agreed to avoid corporal punishment. Allegations that either parent choked Peter were not substantiated, as were allegations of Timothy sleeping naked with Rita and of Timothy leaving Rita alone. The allegation of Gordon biting Rita was unsubstantiated, based on an interview with Gordon and Rita and on the observation of no marks on Rita's wrist. Mr. Brown expresses concern about the level of conflict that the children were exposed to, and he says that the children do not have a clear idea about the schedule for parenting time. He says that there was no concrete evidence of alienation, but he believes that Maria needs to separate her negative feelings about Timothy from the children's relationship with their father, and Timothy needs to separate his negative feelings about Maria from Peter's relationship with her. Mr. Brown states that Peter has not actually rejected his mother, as he reportedly stayed with her this month and said he enjoyed his time with her. Mr. Brown recommends counseling for both older children so that they can have a neutral professional to help them cope with their parents' conflict. Mr. Brown says that Timothy was unhappy with CPS because it did not verify his allegations, and he reports that Timothy hung up on him as he was trying to report the findings of the investigation.

Peter and Rita both told the evaluator that they liked spending time with both parents and that they would turn to whichever parent was closer if they were hurt or upset.

Reflecting During the Evaluation

At this point, the evaluator is part way through the evaluation, and there is the opportunity to reflect on what has been learned to determine what information is missing or needs to be cross-checked to be able to get better convergence and divergence on the issues. The new data will need to be included in revisions of the preliminary decision tree and the preliminary hypotheses, as the evaluator reflects on them.

One warning is that sometimes there may seem to be multiple sources of information, but they are actually the same data repeated by several sources. For example, Maria recently may have told several people that Timothy has been abusive, but they did not see any bruises or witness any aggression. Those people are not actually providing multiple and independent confirmation of the reality of Timothy's alleged abuse. They are all providing the same data about Maria's contention that Timothy has abused her. Interviewing of collaterals needs to be carefully focused on what they actually witnessed as opposed to what they were told. On the other hand, witnesses who were told about abuse at the time it was occurring may be considered to be providing information about how Maria perceived the events contemporaneously to their occurrence.

From this updated information, the evaluator can now see several additional issues to be investigated within the scope of "best interests": possible child abuse by Timothy and Maria, possible mental health problems in Maria, possible abuse by maternal grandparents, and a possible criminal history for Timothy. Some of these issues will use data sources already identified, but new data sources may need to be identified. The additional points to explore are delineated in Table 4.1 below.

From here, one will revise the hypotheses and then the decision tree to include the new issues. This will ensure that none of the issues gets left out of consideration and will provide a template for looking at the complex causal links and interactions among the issues.

Revised Hypotheses and Decision Tree

As you may recall, the original hypotheses are found in Chapter 3. Those original hypotheses will now be revised, shown in Table 4.2, as the new information is examined.

Based on the combination of the preliminary hypotheses created in Chapter 3 and on the revised hypotheses noted above, the evaluator is now ready to add to the revised decision tree on which the optimal parenting plan for the children's safety and the well-being for this family will be based, see Figure 4.1. It is

---

Table 4.1 Points to Explore and Where to Get More Data About the New Issues

Additional Points to Explore	Places to Look for Information
Children's Special Needs/Issues	
Peter: Academic issues	School records, teacher interviews
Interest in sports vs. music	Interview coaches, other parents
	Interview Peter
	Interview prospective music teacher
Rita: Attachment/Separation	Observe a transition between parents
	Interview collateral witnesses
	Interview day care providers
Sarah: Attachment/Separation	Observe a transition between parents
	Observe parent-child behavior
	Interview day care providers
Parent Issues	Substance abuse, past and current
	Drug and alcohol testing of both parents
	Review motor vehicle records
	Interview parents
	Interview medical providers
	Review criminal records
Grandparent Issues	
Availability for care	Interview grandparents
Concerns about abuse	Interview parents
	Interview children
	Interview collateral witnesses

Table 4.2 Hypotheses for the Case of Timothy, Maria, and Family

<u>Topic of Concern</u>	<u>Hypothesis Number</u>	<u>Hypothesis</u>
Safety		
IPV? Child abuse? Neglect? Substance use?	S-1	Timothy has problems with anger management and aggression, leading him to be verbally abusive and controlling with Peter and physically and verbally abusive with Maria.
	S-2	Timothy has a problem with alcohol abuse or dependence.
	S-3	Maria has a problem with prescription medication abuse or dependence.
	S-4	Maria's physical discipline of Peter is abusive.
Child		
Child's perspective? Ages & stages? Adjustment and resiliency? Relationship history?	C-1	The younger girls are reacting to separation from their mother as an attachment figure.
	C-2	The younger girls are afraid of their father.
	C-3	Peter's anxiety is related to the parental conflict and/or Maria's abuse.
Parent		
Mental health? Personal history? Parent-child relationship? Parent-parent relationship?	P-1	One or both parents is fabricating allegations for the litigation advantage.
	P-2	Maria has mental health problems leading her to be verbally and physically abusive with Peter and enmeshed with Rita and Sarah.
	P-3	Maria's depression is the result of her experience of domestic violence.
	P-4	One or both parents is engaged in restrictive gate-keeping: Timothy with Peter and Maria with Rita and Sarah.

at this point that the evaluator has a full picture of the family and he can begin to hold up each issue to the light and can begin to contemplate the myriad of interactions between the issues. The multiple hypotheses and decision tree approach allows the evaluator to do such.

In the next chapter, the authors will begin organizing the collected data according to the revised hypotheses and decision tree. Before doing that and before closing the door to the data collection phase, it is important for the evaluator to first read and then reread all of the case notes, court materials, collateral letters, and interview notes to provide a good understanding of the case. This way he or she can begin moving towards the analysis of the data. If there are missing data and/or gaps in evidence based on the review of materials, it may be necessary to return to additional data collection and then to update the decision tree and hypotheses statements as needed, once again. As the reader can see, the decision tree for a systematic process of conducting PPEs is a dynamic one.

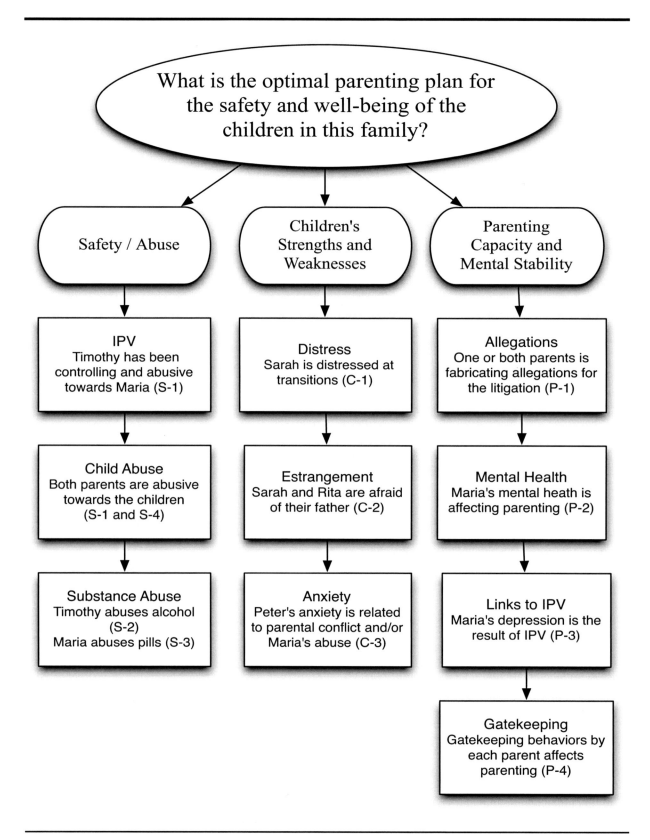

Figure 4.1 A Revised Decision Tree of the Optimal Parenting Plan for the Safety and Well-Being of the Children in This Family

Summary

- The chapter reviewed data collection methods and continuing to collect more data as more questions are raised.
- The chapter reviewed suggestions regarding technological methods of recording the elements of the evaluation: audio and video recording and taking notes on a computer. It also reviewed the notifications about those methods in the initial contract for services.
- Using the case example, the chapter discussed and demonstrated organizing the new information, as it comes in, into a revised decision tree to allow for more refinement in the analysis and synthesis to come.

Annotated Bibliography

Acklin, M. W., & Cho-Stutler, L. (2006). The science and art of parent-child observation in child custody evaluation. *Journal of Forensic Psychology Practice, 6*(1), 51-62.

The authors suggest that the observation of parent-child interaction is a core function in PPEs with potential to yield rich and relevant information concerning both parents and children. The authors introduce behavioral science concepts, research findings, and practical procedures for child custody evaluators with a focus on office-based parent-child observation.

Ash, P., & Guyer, M. J. (1991). Biased reporting by parents undergoing child custody evaluations. *Journal of the American Academy of Child & Adolescent Psychiatry, 30*(5), 835-838.

The authors tested the hypothesis that a parent undergoing a PPE will bias his or her report of the child's symptoms in a direction that supports the parent's aim in the litigation. Parents in 196 court-ordered child custody evaluations rated their children using the Child Behavior Checklist. For the comparison group, 34 additional families undergoing evaluations of visitation disputes and 15 families with custody/visitation disputes complicated by sexual abuse allegations were used to test alternative explanations of the findings. Results support the hypothesis that parental bias was present and quantifiable. Parental distortion seemed to be less on ratings of less ambiguous externalizing behaviors of the child than on ratings of the child's internal state.

Austin, W. G. (2002). Guidelines for utilizing collateral sources of information in child custody evaluations. *Family Court Review, 40*(2), 177-184.

The author underscores that the collateral information is vital to the process of trying to assess the credibility and validity of information obtained from the primary parties in a dispute. It is suggested that information that is from more neutral parties has higher credibility, and when the party has access to key information it produces more discriminant validity. When a source with high discriminant validity agrees with information from a primary party, then it enhances the convergent validity on an issue or hypothesis. The author suggests that gathering data from collateral sources and using a system to evaluate their usefulness on confirmation of hypotheses is a necessary part of the emerging forensic-clinical-scientific child custody evaluation paradigm.

Bow, J. N. (2010). Use of third party information in child custody evaluations. *Behavioral Sciences & the Law, 28*(4), 511-521.

This article reviews the use of third party information and its potential to increase the accuracy and usefulness of child custody evaluations. Legal and admissibility issues are reviewed, along with the types of third party information commonly utilized. Factors impacting such data sources are discussed as well as the importance of determining the degree to which independent sources point to the same conclusion. Suggestions are provided for selecting, contacting, and interviewing collateral sources, and ways of assessing, utilizing, and reporting collateral data are described.

Darlington, Y. (2006). Experiences of custody evaluation: Perspectives of young adults who were the subject of family court proceedings as children. *Journal of Child Custody: Research, Issues, and Practices, 3*(1), 51-66.

This article reports on a retrospective qualitative research study of young adults' views of participating in PPEs in Australia. The authors conducted in-depth interviews with the participants who were between the ages of 18 to 26 at the time of the interviews. Participants described their recollections of being interviewed as children, and they provided suggestions for ways in which professionals working with children in this context might make the process easier for children.

Gould, J. W. (2005). Use of psychological tests in child custody assessment. *Journal of Child Custody: Research, Issues, and Practices, 2*(1/2), 49-69.

This article describes a functional, comprehensive approach to the use of psychological tests and measures in a child custody evaluation. The author describes a conceptual framework to be used in choosing assessment techniques that are used to assess functional aspects of parenting competencies and other related variables that are helpful in creating a reliable foundation from which to generate opinions about custodial placement and visitation access. The author also provides practical examples of how psychological test data might be presented in an advisory report to the court.

Hynan, D. J. (1998). Interviewing children in custody evaluations. *Family and Conciliation Court Review, 36*(4), 466-478.

The author opines that child interviews are a central part of custody evaluations that affect many families, and ways to maximize their accuracy and usefulness are discussed. Empirical research on children of divorce is reviewed and considered within the context of collecting interview data. Information about child interviews from the custody evaluation literature is reviewed, as are relevant research findings about the accuracy of children's statements. Implications for practice are proposed that integrate research findings and recommendations from the literature.

Newton, S. (2011). Obtaining and analyzing school-related data in a child custody evaluation. *Journal of Child Custody: Research, Issues, and Practices, 8*(3), 189-211.

The author notes that parenting plan evaluators routinely collect data about the academic performance and classroom behavior of the children involved, yet little has been written about the best ways to collect this important data given that teachers and school personnel are important collateral sources of information. Currently, guidelines for the systematic collection of school data do not exist. In this article, an overview of the data collection process regarding school records and the areas of consideration relevant to a PPE are presented and organized.

Powell, M. B., & Lancaster, S. (2003). Guidelines for interviewing children during child custody evaluations. *Australian Psychologist, 38*(1), 46-54.

This paper offers a brief review of the current literature related to the interviewing of children during PPEs and provides a series of recommendations for evaluators. These recommendations are organized under the following headings: (a) establish rapport using broad, open-ended questions; (b) make the purpose and ground rules of the interview clear to the child; (c) allow the child's perspective be heard without expecting an outright custody preference; (d) demonstrate a willingness to consider all reasonable perspectives or hypotheses about what has occurred; (e) try not to exacerbate the child's stress or guilt; (f) pursue all possible explanations for a child's report, irrespective of whether there are clear signs of "coaching" or contamination; (g) obtain appropriate training in the use of forensic interviewing techniques; and (h) engage in research on the impact of children's participation in custody cases.

Chapter 5

The Data Matrix: Organizing the Data

By the time that the evaluator sits down to begin the data analysis, a preliminary decision tree has been formed and organization of the data has begun. With all of the data collected, the evaluator then begins to move into the phase of data analysis. At this point, it is essential to separate different levels of inference so as to separate observations from thinking about these observations and so as to present these distinctions in a clear way to the reader. In this chapter, the authors provide a framework for considering the different levels of inference and for following a method to analyze and synthesize the data.

Levels of Inference

Definitions

In a seminal article that outlines these distinctions, Tippins and Wittmann (2005) described a hierarchy of four levels of inference that are relevant in parenting plans for children postseparation and postdivorce. Level I refers to the observational level—what the evaluator sees "without the addition of higher level abstraction" (p. 194). These are the data that are factual where no inferences are being made about the data. Level I observations can include results from drug testing (the father scored positive for the presence of methamphetamine), specific results from psychological testing (there is a significant elevation on Scale 4 in the mother's MMPI-2), or results from documents presented (the father asserts that he was the best parent because of his religious practices), as well as the evaluator's own observations (the child sat in close proximity to the father and made eye contact with the father).

Level II inferences are the conclusions made about the observed facts of the case, the psychology of the family, or the individual family members. These inferences are low-level ones about these facts and observations, but they are without regard for the implications that these low-level inferences may have on the conclusions for specific custody decisions. Level II inferences do not involve considerations of interactions between and among factors. In the example of "the child seems to respond positively to the mother in her interactions," there is an inference being made about the quality of the mother's parenting based on the observed interactions she has with the child, but there is no suggestion about how these interactions may play out within the context of a recommended parenting plan.

Level III is the level at which the evaluator describes conclusions about broader custody-specific constructs, integrating the conclusions about individual elements of psychological functioning that were made at Level II. Examples of Level III opinions might be, "The father's abuse of methamphetamine is causally related to his episodic violent behavior toward the children and their mother, and the children are at risk of harm when they are with him." The statement is not yet about what should be done as a recommendation, but it does integrate several psychological conclusions into a larger opinion.

Level IV conclusions are those that can be characterized as recommendations about the psycholegal questions facing the court—what should be done with and for the family. For example, "The child should be in the primary custody of the mother until he is 5 years old," or "The father should make all educational and medical decisions." The highest level of abstraction, of inference from the data, comes in the recommendations to the court and the parents about what should happen. These are what Tippins and Wittmann (2005) call Level IV inferences.

There is controversy about making Level IV recommendations. There are at least two primary reasons that some legal and some psychological experts have stated that mental health professionals should never offer recommendations to the court. (In 2005, the *Journal of Child Custody* devoted a special issue to this topic). Recommendations address the ultimate issue before the court, and there are jurisdictions in which judges do not want evaluators to issue such recommendations, which are seen as the sole province of the court. Also, Tippins and Wittmann (2005) joined with other scholars (Karras & Berry, 1985; Melton et al., 1997), suggesting that custody evaluators should avoid making recommendations to the courts because there is less evidence available to support conclusions at each higher level of abstraction. They suggest that Level IV inferences lack the "generalizability" and "predictive validity" needed to provide the court with recommendations of what will happen in the future. In the absence of sound empirical evidence, they suggest that recommendations are limited by the evaluator's inability to consider and synthesize extremely complex interactions of factors necessary to make valid predictions that underlie parenting plan recommendations. When there is scant research basis for a conclusion, there is a greater risk that conclusions will be reached based on bias, personal values, or other nonscientific reasoning.

In contrast, others have suggested that child custody evaluators should present expert recommendations because information and observations underlying recommendations can incrementally increase the validity of judicial opinions (M. J. Ackerman & M. Ackerman, 1997; Clark, 1995). In addition, despite the limitations noted above, most courts want to know the evaluator's opinion about what "should" be done and will be heartily disappointed not to get a recommendation.

Because the logical and the empirical connections between the levels are not known or precise, however, there is much room for error and bias in moving up the chain of inference to decision making. While recommending is an important function for an evaluator in most cases, the best practice is to make each level of inference transparent. The court (and others) must be able to see the data, understand the decision-making process that went into organizing clusters of facts into opinions, and then understand the construction of these themes that were combined to support the higher level conclusions and ultimate recommendations. Using this systematic process, the court may not agree with the evaluator's recommendations (e.g., the judge has additional information not considered at the time of the evaluation), but it can use the data at the lower levels of inference to better understand the evidence relied on by the evaluator at the time of the report. So even though the recommendations can be disputed or confirmed by the court, systematically presenting the data in a clear and transparent way can help clarify the basis of the dispute or it can provide confirmation of the evaluator's recommendations.

There are several problems that arise when evaluators confuse the levels of inference that they are presenting to the court. One is that there is little transparency, so neither the family members nor the court knows the basis for the opinions offered. Another is that the evaluators are less conscious and rigorous than they would be if they had described the Level I data and then determined what the meaning and implications of those data were. Thirdly, it is easier and more effective to compare behaviors and/or observations with the relevant social science research before moving on to more abstract concepts and more complex combinations of observations about which there is usually less relevant research.

Learning to Use the Levels of Inference

The authors have been concerned about the many reports that they have reviewed in which these inferential levels are mixed. In fact, it is often the case in the authors' experience that the first level of observed data is not described at all, but instead the psychological inferences and conclusions are presented as though they were simple facts rather than opinions. These inferences are generally presented in report sections called "Behavioral Observations" or "Parent-Child Observations," but actually they are statements such as, "Child appeared strongly attached to Mother," without any reference to the observations on which that opinion was based. Indeed, writers of these reports do not indicate any recognition that they are offering inferences or opinions rather than observations.

As described in Chapter 2, cognitive psychologists have described the ways that humans think in "fast" and intuitive ways, reaching conclusions without awareness of how they did so (Kahneman, 2011). This human tendency may account for the practice of confounding fact and opinion that is so common in PPEs. It is the responsibility of each custody evaluator to train himself or herself to concentrate on initial sensory-based observations before making inferences and constructing conclusions and then to describe the initial sensory-based observations and the inferences and then the conclusions in differentiated terms.

While writing the data/observation section, the evaluator can check for alleged "data" that have been proffered by one of the parents or by the attorneys but that have not been supported by the evidence gathered in the evaluation. If the gratuitous or unsupported data were contained in the original pleadings or in the referral questions, it will be important to describe the ways that these data were investigated and what the findings were, first in a concrete description and then in a conclusion. If not crosschecked, the material in the pleadings and declarations can only be understood as the contentions and allegations of the parties and not as evidence.

Parenting Plan Evaluation Matrix

The data collected in complex evaluations can be complicated, complex, and difficult to record. The Parenting Plan Evaluation Matrix was developed as a tool for evaluators to do just that—keep track of the data. The evaluator enters the Level I data from direct observations into the matrix. Once all data have been entered into the evaluation matrix at Level I, the evaluator can then begin analyzing the data for reliability, validity, and weight of the observations before moving on to higher levels of abstraction for opinions and recommendations. The Parenting Plan Evaluation Matrix for Level I data follows in Table 5.1, and a full-page blank one can be found in Appendix D at the end of this book for evaluators to copy and fill out for each PPE case he or she has.

Working With the Parenting Plan Evaluation Matrix

Most of the entries on the matrix are common factors considered in an evaluation, and many of these factors were defined in Chapter 2. Here, there are examples of how evaluators would include the Level I evidence in the case example presented in Chapter 3. Table 5.2 is a description of the way that each cell in the grid would be filled in for the first three areas of concern: IPV, Child Abuse, and Substance Abuse. It should be noted that for the purposes of explanatory clarity, the information was entered into the matrix in more detail than one would need to use in a real-life case. It is more likely to be useful with a few words about a piece of evidence that would remind the evaluator of it, rather than a fully elaborated description. The latter would make the matrix extremely long, unwieldy, and overwhelming—the very thing that the process is intended to prevent.

The Parenting Plan Evaluation Matrix has two parts. The first part of the matrix contains only Level I inferences—observational data without any kind of inferences. This would include mother's evidence, father's evidence, the child or children's evidence, collateral evidence, and the evaluator's evidence. This matrix does not include inferences, opinions, or recommendations. The initial matrix has only direct observations or data as presented directly by the parties.

The second part of the matrix has Level II and Level III inferences included and will be presented in Chapter 6. The second part of the matrix includes a summary of the evidence, an assessment of the reliability and validity of the evidence, and opinions and inferences that are generated from the first two. This second matrix is the result of analysis and synthesis of the data and includes what Tippins and Wittmann (2005) have called Level II and Level III inferences.

Table 5.1 Parenting Plan Evaluation Matrix I: Data

Source of Concern	Mother's Evidence	Father's Evidence	Children's Evidence	Collateral Evidence	Evaluator's Evidence
Intimate Partner Violence or Domestic Violence					
Child Abuse/ Maltreatment and/or Neglect					
Substance Abuse					
Mental Health					
Children's Adjustment					
Children's Preferences					
Parenting Competency					
Coparenting Capacity					
Relocation					
Other Issues					

The question might be raised as to where in the different matrices the evaluator should put psychological testing. What we are calling the first part of the data matrix, Parenting Plan Evaluation Matrix: Level I Data, would include a parent's clinically significant scores (without any inference about the potential implications of these scores on parenting). An example of this would be, "Mother had elevations on the MMPI-2 validity scales K and S with T-scores of 75 and 82." Any inferences about the meaning of those scores would be found in the second part of the data matrix, which is further described in Chapter 6. Any opinions about the interface between these scores and other data collected about the parent's behaviors would be part of subsequent analysis and ultimately the synthesis of the data—the process that is also further described in Chapter 6. In this hypothetical example, whether the mother's scores on these two validity scales (as originally listed in the Parenting Plan Evaluation Matrix: Level I Data chart) coupled with other data, ultimately affects the synthesis of the data and the parenting plan recommendations is something that is unknown at the point that the evaluator is entering the factual data into the first matrix as in the one found in Table 5.1.

The process of filling in all of the different cells is to describe the different sources of information that create the foundation for later analysis and synthesis of the data. The Parenting Plan Evaluation Matrix allows the evaluator to have present in one picture at one time many sources of data about a given issue in the family. The organization of multiple sources yields clearer and deeper descriptions of the families and helps the evaluator "to reveal inconsistencies, fabrication and inaccuracies in or confirm the primary data obtained from family members" (Austin, 2002, p. 178). As the evaluator relies upon multiple sources of information about the same issue, he or she is engaging in what is called triangulation of the data. Something is clearly more reliable if it comes from several independent sources. This kind of triangulation sets the foundation for the analysis at what Tippins and Wittmann (2005) have described as Level III inferences, that is, when custody-related conclusions about the parents, the children, or the family are formed.

It also happens that sometimes the data do not converge. Instead, there may be data sources that appear reliable but that point in different directions. It is important for the evaluator to work to make whatever sense he or she can of the contradictions. There may be an explanation for two disparate and seemingly contradictory facts that will be very important in understanding the family dynamics. It is important for the evaluator to describe his or her thought processes in regards to the data that do not converge so that the reader can understand better how the evaluator came to their conclusion. Where there is more than one way to interpret the data that the evaluator has, it is important to describe both interpretations and to explain why the evidence leads to the conclusion reached. It is also important to be cautious not to suggest alternative conclusions if they are not supported by the evidence.

In this book, the authors emphasize the importance of keeping the data collection and the reporting of it (Chapter 5) separate from the analysis and synthesis of the data (Chapter 6). It should be separate conceptually, and further it should be kept separate in the evaluation itself. Further, there are two distinct matrices presented in this book, the first one being the Parenting Plan Evaluation Matrix: Level I Data and the second being the Parenting Plan Evaluation Matrix: Summary, Analysis, and Synthesis.

The evaluation matrix is organized around the relevant issues in a given case that were identified at the start of the process and added to during the course of the evaluation, including issues such as IPV or domestic violence, child abuse or maltreatment, substance abuse, mental health, child's adjustment, child's preferences, parenting competency, coparenting capacity, relocation, and other issues including high levels of parental conflict and gatekeeping. The goal is for the evaluator to take each of the main issues in a given case and to enter data into the matrix—first into the matrix with Level I data only, and then once that has been completed, into the matrix for summary, analysis, and synthesis. A blank version of both matrices for the reader's use in his or her practice can be found in the Appendices D and E at the back of the book.

The Parenting Plan Evaluation Matrix
For Maria, Timothy, and Family

The authors will now describe the Parenting Plan Evaluation Matrix: Data for the case example of Maria, Timothy, and family. A copy of the Parenting Plan Evaluation Matrix for Maria, Timothy, and Family can be found in Table 5.2. The factors considered in this matrix include IPV or domestic violence, child abuse or maltreatment, and substance abuse. In the case example of Maria, Timothy, and family, these three issues do not exhaust the issues in the case as a whole, but they are the demonstration variables that the authors are using.

Intimate Partner Violence or Domestic Violence

In our case there were allegations of IPV or domestic violence.

- *Mother's evidence:* Maria alleges that Timothy was verbally and physically aggressive during the marriage and after the separation. She reports that he has kicked her and dragged her down the stairs by her hair and choked her. She states that the children have been exposed to the violence. Maria alleges that Timothy struggles with anger management and often loses his temper.

- *Father's evidence:* Next, moving across the row to the next cell to the right, there is a place for the father's evidence. Timothy denies that he was ever abusive towards Maria. He says that it is Maria who has been abusive towards him. He provides no details of Maria's alleged abuse.
- *Child's evidence:* Peter says that his parents have always argued a lot and that both of them yell, hit, and push each other.
- *Collateral evidence:* Paternal grandfather, Nicholas, says that he has not seen violence between the parents, but he reports that Maria "yelled a lot" at Timothy and the children. Maternal grandfather, Gordon, reports that he was aware of the conflict between the parents for a number of years, describes Timothy as "very aggressive and violent," and says that Timothy screamed at Maria and the children. Gordon reports that he called the police a year ago because Timothy came to his house with an aggressive demeanor and demanded to get into the house. Dr. Connoly, Maria's psychiatrist, states that Maria reported serious abuse by Timothy, including severe verbal abuse in front of the children. Dr. Connoly reports that there was an incident 8 years ago in which Timothy hit Maria on the head. He says that Timothy attended a meeting with him but refused to talk about the marital relationship and used the opportunity to berate the field of psychiatry and all psychiatrists as "quacks." There were several police calls to the home, but no charges were filed until just at the time of separation. Timothy was charged with assault and pled guilty to a lesser charge. There is a 1-year protective order in place prohibiting contact between Timothy and Maria. There were elevations on scales 4 and 9 of Timothy's MMPI-2 and four Aggressive Content Responses on the Rorschach.
- *Evaluator's evidence:* There are no evaluator observations of violence or aggression.

Maltreatment and/or Neglect (Child Abuse)

The second concern arises because both parents allege that the other is abusive toward the children.

- *Mother's evidence:* Maria reports that Timothy displays anger and aggression toward Peter, including calling him a "sissy" for wanting to take music lessons. She reports that Peter has cried as a result of Timothy's frustration with him. She told CPS that Timothy exposed the children to the parental conflict and drove dangerously in the car when he was drinking or when he was angry, endangering the children. Maria says that Timothy was sleeping naked in bed with Rita.
- *Father's evidence:* Timothy reports that Maria is physically and verbally abusive towards Peter. Timothy reports that Maria has hit Peter, has dragged him up the stairs, and has thrown him around. According to Timothy, Peter has called him from his mother's asking to be picked up early because of Maria's abusive behavior. Timothy told CPS that Maria was mentally unstable, that she had initiated the marital conflict, and that she had involved the children in it.
- *Children's evidence:* About this concern, the children have some evidence to provide. Peter reports that Maria has hit him on the buttocks when she was frustrated over his homework. He reports that he had refused visits because of wanting to avoid her abuse. The last time, he said, was 2 months ago when she hit him "over and over" at least 10 times. He said that his father told him to tell the interviewer about his mother's abuse. Rita says that her father told her to tell the evaluator that her mother hits her and Peter. She says that her mother had hit her one time, 4 days earlier, on the cheek, causing her to bleed. She says that her mother never hit her anywhere else, but she did say that she saw her mother hit Peter on the head. Peter reports that he is not afraid of either parent.
- *Collateral evidence:* In terms of collaterals, Dr. Connoly reports that Maria is working on not yelling at the children. CPS verified the presence of adult conflict and concluded that there was a moderate level of harm to the children from their exposure to it. CPS did not substantiate the allegation that Timothy was sleeping naked with Rita. No collateral confirmed that Timothy drives dangerously.
- *Evaluator's evidence:* The evaluator has not witnessed child abuse but has observations nonethe-

less. When Rita told about being hit on the cheek hard enough to draw blood 4 days earlier, she pointed to the spot, but the evaluator did not see any mark, scab, or scar. Timothy reported that he had told his children to report to the evaluator that their mother had hit them. Timothy came to the school when Peter was scheduled to be interviewed to provide guidance for Peter about being sure to report the alleged hitting by Maria. The children told the evaluator that they generally want to continue contact with both parents, and they talked specifically about ways that they rely on and turn to both parents for support.

Substance Abuse

Substance abuse is alleged as a concern with both parents, and here the evaluator will lay out the evidence regarding each parent separately. Maria's allegation that Timothy drinks heavily on a daily basis will be explored first.

- *Mother's evidence:* Maria says that Timothy drinks three to four beers a day, and he becomes easily agitated and the children are fearful when he is drinking.
- *Timothy's evidence:* Timothy denies that he has a drinking problem and refuses to discuss or elaborate on the four convictions except to describe them as "misunderstandings."
- *Children's evidence:* The children did not provide any statements about their father's alleged drinking.
- *Collateral evidence:* The collateral evidence was extensive. Timothy's criminal record shows that Timothy had four drinking-related convictions (two for driving under the influence, one for public intoxication, and one for disturbing the peace), and he was found guilty on all four.
- *Evaluator's evidence:* The evaluator observes that Timothy drank four beers during the 90-minute home visit, and he appeared somewhat impaired. He refused to talk about his history of drinking-related convictions, saying just that they were "misunderstandings."

Timothy's allegation that Maria abuses prescription medications will be explored next.

- *Mother's evidence:* Maria denies ever misusing prescribed drugs and says that she always takes them as instructed. She says that she took Ritalin briefly several years ago when Dr. Connoly thought that she might have adult Attention-Deficit/Hyperactivity Disorder. She reports that she did not find it helpful and discontinued use after 2 months.
- *Father's evidence:* Timothy says that Maria takes Ritalin to keep up her performance at work. He says that she becomes moody, irritable, and "snappy" towards the family. Timothy reports that he overheard Maria contact the pharmacy 11 times in one night, yelling and swearing because they would not refill her prescription.
- *Children's evidence:* Again the children did not offer evidence about this concern.
- *Collateral evidence:* There is a little collateral evidence that corroborates the allegation. Dr. Connoly reports that Maria seems to be taking her medication as prescribed. He confirms the brief trial use of Ritalin 3 years ago. The records from the pharmacy do not show a pattern of misuse of any medications. There was no record of repeated, drug-seeking telephone calls.
- *Evaluator's evidence:* The evaluator did not observe Maria to be under the influence of any substance during the interviews and/or the home visit.

The reader is reminded that the data just described for the aforementioned areas of concern have been entered into the Parenting Plan Evaluation Matrix (Table 5.2).

Table 5.2 Parenting Plan Evaluation Matrix I: Data for Maria, Timothy, and Family *(continued)*

Source of Concern	Maria's Evidence	Timothy's Evidence	Children's Evidence	Collateral Evidence	Evaluator's Evidence
Intimate Partner Violence or Domestic Violence					
Concerns that Timothy is violent and struggles to manage his anger.	Maria alleges that Timothy was verbally and physically aggressive during the marriage. She reports that he kicked and dragged her down the stairs by her hair and that he choked her. She reports that the children have been exposed to violence. Maria alleges that Timothy struggles with anger management, losing his temper with the children and with her.	Timothy denies that he was ever abusive towards Maria. He says that it is Maria who has been abusive towards him.	Peter says that his parents have always argued a lot as both yelled, hit, and pushed each other.	Paternal grandfather, Nicholas, says that he has not seen violence between the parents, but he reports that Maria "yelled a lot" at Timothy and the children. Maternal grandfather, Gordon, reports that he was aware of conflict between the parents for a number of years. He describes Timothy as "very aggressive and violent" and describes Timothy screaming at Maria and the children. Gordon also reports that he called the police a year ago because Timothy came to his house with an aggressive demeanor and demanded to get into the home. Dr. Connoly, Maria's psychiatrist, states that Maria reported serious abuse by Timothy, including severe verbal abuse in front of the children. Dr. Connoly reports that there was a domestic violence incident 8 years ago in which Timothy hit Maria on the head. Timothy attended a meeting with Dr. Connoly and took that opportunity to berate the field of psychiatry, suggesting that all psychiatrists are "quacks." Dr. Connoly states that Timothy was hostile during the meeting and that he did not seem willing to talk about relationship issues. There were several incidents of contact with police. Charges were filed on one occasion and Timothy pled guilty to disturbing the peace.	None observed

Table 5.2 Parenting Plan Evaluation Matrix I: Data for Maria, Timothy, and Family

Source of Concern	Maria's Evidence	Timothy's Evidence	Children's Evidence	Collateral Evidence	Evaluator's Evidence
Child Abuse/Maltreatment and/or Neglect					
Concerns that both parents have been abusive towards the children.	Maria reports that Timothy displays anger and aggression towards Peter. She reports that Timothy referred to Peter as a "sissy" for wanting to take music lessons. Maria reports that Peter has cried as a result of Timothy's frustration towards him. Maria reported to CPS allegations that Timothy exposed the children to interparental conflict and that he was driving dangerously in the car. She also reported that he was sleeping naked in the bed with Rita.	Timothy reports that Maria is physically and verbally abusive towards Peter. Timothy reports that Maria has hit Peter, has dragged him up the stairs, and has thrown him around. He reports that Peter called him asking to be picked up from Maria's due to her abusive behaviors. Timothy reported to CPS that Maria was mentally unstable, that she was initiating the conflict, and that she was involving the children.	Peter discloses that Maria has hit him sometimes on the face, stomach, and buttocks. He reports that this was due to Maria's frustration over homework. He reports that he was refusing visits because of this. He reports that the last time was 2 months ago when she hit him "over and over" up to 10 times. Rita says that her father told her to tell the evaluator that her mother hits both her and Peter. Rita says that her mother hit her on the cheek 4 days ago and made her bleed. Rita pointed to her cheek. (No visible injury or mark was noted.) She says that her mother did not hit her anywhere else. She also states that she has seen her mother hit Peter on his head and that his head was bleeding. Peter reports that he is not afraid of either parent and would turn to both of them for support.	Dr. Connoly reports that Maria is working on not yelling at the children. CPS verified the presence of adult conflict and the presence of moderate levels of emotional harm from the conflict by both parents towards the children. Allegations regarding Timothy sleeping naked with Rita were not substantiated. No collateral evidence confirms that Timothy drives dangerously with the children in the car. CPS reports that Peter is not rejecting his mother, has been staying with Maria, and says he does not fear her.	No abusive behavior was observed by the evaluator. The evaluator was informed by Peter that his dad had instructed him to say that his mother hit him. The evaluator did not see a mark on Rita's cheek where she said that her mother very recently hit her.

Table 5.2 Parenting Plan Evaluation Matrix I: Data for Maria, Timothy, and Family *(continued)*

Source of Concern	Maria's Evidence	Timothy's Evidence	Children's Evidence	Collateral Evidence	Evaluator's Evidence
Substance Abuse					
Timothy's Alcohol Use, Misuse, Abuse, Dependence					
Maria alleges that Timothy has a drinking problem.	Maria states that she has had long-term concerns regarding Timothy's drinking. She reports that he drinks 3 to 4 beers per day. She states that while drinking, Timothy becomes easily agitated, yells, and is physically aggressive. She reports that the children are fearful of their father when he is drinking.	Timothy refuses to elaborate on the historical criminal charges and describes them as "misunderstandings."	The children report no evidence regarding substance use.	Criminal records show that Timothy has had four drinking-related charges: two driving under the influence charges from 2 and 4 years ago. Two years ago, Timothy was convicted of a charge of public intoxication and another charge of disturbing the peace.	Timothy drank four beers during the home visit of 90 minutes. He appeared impaired to the evaluator.
Maria's Prescription Drug Use, Misuse, Abuse, Dependence					
Timothy alleges that Maria abuses Ritalin.	Maria denies having substance use issues and states that she takes her medication as prescribed. She states that she took Ritalin briefly a few years ago and stopped after 2 months.	Timothy reports that Maria takes Ritalin to keep up her performance at work. He reports that she becomes moody, irritable, and "snappy" towards the family. He reports that he overheard Maria contact the pharmacy 11 times in one night, yelling and swearing because they would not refill her prescription.	The children report no evidence regarding substance use.	Dr. Connoly reports that Maria appears to be taking her medication as prescribed. He reports that Maria was prescribed Ritalin for a few months several years ago and has not taken it since, to his knowledge. Pharmacy records do not show Ritalin use within the past 3 years.	Maria did not appear to be under the influence of any substance when in the presence of the evaluator.

Summary

- Organizing and analyzing data are among the most complicated activities for the evaluator, who faces hundreds of pages of information (notes, documents, test scores, emails, etc.).
- Following Tippins and Wittmann's (2005) model of levels of inference, the evaluator can sort his or her observations, make inferences about them, and form opinions from the inferences.
- This chapter presented a systematic method for assembling the observations and facts and for placing them into a Parenting Plan Evaluation Matrix—first for data only, and then in Chapter 6 for a summary, analysis, and synthesis of the evidence.

Annotated Bibliography

Ellis, E. M. (2000). *Rationale and Goals of the Custody Evaluation.* Washington, DC: American Psychological Association.

The author provides an overview of the theoretical and scientific basis for the custody evaluation—the goals, rationale, elements, and use of psychological tests. The author provides a discussion of some principles for organizing the data and reaching conclusions within the evaluation.

Gould, J. W., & Stahl, P. M. (2001). Never paint by the numbers: A response to Kelly and Lamb (2000), Solomon and Biringen (2001), and Lamb and Kelly (2001). *Family Court Review, 39*(4), 372-376.

The authors opine that a number of decision rules are needed in applying the guidelines for overnight visits and that there should not be one guideline created for all situations. They suggest that parenting plan evaluators must consider all factors relevant to the situation, including a history of caretaking, attachment history, parents' strengths and weaknesses, child temperament, parental communication, and caregiving by others.

Vertue, F. M. (2011). Applying case study methodology to child custody evaluations. *Family Court Review, 49*(2), 336-347.

The author proposes a scientifically based, integrative, methodological framework within which existing methods might be situated. In this article, the case study methodology is proposed as an appropriate methodological framework for PPEs. The application of this methodology is explicated with particular attention being paid to the methodological tasks of data collection and data interpretation. An orienting model is proposed to guide the collection of data, and strategies are described for applying population-level research findings to individual cases in the form of risk and resilience models. Finally, coherence, analogy, and making methodology explicit are proposed.

Chapter 6

Connections and Synthesis

In this chapter, there is a progression from the earlier data collection and organization to analysis and synthesis. Whereas analysis involves taking something apart, holding the pieces up to the light, and examining them, synthesis involves putting the pieces together to present the whole case and to provide an understanding of the family dynamics and of its functioning and needs, all eventually leading to appropriate recommendations.

Chapter 4 was about how to do data collection, and Chapter 5 was about the first phase of the analysis, which is to organize the facts and identify the issues. The next phase of data analysis, to be described in this chapter, involves summarizing the data and examining it for validity, creating inferences about those issues that are entered into the Parenting Plan Evaluation Matrix II: Analysis and Inferences. This is followed by further analysis and synthesis, involving the generation of themes to describe the data, which also will be described and shown in a third Parenting Plan Evaluation Matrix III: Themes, Analysis, Synthesis (Recommendations), and Accountability. The development of recommendations will be examined even further in Chapter 7.

Updating the Hypotheses and the Decision Tree

First, the evaluator looks at the information from the continuing evaluation process to amend the hypotheses. In Table 6.1, the hypotheses are organized according to the major topics of concern for this case: safety, child issues, and parent issues, and they are phrased as affirmative statements to be investigated, although the determination of whether the hypotheses are confirmed or not is yet to be done.

A new decision tree also is created with the updated data. This revised decision tree (see Figure 6.1) includes the data gathered and reported in the text in Chapter 5 and described in the Parenting Plan Evaluation Matrix I in Chapter 5. The factors that appear to be relevant in this case are now clustered and visible in one diagram.

Parenting Plan Evaluation Matrix: Summary, Analysis, and Synthesis

Once the collected data are entered into the Parenting Plan Evaluation Matrix, the evaluator turns to a separate process: the summary, analysis, and synthesis of the data. A chart that assists in that is found in Table 6.2, and a blank one for use by evaluators in their practices is found in Appendix E at the end of this book.

Table 6.1 Hypotheses for the Case of Timothy and Maria and Family

Topic of Concern	Hypothesis Number	Hypothesis
Safety		
IPV? Child abuse? Neglect? Substance use?	S-1	Timothy has problems with anger management and aggression, leading him to be verbally abusive and controlling with Peter and physically and verbally abusive with Maria.
	S-2	Timothy has a problem with alcohol abuse or dependence.
	S-3	Maria has a problem with prescription medication abuse or dependence.
	S-4	Maria's Physical discipline of Peter is abusive
Child		
Child's perspective? Ages & stages? Adjustment and resiliency? Relationship history?	C-1	The younger girls are reacting to separation from their mother as an attachment figure.
	C-2	The younger girls are afraid of their father.
	C-3	Peter's anxiety is related to the parental conflict and/or Maria's abuse.
Parent		
Mental health? Personal history? Parent-child relationship? Parent-parent relationship?	P-1	One or both parents is fabricating allegations for the litigation: Maria about IPV and Timothy about the abuse of Ritalin.
	P-2	Maria has mental health problems leading her to be verbally and physically abusive with Peter and to be enmeshed with Ruth and Sarah.
	P-3	Maria's depression is the result of her experience of domestic violence.
	P-4	One or both parents is engaged in restrictive gate-keeping: Timothy with Peter and Maria with Rita and Sarah.

The new matrix could be conceptualized as a continuation of the first one. It is important, though, to keep them separate. As we said in Chapter 5, a significant and unfortunately common problem in PPEs occurs when the data is confused with the evaluator's inferences and opinions. Putting data in the first matrix and then putting a summary in the second matrix is a good start to resolving this problem; an analysis and synthesis will follow in the second matrix.

In the left column, the evaluator lists the issues in the case as they were listed in the first matrix (found in Table 5.2: Intimate partner violence or domestic violence, child abuse/maltreatment and/or neglect, and substance abuse). To the right, in columns, are the following: Summary of the evidence, analysis of evidence (reliability and validity), and synthesis of evidence (inferences).

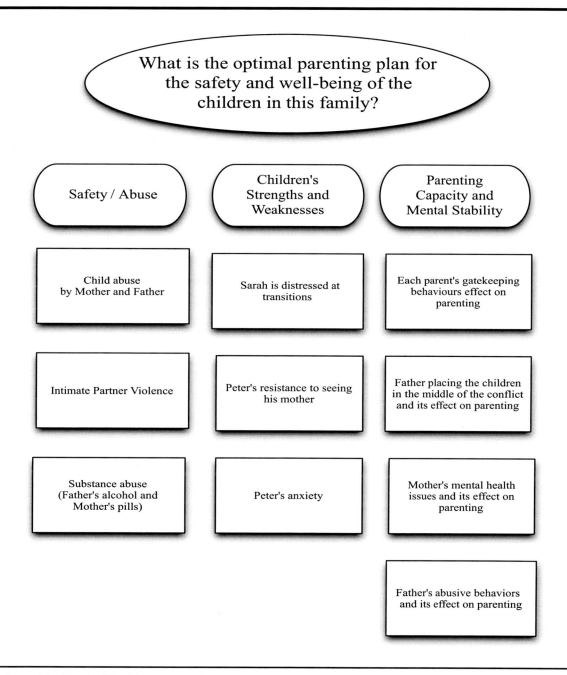

Figure 6.1 A Revised Decision Tree Provides the Factors to Be Considered Once the Decision Tree Has Been Modified

Using the data from the Matrix-Phase 1, the authors will summarize the evidence for the three issues that were chosen as examples, describe the reliability and validity of evidence about those issues, and finally outline the Level II inferences (synthesis) that arise from the summaries and the assessments of evidence. These inferences will be entered in the Evaluation Matrix II: Analysis and Synthesis. In this demonstration, this second matrix could be considered a logical continuation of the first, with movement into Level II inferences as the evidence is summarized and evaluated and as inferences are formed and formulated into opinions.

Table 6.2 Parenting Plan Evaluation Matrix II: Summary, Analysis, and Synthesis

Source of Concern	Summary of Evidence	Analysis of Evidence: Reliability & Validity	Synthesis of Evidence: Inferences
Intimate Partner Violence or Domestic Violence			
Child Abuse/Maltreatment and/or Neglect			
Substance Abuse			
Mental Health			
Children's Adjustment			
Children's Preferences			
Parenting Competency			
Coparenting Capacity			
Relocation			
Other Issues			

The Parenting Plan Evaluation Matrix for Maria, Timothy, and Family: Summary, Analysis, and Synthesis

In the previous chapter, the current case was described in the Parenting Plan Evaluation Matrix I: Data. The data from that matrix is now summarized, analyzed, and synthesized (see Table 6.3) for the three issues (IPV or domestic violence, child abuse/maltreatment and/or neglect, and substance abuse) described in the first data matrix. Again, these three issues do not exhaust the issues in the case as a whole, but they are the demonstration variables that the authors are using. There are other relevant issues not shown in the example here, including mental health, child's adjustment, child's preferences, parenting competency, co-parenting capacity, relocation, high levels of parental conflict, and gatekeeping. A sample of some of the Level I data is found in Table 5.2.

Intimate Partner Violence or Domestic Violence

The first issue considered was IPV, for which we have the following summary, assessment of reliability and validity (analysis), and inferences (synthesis).

- *Summary of the evidence:* Maria alleges significant domestic violence against Timothy, and she had reported these concerns to her psychiatrist in an ongoing way. Maria also alleges that Timothy is verbally aggressive towards Peter. Timothy denies abusing Maria or the children. There are extended family members who support each parent's view. Peter reports extensive yelling and mutual hitting and pushing. There are a number of reports by the police where they came out to the parents' homes, and there was one arrest with a conviction for disturbing the peace.

- *Reliability and validity:* There are accusations of IPV from both sides, but there were criminal charges filed against Timothy, not Maria. The police reports are reliable as independent sources, but they are somewhat limited in the information that they contain. The evidence from the grandfathers is of dubious reliability and validity due to their alliances with their respective adult children. Peter's evidence is somewhat reliable as there was no apparent coaching from his parents on this subject. Reliability and validity are related to the weight that one might want to give to the evidence. The question becomes how much meaning will this piece of evidence bring to the overall understanding of the issues in the family? For this first area of concern, the most weight is given to the police reports, with less weight given to the other collaterals as they all have investments in one parent or the other.

- *Level II inferences for intimate partner (or domestic) violence:* Based on Maria's report, Timothy's psychological test findings, and some of the collaterals' statements, Timothy appears to have problems with anger management and occasionally with outbursts that have the potential for violence. It appears that there may be a pattern of coercive control, given that Timothy has attempted to control the children and to harass Maria with false allegations of drug abuse. The implications of these findings about the first concern and the integration with other conclusions will be discussed later in this chapter.

Child Abuse/Maltreatment and/or Neglect

The second concern was about child abuse, with allegations against both parents.

- *Summary of evidence:* The evidence can be summarized briefly. Both parents allege that the other is abusing the children. Peter states that his mother hits him repeatedly, but he also says that he likes to be with both of his parents. He reports that his father had apparently instructed the two older children to say that their mother hit them. Rita reports some concerns about her mother but not her father. CPS did not substantiate any of the allegations except for the presence of adult conflict. The mother acknowledges that she used physical discipline with Peter and that she "yells and screams" too much.

- *Reliability and validity:* The reliability and validity of the evidence collected is marginal. CPS did not substantiate the allegations and the evaluator did not observe a mark consistent with Rita's story about her mother hitting her. The validity of Peter's evidence for child abuse is weak based on both of the older children's reports that their father had coached them. Maria admits using physical discipline, consistent with Peter's apparently spontaneous comments. Dr. Connoly says that Maria is trying to stop yelling at the children, suggesting an apparent problem with verbal abuse. The weight of the evidence about physical abuse is equivocal. Evidence from CPS and from Dr. Connoly have the most weight because they are independent. The evaluator's observations have some weight as independent and neutral. The children's reports of abuse are given some weight but not a great deal because of the degree to which those reports appear to have been directed by Timothy. Maria's evidence, because it is against her own interests, is given considerable weight.

- *Level II inferences for child abuse:* Maria has been harsh in her punishment of Peter. She is mildly to moderately depressed (from other data not included in the four issues in this matrix). There is no evidence that Timothy is abusing his children physically, and the major emotional abuse appears to be in his involving the children in the divorce disputes. There is some evidence that he may be undermining Peter's relationship with his mother and may be encouraging Peter to be aggressive at school, which are elements of poor parenting.

Substance Abuse

The third area of concern was substance abuse, with allegations against both parents. These will be handled separately to keep them clear. Maria's allegation that Timothy drinks heavily on a daily basis will be explored first.

- *Summary of the evidence:* The summary of the evidence includes that there were allegations by Maria, a history of alcohol-related criminal offenses, and the direct observation of drinking by the evaluator.
- *Reliability and validity:* In terms of the reliability of the evidence, one could worry about the reliability and validity of Maria's evidence, but her allegations are supported by independent evidence from the criminal record, and Timothy's behavior of minimizing the four events as "misunderstandings" is consistent with possible alcoholic denial of a substance abuse problem. The evaluator's observation of drinking four beers during the home visit is also considered highly valid and reliable. The weight of the evidence is on the independent criminal records, the evaluator's own observation, and Maria's account to the extent that it is supported by the independent evidence.
- *Level II inferences for Timothy's substance abuse:* It is highly likely that Timothy abuses alcohol. It is not clear from these data whether his alcohol abuse interferes substantially with his parenting.

Timothy's allegation that Maria abuses prescription medications will be explored next.

- *Summary of the evidence:* The summary of the evidence is that the only evidence regarding Maria's alleged substance abuse comes from Timothy's reports.
- *Reliability and validity:* The weight given to Timothy's evidence is low in the absence of supporting evidence. The weight given to Maria's evidence is high because it is supported by the pharmacy records and by her psychiatrist's statements.
- *Level II inferences for Maria's substance abuse:* The conclusion is that Maria does not appear to be misusing prescription drugs and that Timothy appears to have created a false accusation against Maria.

The summaries, determination of reliability and validity, and inferences are entered onto the chart, shown in Table 6.3.

Creating Understandings That Integrate the Facts and Conclusions and Can Lead to the Creation of Parenting Plans

Themes represent the points at which several areas of concern converge. They may contribute additional force to a problem area, they may complicate the understanding of or the potential interventions for the problem, or they may provide some mitigation. A common interaction, for example, is between reciprocal allegations of gatekeeping and of child abuse where there is an identified problem of a child-parent relationship disruption that has several sources. Mental health issues (in parents or in children) can introduce a third source of complexity to that same theme, as can substance abuse or IPV. The evaluator is charged with the task of describing the factors that contribute to or complicate the problems that have been identified in the

Table 6.3 Parenting Plan Evaluation Matrix II: Summary, Analysis, and Synthesis - Case of Maria, Timothy, and Family

Source of Concern	Summary of Evidence	Analysis of Evidence: Reliability and Validity	Synthesis of Evidence: Inferences
Intimate Partner Violence or Domestic Violence			
Concerns that Timothy has been controlling and Violent toward Maria.	Maria alleges significant domestic violence against Timothy, and she had reported these concerns to her psychiatrist in an ongoing way. Maria also alleges that Timothy is verbally aggressive towards Peter. Timothy denies abusing Maria or the children. There are extended family members who support each parent's view. Peter reports extensive yelling and mutual hitting and pushing. There are a number of reports by the police where they came out to the parents' homes, and there was one arrest with a conviction for disturbing the peace.	There are reports of IPV from both sides, but there were criminal charges filed against Timothy, not Maria. The police reports are reliable as independent sources, but they are somewhat limited in the information that they contain. The evidence from the grandfathers is of dubious reliability and validity due to their alliances with their respective adult children. Peter's evidence is somewhat reliable as there was no apparent coaching from his parents on this subject. Reliability and validity are related to the weight that one might want to give to the evidence. The question becomes how much meaning will this piece of evidence bring to the overall understanding of the issues in the family? For this first area of concern, the most weight is given to the police reports, with less weight given to the other collaterals as they all have investments in one parent or the other.	Timothy appears to have problems with anger management and occasionally with outbursts that have the potential for violence. This inference is based on Maria's report, his psychological test findings, and some of the collaterals' statements. It appears that there may be a pattern of coercive control, given that he has attempted to control the children and to harass Maria with false allegations of drug abuse.

Table 6.3 Parenting Plan Evaluation Matrix II: Summary, Analysis, and Synthesis - Case of Maria, Timothy, and Family *(continued)*

Source of Concern	Summary of Evidence	Analysis of Evidence: Reliability and Validity	Synthesis of Evidence: Inferences
Child Abuse/Maltreatment and/or Neglect			
Concerns that both parents have been abusive toward the children.	The evidence can be summarized briefly. Both parents allege that the other is abusing the children. Peter states that his mother hits him repeatedly, but he also says that he likes to be with both of his parents. He reports that his father apparently instructed the two older children to say that their mother hits them. Rita reports some concerns about her mother but not her father. CPS did not substantiate any of the allegations except for the presence of adult conflict. The mother acknowledges that she used physical discipline with Peter and that she "yells and screams" too much.	The reliability and validity of the evidence collected is marginal. CPS did not substantiate the allegations, the evaluator did not observe a mark consistent with Rita's story about her mother hitting her, and the validity of Peter's evidence is weak based on both of the older children's reports that their father had coached them. Maria admits using physical discipline, consistent with Peter's apparently spontaneous comments. Dr. Connoly says that Maria is trying to stop yelling at the children, suggesting an apparent problem with verbal abuse. The weight of the evidence about physical abuse is equivocal. Evidence from CPS and from Dr. Connoly have the most weight because they are independent. The evaluator's observations are independent and neutral. The children's reports of abuse are given some weight but not a great deal because of the degree to which those reports appear to have been directed by Timothy. Maria's evidence, because it is against her own interest, is given considerable weight.	Maria has been harsh in her punishment of Peter. She is mildly to moderately depressed (from other data not included in this shortened matrix). Peter is somewhat estranged from his mother, and the poor relationship between them may be exacerbating Maria's depression, which is also impairing her ability to discipline her son appropriately. There is no evidence that Timothy is abusing his children physically, and the major emotional abuse appears to be in his involving the children in the divorce disputes. There is some evidence that he may be undermining Peter's relationship with his mother and may be encouraging Peter to be aggressive at school, which are elements of poor parenting.

Table 6.3 Parenting Plan Evaluation Matrix II: Summary, Analysis, and Synthesis - Case of Maria, Timothy, and Family *(continued)*

Source of Concern	Summary of Evidence	Analysis of Evidence: Reliability and Validity	Synthesis of Evidence: Inferences
Substance Abuse			
Concerns that Timothy is abusing alcohol.	The summary of the evidence includes that there were allegations by Maria, a history of alcohol-related criminal offenses, and the direct observation of drinking by the evaluator.	In terms of the reliability of the evidence, one could worry about the reliability and validity of Maria's evidence, but her allegations are supported by independent evidence from the criminal record, and Timothy's behavior of minimizing the three events as "misunderstandings" is consistent with possible alcoholic denial of a substance abuse problem. The evaluator's observation of drinking four beers is also considered highly valid and reliable. The weight of the evidence is on the independent criminal records, the evaluator's own observation, and Maria's account to the extent that the independent evidence supports it.	It is highly likely that Timothy abuses alcohol. It is not clear from these data whether his alcohol abuse interferes substantially with his parenting.
Concerns that Maria is abusing prescription medications.	The summary of the evidence is that the only evidence regarding Maria's alleged substance abuse comes from Timothy's reports.	The weight given to Timothy's evidence is low in the absence of supporting evidence. The weight given to Maria's evidence is high because the pharmacy records and her psychiatrist's statements support it.	The conclusion is that Maria does not appear to be misusing prescription drugs and that Timothy appears to have created a false accusation against Maria, perhaps to counter her allegations about his alcohol abuse or to gain an advantage in the litigation.

case. Wherever possible, the evaluator should identify the causal relationships and the sequential order in which interventions should occur if they are known.

The evaluator turns to filling in the third matrix, the Parenting Plan Evaluation Matrix III: Themes, Additive/Synergistic/Antagonistic, Parenting Plans and Accountability. This matrix contains Levels II, III, and IV inferences. From left to right, there are themes (Level II Inference: Analysis), a place to analyze whether the issues are additive, synergistic, or antagonistic (Level III Inference: Analysis), and parenting plan implications (Level IV Inference: Synthesis). That is followed up by a column for information about how to keep the parties accountable for follow-through in interventions on any given issue.

Themes

Safety Issues

Within the safety cluster of issues, a theme emerged relating to Timothy's difficulties: He has an alcohol abuse problem and a problem with anger, sometimes leading to violence. These two problems are likely to be synergistic, based on research that suggests that substance abuse is sometimes a factor in increasing the risks of domestic violence. It is also possible that both the drinking and the violence are associated with a third factor that is not known at this point, for example, problems with his attachment relationships.

There is also a theme relating to Maria's difficulties within the safety cluster: She has been harsh in her punishment of Peter and has been losing her temper and yelling at the children. While the mental health concerns were not included in this chart, her depression is likely to be implicated in her abusive discipline of Peter. Research has suggested that maternal depression is often associated with problems in parenting and with insecurity and anxiety in children. There is another potential factor that may have a bearing on Maria's parenting problems, arising from her experiences as a victim of domestic violence, which has been associated in the research with disruptions in parenting.

Child Issues

The next category is child issues. Peter has been anxious since he was quite young, and his symptoms have been attributed to the level of conflict in the home. His father's alcohol abuse, anger, and violence, and his mother's harsh punishment are likely to be contributory factors in his anxiety. Rita and Sarah are somewhat frightened by their father, and Sarah clings to her mother at transitions. Sarah is likely to be re-acting to anxiety about separation from her mother as her attachment figure and both girls may be reacting to their mother's depression and/or fear of her father's anger and behavior when drinking, although the girls

Table 6.4 Parenting Plan Evaluation Matrix III:
Themes, Analysis, Synthesis (Recommendations), and Accountability

Themes (Level II Inferences: Analysis)	Additive? Synergistic? Antagonistic? Direction? (Level III Inferences: Analysis)	Parenting Plan Implications and Recommendations (Level IV Inferences: Synthesis)	Accountability
Safety			
Child Issues			
Parent Issues			

would not be likely to identify alcohol use itself at their ages. Rita may be afraid of her father, and/or she may be fearful of leaving her mother's proximity.

Parent Issues

The last category to be examined among those in this demonstration is parent issues. Maria is mildly to moderately depressed, and Peter has been estranged from her probably because she loses her temper with him and because his father appears to undermine the mother-son relationship. It is likely that her depression contributes to her irritability and difficulty controlling her temper. Her poor relationship with Peter probably contributes to her depression. She may be clinging to the younger girls for comfort for herself.

Timothy has been very negative about Maria and her parenting and has made false allegations, possibly out of a wish to deflect attention from his own alcohol use or out of anger at Maria and a wish for revenge.

As the Issues Interact, Are They Additive, Synergistic, Antagonistic?

In the next space, for each theme, the evaluator can enter his opinion about whether the issues within the theme are additive, synergistic, or antagonistic.

What Are the Parenting Plan Implications or Recommendations?

Finally, for each theme there is a space to describe the parenting plan implications of the findings about that theme, recommendations for parenting access, and interventions to improve family functioning. These will be discussed in more detail in Chapter 7.

How Is Accountability Maintained?

In the last column to the right, there is space to describe a means to establish accountability for follow-through with the parenting plan.

To demonstrate the process, the table has been filled out for the first three themes that have been used as an illustration (Table 6.5). Clearly in a real case, there would be many other issues and themes to consider in the final analysis and in Chapter 7, a complete matrix is presented.

Again, though, for the purposes of simplicity and illustration, the authors have chosen a few themes.

Table 6.5 Parenting Plan Evaluation Matrix III: Case of Maria, Timothy, and Family

Themes (Level II Inferences: Analysis)	Additive? Synergistic? Antagonistic? Direction? (Level III Inferences: Analysis)	Parenting Plan Implications and Recommendations (Level IV Inferences: Synthesis)	Accountability
Safety			
Lack of safety. Timothy S-1. Timothy has a problem with anger and is sometimes violent. S-2. Timothy has a problem with alcohol abuse or dependence.	These factors are likely to be synergistic, with each potentially exacerbating the other. There is no clear causal direction.	Timothy and Maria should have no face-to-face exchanges. He should attend anger management treatment, concurrent with treatment for alcohol abuse and individual counseling. Overnights should be added with younger girls after 90 days if he is sober, committed, and visits have gone well.	There should be a mechanism by which the records of Timothy's attendance at 12-step meetings, at anger management, and at counseling can be collected and provided to someone in authority (minor's counsel, parenting coordinator, court personnel).
Lack of safety, Maria S-3. Maria has no problem with abuse of presription medications.		No intervention necessary.	
S-4. Maria's physical discipline of Peter is abusive.	These factors are synergistic with other concerns not in this chart, such as depression. Possibly also associated with history of domestic violence and Timothy's efforts to undermine her authority.	Maria should attend a parent education program with emphasis on appropriate discipline for preteens. She should continue treatment for her depression.	There should be a mechanism by which records of Maria's attendance at parent education and at her psychiatrist can be collected and provided to someone in authority.

Table 6.5 Parenting Plan Evaluation Matrix III: Case of Maria, Timothy, and Family *(continued)*

Themes (Level II Inferences: Analysis)	Additive? Synergistic? Antagonistic? Direction? (Level III Inferences: Analysis)	Parenting Plan Implications and Recommendations (Level IV Inferences: Synthesis)	Accountability
Child Issues			
C-1. Both girls resist leaving their mother and are likely reacting to the threatened loss of their mother as an attachment figure.	Maria's depression may contribute to their insecurity.	Maria should be given advice about helping support both girls' ability to separate from her appropriately for their respective ages. Maria should continue treatment for depression.	Both parents should be responsible for helping the girls make the transition from mother to father when it is scheduled.
C-2. Both girls are afraid of their father. Their anxiety is likely to be related to their father's anger and also possibly to his alcohol abuse as well as to their mother's anxiety about their safety.	The girls may also be frightened by their father's use of alcohol and by their having witnessed domestic violence. Their mother's anxiety about their safety with their father may be contributing to their fearfulness.	To help the girls' anxiety and Maria's, Timothy needs to improve his self-control. The interventions for Timothy should be in effect for 90 days before any attempt is made to start overnights with him. Maria needs to be helped to distinguish her realistic fears from her unrealistic fears as Timothy becomes sober and peaceful.	There is accountability for Timothy's sobriety and anger management attendance in the factors listed above.
C-3. Peter is anxious and sometimes resists going to his mother's home. His anxiety is likely to be related to the parental high conflict as well as to his mother's harsh punishments.	Peter's anxiety may be worsened by separation from his mother and sisters and by exposure to his father's anger.	After his mother is engaged in her parenting course, Peter should resume spending substantial time at her home. He and both of his parents should begin family therapy to repair the relationship between mother and son if that is necessary to ensure the contact. Peter should resume individual treatment for his anxiety.	Both parents should be responsible for keeping Peter away from the conflict and for his regular time spent with his mother. Records of his compliance with visits to his mother should be kept and provided to someone in authority.

Table 6.5 Parenting Plan Evaluation Matrix III: Case of Maria, Timothy, and Family *(continued)*

Themes (Level II Inferences: Analysis)	Additive? Synergistic? Antagonistic? Direction? (Level III Inferences: Analysis)	Parenting Plan Implications and Recommendations (Level IV Inferences: Synthesis)	Accountability
Parent Issues			
P-1. Evidence supports the fact that Timothy has been angry, sometimes violent, and controlling. Evidence does not support the contention that Maria is abusing prescription medication (Ritalin). It appears that Timothy is trying to make Maria look bad, perhaps for a litigation advantage.	Timothy may have made the allegation about Ritalin to deflect attention from his own alcohol use or to get even with Maria for leaving him by taking the children away from her.	Timothy's individual counseling as recommended above should also be directed toward helping him to improve his ability to coparent. The court will need to order him to support Maria's custodial time with Peter. Given his apparent willingness to lie about Maria, his future allegations should be carefully scrutinized.	Records of attendance and engagement in coparent counseling should be collected as well as records of Peter's compliance with timeshare orders and provided to someone in authority.
P-2. Maria has been mildly to moderately depressed, and it is likely that her depression contributes to her irritability and poor self-control of her anger.	It is possible that Maria keeps the younger girls with her for her own comfort and because she identifies with their difficulty going with their father and away from her.	Her depression is not serious enough to warrant changes in the timeshare. Maria needs to continue with her therapy with some focus on learning better self-soothing techniques and possibly on medications with her psychiatrist. She needs to work with the parent education program and the coparent counselor as described above.	Maria's attendance at her therapy and at coparenting counseling should be recorded and provided to someone in authority.
P-3. It is not likely that Maria's depression is primarily the result of the IPV because it has been very longstanding.	Maria's depression may have been worsened by the IPV with the accompanying feelings of helplessness and/or by the poor relationship with Peter.	No interventions are necessary other than those already put in place for her continuing psychiatric treatment and for working to improve her relationship with Peter.	Accountability is described above.

The Interactional Nature of the Analysis

One of the characteristics shared by families and PPEs that is emphasized in this book is complexity—the fact that different factors interact with one another to amplify or diminish or alter one another. Those interactions must also be described and understood. In keeping with the theme of making the processes of thinking concrete and visual, in this chapter the reader will find examples of ways to describe interactions between factors and then examples from the case example.

It has been the point of this book to provide methods for organizing and analyzing and synthesizing the facts that are the basic level of the PPE. But it is also the authors' intention to provide some guidance about ways to analyze and represent to the parents, their attorneys, and the court the complex interactions of these factors.

One can write linear descriptions, such as "Mother's major depression increases the risk of her irritability in her reactions to the father and increases the risk of neglect of her young children, while those risks are diminished by her compliance with her treatment program and by the close relationship she has with her psychiatrist."

One can also draw diagrams, like Venn diagrams, showing each issue or factor in a circle, in a stylized way as independent (not touching other circles), completely identical with one another (almost completely overlapping), or as interacting with one another but having aspects of independent effect on the family. An example of such a diagram is in Appendix G.

An example of the former situation might be a child's particular talent at music or sports and a parent's problems with substance abuse. One could imagine a situation in which these two realities have little impact on one another, but in another situation, the parent's substance abuse problem might lead to the child missing lessons or sports practice or games so there would be some overlap.

An example of the second situation could be a child's enmeshment with a parent and the parent's major mental illness, leading the parent to depend entirely on the child for continued feelings of well-being and the child to depend entirely on the parent for feelings of security. Those two facts might well be so closely entangled that it is difficult or impossible to separate the issues and to look at them individually.

An example of the third situation might be a child's anxiety and depression and difficulty trusting anyone in or out of the family when there has been a history of family violence. There may be ways in which the child's anxiety and depression might be the result of many things, from the divorce or exposure to domestic violence. But there is likely to be some area in which the circles would overlap, where the exposure to violence exacerbates the child's emotional problems; perhaps the child's emotional problems make it more difficult for the violent parent to respond more appropriately to the child, and the mistrust keeps the child from turning to the nonviolent parent for help.

The point of working to visualize the interactions and dynamics of the factors is that the individual issues in a family are not unitary. They are not isolated. They are rarely all-or-nothing. The grids that we have drawn could and probably should be visualized as three dimensional, with interactional arrows going in many directions. As we can think in these complex ways, we will improve out abilities to help the overwhelmed families that we are seeing and evaluating.

We can begin to visualize a system somewhat as one learns to play three-dimensional games of tic-tac-toe or checkers. In three-dimensional checkers, each square has interactions not only with those squares that abut the four sides, but also with squares that are above and below. If we can picture such a game board in three dimensions, we can imagine a child on one square who is affected by his parent's separation, by his own learning differences and need for special help, by the school's inability to provide appropriate resource help, by his father's wish that he be perfect and have no problems, by his father's blame of the mother for the boy having school problems, by the mother's overly helpful support that undermines the boy's wish for mastery and independence, and by the mother's blame of the father and of the school for not understanding her "special" son. The father's distrust of the mother may affect the father by making him more impatient with his son's slowness in learning. The mother's distrust of the father may make her more inclined to coddle the boy and "let him off the hook" for doing his homework. In a case like this, each parent may believe that he or she knows what is best for the boy, and each parent is certain that he or she should be the primary parent to provide what the boy needs. But things are not so simple as the parents may wish. One can add in factors such as the boy's peer relationships in the current school, his interest in and talent for sports, and the location of the teams that will be the best fit for him. There may be financial problems in the parents' lives that will complicate school choice or the future residential options for each parent. There may be stepparents and stepsiblings with whom he has relationships of greater or lesser success. Now the three-dimensional checkerboard is full of factors that impact the boy and that he impacts in turn.

The evaluator's report is going to be linear because it is a written document, and few evaluators will be able to draw effective visual presentations of their findings in the case. But it may be possible for one to form the image of the factors that are operative, to define those factors in one's own mind as clearly as possible, and to convey to the court as much of the complex web of factors as one can. Then the evaluator can describe recommendations that take the greatest number of the most relevant factors into account, according to the priority that he assigns the identified factors. The parents or the court can look independently at the identified factors and at the priorities assigned by the evaluator.

In the hypothetical case described just above, the most relevant factors may be the school's inability to help the boy, the father's inability to recognize that the boy needs support and help, and the mother's overly helpful, intrusive support, plus the boy's talent for sports that provides a strong identity and self-esteem. These factors may, together, point to a residential schedule that maximizes the opportunities for the child to feel valued and successful and to interventions that can assist both parents in providing both more support and more demands.

Summary

- This chapter provides the structure of the proposed system for an evaluator to use to sort the factors that will inform his opinions and recommendations.
- The steps include clustering the issues into themes, organizing them into a new and probably final decision tree, and forming an opinion about the list of hypotheses.
- From those themes, a chart was proposed for explicitly laying out the conclusions about the connections between issues and the implications for the parenting plan and any interventions that might be recommended.

Chapter 7

Finishing the Synthesis, Making Parenting Plan Recommendations

Parenting Plan Recommendations for Maria, Timothy, and Family

In the last chapters, the case study of Timothy and Maria was described using the matrices for Levels II, III, and IV. In this chapter, the matrices will be completed for the relevant concerns for the family. After the case example, we will outline some general principles about report writing, parenting plans, and interventions that are often needed and useful in PPEs.

Summary of Factors Not Considered to Date

In prior chapters, for the current example, we have used three issues to demonstrate how to make multiple hypotheses and how to use the evaluation matrices. Thinking about these issues generated a number of questions that helped to guide our analysis and synthesis of the pertinent issues. We had selected three factors to highlight and to show as examples of how evaluators should plan, organize, analyze, and synthesize the data. But other factors that have not been considered in our examples also contribute important information when considering the overall parenting plan recommendations for this family, and they are included at this point in the final series of charts, as we describe the recommendations. The additional factors not yet written into the matrices for Timothy, Maria, and their children include:

- the concerns regarding the parents' inability to protect the children from violence and abuse (parental fitness concerns such as domestic violence, substance abuse, or mental health problems);
- the age and development of each of the three children;
- the children's relationship with both parents and the potential factors that may have created a strain in these relationships (Austin, 2011);
- the special needs of the children; and
- the lack of communication between the parents and the longstanding inability to cooperate free from violence and abuse.

The complete set of hypotheses for the family is shown in Table 7.1.

Table 7.1 Complete Hypotheses for the Case of Timothy and Maria and Family

Topic of Concern	Hypothesis Number	Hypothesis
Safety		
IPV? Child abuse? Neglect? Substance use?	S-1	Timothy has problems with anger management and aggression, leading him to be verbally abusive and controlling with Peter and physically and verbally abusive with Maria.
	S-2	Timothy has a problem with alcohol abuse or dependence.
	S-3	Maria has a problem with prescription medication abuse or dependence.
	S-4	Maria's Physical discipline of Peter is abusive
Child		
Child's perspective? Ages & stages?	C-1	The younger girls, Rita and Sarah, are reacting to separation from their mother as an attachment figure.
Adjustment and resiliency?	C-2	The younger girls are afraid of their father.
Relationship history?	C-3	Peter's anxiety is related to the parental conflict and/or Maria's abuse.
Parent		
Mental health? Personal history? Parent-child relationship?	P-1	One or both parents is fabricating allegations for the litigation: Maria about IPV and Timothy about the abuse of Ritalin.
Parent-parent relationship?	P-2	Maria has mental health problems leading her to be verbally and physically abusive with Peter and to be enmeshed with Rita and Sarah.
	P-3	Maria's depression is the result of her experience of domestic violence.
	P-4	One or both parents is engaged in restrictive gate-keeping: Timothy with Peter and Maria with Rita and Sarah.
Children's Adjustment		
	CA-1	Peter's anxiety is due to witnessing his father's violence against his mother.
	CA-2	Peter's anxiety is due to his exposure to his parents' conflicts.
	CA-3	Rita is afraid of her father due to his violence and alcoholism.
Children's Preferences		
	CP-1	Peter wants to live with his father.
	CP-2	Rita wants to live with her mother and visit her father.
Parenting Competency		
	PC-1	Timothy is not competent in day-to-day parenting.
	PC-2	Timothy's coercive control and domestic violence make him a poor parent.
	PC-3	Maria is abusive and angry as a parent.
Coparenting Capacity		
	CpC-1	Both parents are engaged in high-conflict behavior.
	CpC-2	Timothy is generating most of the conflict and communication problems.
	CpC-3	Maria is generating most of the conflict and communication problems.

Table 7.1 Complete Hypotheses for the Case of Timothy and Maria and Family *(continued)*

Topic of Concern	Hypothesis Number	Hypothesis
Gatekeeping		
	G-1	Timothy is restricting Peter's access to time with his mother.
	G-2	Timothy is restricting Peter's access to his mother to protect him from child abuse.
	G-3	Maria is restricting Rita and Sarah's access to time with their father.
	G-4	Maria is restricting the girls' access to their father to protect them from danger from Timothy's alcohol abuse and/or his anger.

Parenting Plan Recommendations for Maria, Timothy, and Family

Early in this book, we emphasized the importance of having a court order that clearly identifies the scope of the evaluation task and the specific questions to be investigated. It is important to review the questions posed in the court order to ensure that each question has been investigated. It is also important not to exceed the scope of the order, an instruction that is emphasized in the 2006 California Supreme Court decision *in re Marriage of Seagondollar*. That is, do not investigate questions that were not identified in the court order as the focus of the evaluation (AFCC Model Standard 12.5; AFCC, 2006). After all of the data are gathered and analyzed, the evaluator should revisit the list of questions in the order that were presented in Chapter 4.

Table 7.2 Referral Questions From Attorneys for the Case of Timothy, Maria, and Children

- What is the best parenting plan for Peter, Rita and Sarah?
- What are each parent's strengths and weaknesses in terms of their parenting of their three children?
- To what degree, if any, has either parent engaged in any kind of abuse, whether that is IPV, substance abuse, and/or child abuse?
- If any abuse has been or is present, what is the nature of the effects of the abuse on the children?
- What is the nature of each parent-child relationship as well as the nature of the parent-parent relationship?
- To what extent does each parent support and/or interfere with the children's relationships with the other parent?

The hypotheses in Table 7.1 correspond to these referral questions in Table 7.2, and the data gathered in the evaluation help to answer the specific referral questions. The recommendations offered are tied to them as well. Before looking specifically at recommendations, we can show the Level II and III inferences and opinions for all the factors and hypotheses. These inferences are in Table 7.3. As the reader can see, the first factors in the list are those that were presented earlier, followed by those that were not written into a full PPE data matrix because of space concerns.

For this family, we can see from the themes identified and outlined in the matrices that there will be very specific recommendations. The Parenting Plan Evaluation Matrix III (Table 7.4) which was presented first in Chapter 6, shows the reasoning leading to the recommendations. As indicated the evaluator will consider the strength of the evidence and organize parenting access plans and interventions for those issues

Table 7.3 Parenting Plan Evaluation Matrix II: Summary, Analysis, and Synthesis - Case of Maria, Timothy, and Family

Source of Concern	Summary of Evidence	Analysis of Evidence: Reliability and Validity	Synthesis of Evidence: Inferences
Intimate Partner Violence or Domestic Violence			
Concerns that Timothy has been controlling and Violent toward Maria.	Maria alleges significant domestic violence against Timothy, and she had reported these concerns to her psychiatrist in an ongoing way. Maria also alleges that Timothy is verbally aggressive towards Peter. Timothy denies abusing Maria or the children. There are extended family members who support each parent's view. Peter reports extensive yelling and mutual hitting and pushing. There are a number of reports by the police where they came out to the parents' homes, and there was one arrest with a conviction for disturbing the peace.	There are reports of IPV from both sides, but there were driminal charges filed against Timothy, not Maria. The police reports are reliable as independent sources, but they are somewhat limited in the information that they contain. The evidence from the grandfathers is of dubious reliability and validity due to their alliances with their respective adult children. Peter's evidence is somewhat reliable as there was no apparent coaching from his parents on this subject. Reliability and validity are related to the weight tht one might want to give to the evidence. The question becomes how much meaning will this piece of evidence bring to the overall understanding of the issues in the family? For this first area of concern, the most weight is given to the police reports, with less weight given to the other collaterals as they all have investments in one parent or the other.	Timothy appears to have probolems with anger management and opccasionally with outbursts that have the potential for violence. This inference is based on Maria's report, his psychological test findings, and some of the collaterals' statements. It appears that there may be a pattern of coercive control, given that he has attempted to control the children and to harass Maria with false allegations of drug abuse.

Table 7.3 Parenting Plan Evaluation Matrix II: Summary, Analysis, and Synthesis - Case of Maria, Timothy, and Family *(continued)*

Source of Concern	Summary of Evidence	Analysis of Evidence: Reliability and Validity	Synthesis of Evidence: Inferences
Child Abuse/Maltreatment and/or Neglect			
Concerns that both parents have been abusive toward the children.	The evidence can be summarized briefly. Both parents allege that the other is abusing the children. Peter states that his mother hits him repeatedly, but he also says that he likes to be with both of his parents. He reports that his father apparently instructed the two older children to say that their mother hits them. Rita reports some concerns about her mother but not her father. CPS did not substantiate any of the allegations except for the presence of adult conflict. The mother acknowledges that she used physical discipline with Peter and that she "yells and screams" too much.	The reliability and validity of the evidence collected is marginal. CPS did not substantiate the allegations, the evaluator did not observe a mark consistent with Rita's story about her mother hitting her, and the validity of Peter's evidence is weak based on both of the older children's reports that their father had coached them. Maria admits using physical discipline, consistent with Peter's apparently spontaneous comments. Dr. Connoly says that Maria is trying to stop yelling at the children, suggesting an apparent problem with verbal abuse. The weight of the evidence about physical abuse is equivocal. Evidence from CPS and from Dr. Connoly have the most weight because they are independent. The evaluator's observations have some weight as independent and neutral. The children's reports of abuse are given some weight but not a great deal because of the degree to which those reports appear to have been directed by Timothy. Maria's evidence, because it is against her own interest, is given considerable weight.	Maria has been harsh in her punishment of Peter. She is mildly to moderately depressed (from other data not included in this shortened matrix). Peter is somewhat estranged from his mother, and the poor relationship between them may be exacerbating Maria's depression, which is also impairing her ability to discipline her son appropriately. There is no evidence that Timothy is abusing his children physically, and the major emotional abuse appears to be in his involving the children in the divorce disputes. There is some evidence that he may be undermining Peter's relationship with his mother and may be encouraging Peter to be aggressive at school, which are elements of poor parenting.

Table 7.3 Parenting Plan Evaluation Matrix II: Summary, Analysis, and Synthesis - Case of Maria, Timothy, and Family *(continued)*

Source of Concern	Summary of Evidence	Analysis of Evidence: Reliability and Validity	Synthesis of Evidence: Inferences
Substance Abuse			
Concerns that Timothy is abusing Alcohol	The summary of the evidence includes that there were allegations by Maria, a history of alcohol-related criminal offenses, and the direct observation of drinking by the evaluator.	In terms of the reliability of the evidence, one could worry about the reliability and validity of Maria's evidence, but her allegations are supported by independent evidence from the criminal record, and Timothy's behavior of minimizing the three events as "misunderstandings" is consistent with possible alcoholic denial of a substance abuse problem. The evaluator's observation of drinking four beers is also considered highly valid and reliable. The weight of the evidence is on the independent criminal records, the evaluator's own observation, and Maria's account to the extent that the independent evidence supports it.	It is highly likely that Timothy abuses alcohol. It is not clear from these data whether his alcohol abuse interferes substantially with his parenting.
Concerns that Maria is abusing prescription medications.	The summary of the evidence regarding Maria's alleged substance abuse comes from Timothy's reports.	The weight given to Timothy's evidence is low in the absence of supporting evidence. The weight given to Maria's evidence is high because the pharmacy records and her psychiatrist's statements support it.	The conclusion is that Maria does not appear to be misusing prescription drugs and that Timothy appears to have created a false accusation against Maria, perhaps to counter her allegations about his alcohol abuse or to gain an advantage in the litigation.

Table 7.3 Parenting Plan Evaluation Matrix II: Summary, Analysis, and Synthesis - Case of Maria, Timothy, and Family *(continued)*

Source of Concern	Summary of Evidence	Analysis of Evidence: Reliability and Validity	Synthesis of Evidence: Inferences
Children's Adjustment			
Concerns that Peter is anxious and distressed. Concerns that Rita and Sarah are fearful.	Peter was diagnosed as anxious at the age of 3. Dr. Becan cautioned the parents 3 years ago that Peter's behavioral issues were due in part to his exposure to family conflict. Rita says that she likes spending time with both parents. CPS worker Brown and the evaluator observed all three children as comfortable with both parents, not fearful. Rita's day care provider says that Rita talked happily about both homes and was happy to see both parents when they picked her up.	The long-term negative impact of being exposed to this conflict is evident by Peter's historical struggles with issues of anxiety and aggression. The observations of the evaluator and CPS worker are seen as reliable. Peter's self-report of distress is seen as reliable. Dr. Becan's opinions are seen as reliable.	Peter is anxious and overtly distressed. He has academic problems that may be related to his level of anxiety. He is suffering from the harsh, abusive punishment he receives from his mother. He is caught in the middle of his parents' conflict, being asked to give evidence against his mother. Given his exposure to domestic violence, there is a possibility that he is protective of his father and identifies with him. Rita is not showing adjustment problems at this time but could be considered at risk given the levels of conflict.
Children's Preferences			
Parents' concerns that the children want to avoid staying with one parent or the other.	Both older children state they want to spend time with both parents.	The evidence is scant that the parents' reports about the children wanting to avoid the other parent are reliable. There appears to be mild preference in Peter for time with his father and in Rita and Sarah for time with their mother but there is not a strong preference.	Other issues in the family will be more important in planning parenting time, since the children want to spend time with both parents.

Table 7.3 Parenting Plan Evaluation Matrix II: Summary, Analysis, and Synthesis - Case of Maria, Timothy, and Family *(continued)*

Source of Concern	Summary of Evidence	Analysis of Evidence: Reliability and Validity	Synthesis of Evidence: Inferences
Parenting Competency			
Concerns that Timothy is not competent as a parent.	Maria has reported concerns regarding Timothy's parenting competency, which Timothy denies. These concerns have not been noted by the evaluator or mentioned by the children. Gordon provides evidence that may support Maria's claim. The other collaterals contacted have not noted the same concerns.	The evidence provided by collateral contacts aside from Maria's family has the most reliability and validity due to their neutral position, however many of the contacts are from short periods of time. The reliability and validity of the children's reports is lessened somewhat by the documented efforts by Timothy to direct their statements, but they are considered reliable and valid to some extent, given that they see their parents most often, and they supported what was observed by the evaluator.	Timothy is probably a good enough parent in terms of day-to-day competency.
Coparenting Capacity			
Concerns that the parents are in conflict and unable to communicate peacefully and effectively.	All evidence supports that the parents are engaging in high conflict. They expose the children to arguments and allegations. Timothy's pattern of coercive control is an important factor in the levels of conflict.	All sources of evidence are convergent and consistent. They can be considered reliable and valid.	The parents are not, at least at the present time, able to work together to coparent cooperatively.

Table 7.3 Parenting Plan Evaluation Matrix II: Summary, Analysis, and Synthesis - Case of Maria, Timothy, and Family *(continued)*

Source of Concern	Summary of Evidence	Analysis of Evidence: Reliability and Validity	Synthesis of Evidence: Inferences
Relocation			
This is not an issue			
Other Issues: Gatekeeping			
Concerns that both parents are gatekeeping, Maria with the younger girls and Timothy with Peter.	Peter is sometimes refusing contact with Maria, which all family members agree on. Maria reports that this is due to interference by Timothy, which is supported by the evidence that Timothy plans other activities during Peter's access time with his mother and asks him to choose. Timothy reports that Maria's abusive parenting causes Peter to resist contact, which is supported by evidence that Maria is harsh and abusive in her punishment of him. Maria is concerned about the safety and well-being of Rita and Sarah when they are with Timothy. There was no evidence that the girls are in dasnger when with Timothy.	Evidence about Timothy's interference in Peter's relationship with Maria is considered reliable and valid. Evidence about Maria's poor parenting and abusive punishment is considered reliable and valid. The younger girls do not appear fearful of their father. The observations of the evaluator, CPS social worker, and day care provider all agree and all can be considered reliable and valid because of their independence and convergence.	Peter is caught in a position of resisting contact with his mother based on both Maria's poor parenting and Timothy's efforts to undermine the mother-son relationship. The girls are not avoiding contact with their father, and Maria appears to be making the effort to be protective given the anger and violence that she has observed and experienced.

Table 7.4   Parenting Plan Evaluation Matrix III:
Themes, Analysis, Synthesis (Recommendations), and Accountability

Themes (Level II Inferences: Analysis)	Additive? Synergistic? Antagonistic? Direction? (Level III Inferences: Analysis)	Parenting Plan Implications and Recommendations (Level IV Inferences: Synthesis)	Accountability
Safety			
Child Issues			
Parent Issues			

that are probably or highly probably true. In the iteration of the process in this chapter, all the issues are taken into consideration.

There is a great deal of evidence that confirms that Timothy has a substance abuse problem, with either dependence or abuse of alcohol. There is also strong evidence that Timothy has trouble controlling his anger—especially when he is drinking—and the pattern of his behavior, even when not drinking, could be seen as coercive control. Therefore, a parenting plan to keep the children safe would work to treat those two problems before one might foresee his having more time with his young daughters, including one or more overnights.

Such a plan would call for Timothy to enter a 12-step alcohol treatment program and at the same time a structured anger management program. After 90 days of sobriety and consistent attendance at and successful engagement in both programs, his time with Rita and Sarah could be increased from the weekdays he sees them now to include one overnight at first. In addition, Timothy should meet with an individual counselor to improve his coparenting and his awareness of his own reactions and his impact on others in his family. All of the counseling should have explicit goals and reasonable ways to assess progress toward those goals. Timothy should sign releases for all of his therapists and group leaders to coordinate treatment for him. Timothy's time with his daughters should be increased as there is evidence of improvement in his treatment and evidence that the visits have been successful. The ultimate schedule may well be a 50-50 timeshare, but that should not be seen as the primary goal from the start.

At the same time, there is evidence that Maria yells and screams at her children and is particularly unable to discipline Peter appropriately. Maria needs parent education about appropriate and positive discipline of a preteen, and she needs to continue her treatment for depression (which is contributing to her losses of control). When she has completed 8 weeks of parent education (concurrent with Timothy's alcohol and anger treatments), she and Peter and Timothy should enter family therapy with the goal of repairing the mother-son relationship, with support from Timothy. Peter should begin to have expanded days and overnights with Maria after family therapy has begun. Maria also needs to work with a parent education counselor around her concerns about separating from her 7-year-old and 2-year-old so that she can support the girls' expanded time with Timothy when it is safe for that to happen.

The children are somewhat symptomatic. Peter should continue in counseling with his individual therapist or psychiatrist, and that person should have releases to speak with the professionals treating the parents. The parents may need a consultation with an infant-parent specialist if Sarah does not develop the ability to separate from her mother more easily, but at this point, her behavior is developmentally normal and does not need intervention.

Table 7.5 Parenting Plan Evaluation Matrix III: Case of Maria, Timothy, and Family

Themes (Level II Inferences: Analysis)	Additive? Synergistic? Antagonistic? Direction? (Level III Inferences: Analysis)	Parenting Plan Implications and Recommendations (Level IV Inferences: Synthesis)	Accountability
Safety			
Lack of safety, Timothy. S-1. Timothy has a problem with anger and is sometimes violent. S-2. Timothy has a problem with alcohol abuse or dependence.	These factors are likely to be synergistic, with each potentially exacerbating the other. There is no clear causal direction.	Timothy and Maria should have no face-to-face exchanges. He should attend anger management treatment, concurrent with treatment for alcohol abuse and individual counseling. Overnights should be added with younger girls after 90 days if he is sober, committed, and visits have gone well.	There should be a mechanism by which the records of Timothy's attendance at 12-step meetings, at anger management, and at counseling can be collected and provided to someone in authority (minor's counsel, parenting coordinator, court personnel).
Lack of safety, Maria S-3. Maria has no problem with abuse of presription medications.		No intervention necessary.	
S-4. Maria's physical discipline of Peter is abusive.	Maria's problem with harsh discipline of Peter is synergistic with other concerns not in this chart, such as depression. It is possibly also associated with history of domestic violence and Timothy's efforts to undermine her authority.	Maria should attend a parent education program with emphasis on appropriate discipline for preteens. She should continue treatment for her depression.	There should be a mechanism by which records of Maria's attendance at parent education and at her psychiatrist can be collected and provided to someone in authority.

Table 7.5 Parenting Plan Evaluation Matrix III: Case of Maria, Timothy, and Family *(continued)*

Themes (Level II Inferences: Analysis)	Additive? Synergistic? Antagonistic? Direction? (Level III Inferences: Analysis)	Parenting Plan Implications and Recommendations (Level IV Inferences: Synthesis)	Accountability
Child Issues			
C-1. The resistance that both girls have to leaving their mother is likely a reaction to the threatened loss of their mother as an attachment figure.	Maria's depression may contribute to their insecurity.	Maria should be given advice about helping support both girls' ability to separate from her appropriately for their respective ages. Maria should continue treatment for depression.	Both parents should be responsible for helping the girls make the transition from mother to father when it is scheduled.
C-2. Both girls are slightly afraid of their father. Their anxiety is likely to be related to their father's anger and also possibly to his alcohol abuse as well as to their mother's anxiety about their safety.	The girls may also be frightened by their father's use of alcohol and by their having witnessed domestic violence. Their mother's anxiety about their safety with their father may be contributing to their fearfulness.	To help the girls' anxiety and Maria's, Timothy needs to improve his self-control. The interventions for Timothy should be in effect for 90 days before any attempt is made to start overnights with him. Maria needs to be helped to distinguish her realistic fears from her unrealistic fears as Timothy becomes sober and peaceful.	There is accountability for Timothy's sobriety and anger management attendance in the factors listed above.
C-3. Peter is anxious and sometimes resists going to his mother's home. His anxiety is likely to be related to the parental high conflict as well as to his mother's harsh punishments.	Peter's anxiety may be worsened by separation from his mother and sisters and by exposure to his father's anger.	After his mother is engaged in her parenting course, Peter should resume spending substantial time at her home. He and both of his parents should begin family therapy to repair the relationship between mother and son if that is necessary to ensure the contact. Peter should resume individual treatment for his anxiety.	Both parents should be responsible for keeping Peter away from the conflict and for his regular time spent with his mother. Records of his compliance with visits to his mother should be kept and provided to someone in authority.

Table 7.5 Parenting Plan Evaluation Matrix III: Case of Maria, Timothy, and Family *(continued)*

Themes (Level II Inferences: Analysis)	Additive? Synergistic? Antagonistic? Direction? (Level III Inferences: Analysis)	Parenting Plan Implications and Recommendations (Level IV Inferences: Synthesis)	Accountability
Parent Issues			
P-1. Maria is not fabricating her fear and her allegations about Timothy's anger and violence, but Timothy apparently fabricated a story about her Ritalin use.	Timothy's false allegatioins may be connected with his high level of anger and his wish to control his wife and family.	Timothy should be ordered to support Maria's relationship with all of the children.	Accountability should follow the plans above with record keeping.
P-2. Maria has been mildly to moderately depressed, and it is likely that her depression contributes to her irritability and poor self-control of her anger and in this way impairs her parenting to some degree.	It is possible that Maria keeps the younger girls with her for her own comfort and because she identifies with their difficulty going with their father and away from her.	Her depression is not serious enough to warrant changes in the timeshare. Maria needs to continue with her therapy with some focus on learning better self-soothing techniques and possibly on medications with her psychiatrist. She needs to work with the parent education program and the coparent counselor as described above.	Maria's attendance at her therapy and at coparenting counseling should be recorded and provided to someone in authority.
P-3. Maria does not have any other mental or emotional illness except for the mild to moderate depression.	There is no mental illness.	No intervention is necessary.	
P-4. It is not likely that Maria's depression is primarily the result of the IPV because it has been very longstanding.	Maria's depression may have been worsened by the IPV with the accompanying feelings of helplessness and/or by the poor relationship with Peter.	No interventions are necessary other than those already put in place for her continuing psychiatric treatment and for working to improve her relationship with Peter.	Accountability is described above.

Table 7.5 Parenting Plan Evaluation Matrix III: Case of Maria, Timothy, and Family *(continued)*

Themes (Level II Inferences: Analysis)	Additive? Synergistic? Antagonistic? Direction? (Level III Inferences: Analysis)	Parenting Plan Implications and Recommendations (Level IV Inferences: Synthesis)	Accountability
Children's Preferences			
CpC-1. Peter wants to live with his father. CpC-2. Rita wants to live with her mother and visit her father.	All three children want to spend time with both parents. None is afraid of either parent.	This factor points toward joint physical and legal custody, absent other factors against it.	Records should be kept of the children's time spent with the parents and of the transitions between the parents, and the records should be provided to someone in authority.
Parenting Competency			
PC-1. Timothy is not competent in day-to-day parenting. PC-2. Timothy's coercive control and domestic violence make him a poor parent.	Timothy's competency is not in question when he is sober and is not provoked, but he is impaired by his alcoholism and his pattern of coercive and controlling violence.	The parenting plans discussed above under domestic violence and substance abuse should be relevant at first. If Timothy successfully completes his treatment in both areas, his parenting time should increase gradually, with a goal of eventually reaching a 50-50 timeshare.	Accountability was described above under domestic violence and substance abuse.
PC-3. Maria is abusive and angry as a parent.	Maria's parenting competency is adequate when she is not in a depressive or angry state. She is also likely to be more effective as a parent when she feels safe from abuse or harassment.	Maria should have primary custody, with support from her therapist, a parenting class, and possibly a parenting coach.	Accountability was described above under parent issues.

Table 7.5 Parenting Plan Evaluation Matrix III: Case of Maria, Timothy, and Family *(continued)*

Themes (Level II Inferences: Analysis)	Additive? Synergistic? Antagonistic? Direction? (Level III Inferences: Analysis)	Parenting Plan Implications and Recommendations (Level IV Inferences: Synthesis)	Accountability
Coparenting Capacity			
CpC-1. Both parents are engaged in high-conflict behavior... CpC-2. Timothy is generating most of the conflict and communication problems. CpC-3. Maria is generating most of the conflict and communication problems.	Both parents are engaged in high-conflict behavior, involving the children and struggling to turn others to their side against the other.	Communication must be written and controlled by use of a website with the potential to be monitored. Transitions must be via neutral space such as day care and school. There can be no face-to-face exchange of children or of information.	The records of the communications between parents should be reviewable by someone in authority.
Gatekeeping			
G-1. Timothy is restricting Peter's access to time with his mother. G-2. Timothy is restricting Peter's access to his mother to protect him from child abuse.	Timothy is restricting Peter's contact with his mother and is working to undermine that relationship. The evidence does not support this as protective gatekeeping. It may be the result of or exacerbated by Timothy's anger and his tendency to want to control his ex-wife and his son.	Timothy must be ordered to support Peter's time with his mother, and the family therapy should focus on helping him support that relationship. Maria must work on improving her parenting, especially in discipline and in managing her frustration and anger. Family therapy should work with this issue from both sides.	Accountability was discussed above.
G-3. Maria is restricting Rita and Sarah's access to time with their father. G-4. Maria is restricting the girls' access to their father to protect them from danger from Timothy's alcohol abuse and/or his anger.	Maria is not restricting Timothy's access to the younger girls, but she may be conveying to them that she fears that they are not safe with him, thus undermining the father-daughter relationships. Her depression may contribute to her wanting to keep the younger girls close.	Maria must work on supporting Rita and Sarah's relationship with Timothy. Family therapy should work with this issue.	Accountability was discussed above.

The evidence does not confirm that either parent is completely fabricating his or her accusations to gain an advantage in the litigation with the exception of Timothy's allegation that Maria is abusing Ritalin, for which there is no corroborating evidence. Timothy appears to be exaggerating Maria's losing her temper and appears to be enlisting the children to tell stories about her abusing them, which is a problem. Maria may be exaggerating her level of fear about the angry and abusive behavior of Timothy, but she has reasons to be fearful to some extent. The counselors who work with the parents should have a copy of this report so that they can work with their clients on regulating their anger and undoing their distortions.

There needs to be accountability with regard to all of the interventions. Timothy can collect signatures from his attendance at the 12-step program. Attendance records from the anger management or batterer's intervention program will be important as well. He should also seek a statement from his counselor in the program about the level of engagement that he is showing in the counseling. Maria should request the same attendance records from her parent education program and statements about her level of engagement from both the educational program and from her individual counseling. These records can be exchanged between attorneys, or a parenting coordinator or a minor's counsel can gather them if there is someone in such a role. The records will be important for accountability and for decision making at each point at which there will be a change in the custodial timeshare, such as increasing overnights.

Whether or not there is a parenting coordinator or minor's counsel, there needs to be some person in authority who can collect and collate the reports from treating professionals and who has the ability to make a report to the court when necessary and appropriate. The parents should not be in the position of collecting evidence on one another, and their attorneys may be too expensive and polarizing to use for that purpose.

The plan calls for quite a lot of intervention, especially during the first phases. If the family does not have the financial resources to pay for private counseling and family therapy and the parenting coordinator or minor's counsel, and if the family does not have insurance that will help to cover the costs, the plan should recommend low-fee resources such as a community clinic for the individual treatment of Timothy and Maria and Peter. The biggest part of the available family resources should be allocated to cover costs of an experienced family therapist who can also serve as a sort of case manager, speaking with all of the other therapists and helping to keep cooperation and communication open and flowing.

The recommendations should be written in phases, with phase 1 being the most restrictive of Timothy's access with the children, followed by phases that gradually step up his access time to the next level as he has success at each level. There needs to be a provision for a return to earlier levels or to the first level if there is an incident of relapse into drinking or an outburst of rage in any context.

General Considerations in Parenting Plans

The reader is reaching the end of the decision tree process described in this book. The ultimate conclusion of this journey is the creation of recommendations for a parenting plan. Earlier in the process there was the planning for the trip, and there has been data collection along the way. The data is kept as separate as possible from anything that follows, that is, separate from any kind of analysis and higher order inferences, including opinions and ultimately separate from this, the recommendations.

One of the primary purposes of the PPE is to make recommendations regarding issues of custody and access of the children with their parents and/or significant caregivers. In Table 7.6 there is a list showing aspects of parenting plan recommendations. Recommendations to the court can also guide decisions regarding how best: to keep children safe, to insulate children from the conflict, to maximize parent-child contact opportunities that are in the interests of the children, to consider the best ways for the parents to communicate about their children (if possible) so that they are both kept up to date about the children's progress, to consider services and resources that may help the parties and/or the children to deal with issues that are impeding healthy reorganization after the separation, and ultimately to provide strategies to help the children adjust to their parents' separation. The recommendations regarding the optimal parenting plan for the children should serve as a guide for both parents to follow so that the parents have the needed structure and guidance.

Recommendations are formal statements that establish how members of the family will function in regards to several aspects of their lives.

Table 7.6 Aspects of Parenting Plan Recommendations

Aspect	*Explained*
Physical custody	• When should the child be in the mother's care? In the father's care?
Transitions	• What should the transitions be like?
Legal custody	• By whom and how are decisions going to be made? • Through what means and in what forum are communications between the parents to take place? • How is information to be shared?
Protect children	• How will the children be kept safe—protected from conflict and violence?
Resolve issues interfering with effective parenting	• What are the issues that are interfering with effective parenting, and what are the interventions to help mediate these problems?
Accountability	• Through what means are the family members going to be kept accountable and to whom are they to be accountable in order that the preceding aspects of the parenting plan recommendations are successfully implemented?

There are many ways to schedule parenting time and to develop parenting plans. Evaluators can find it helpful to consider suggested recommendations for parenting plans (e.g., the use of communication log books for parents who are unable to communicate face-to-face), but each recommendation should be vetted for relevance, applicability, and utility for the specific case in question.

There are several guidelines that have been created for physical custody or parenting plan arrangements that can be helpful if used carefully. A sample of those follows in Table 7.7.

As tempting as it may be to use a cookie-cutter approach to PPEs, such practices often fail to capture the unique aspects of a given family. Some states have presumptions about custody; sometimes it is for joint legal and physical custody, or sometimes it is a rebuttable presumption that custody should be awarded to the nonviolent parent where there has been a finding of domestic violence. The problem is that presump-

---

Table 7.7 Parenting Plan Development

Name	*URL*
Alaska Court System, Model Parenting Agreement	www.state.ak.us/courts/forms/dr-475.pdf
Arizona's Guide for for Parents Living Apart, Arizona Supreme Court	http://www.supreme.state.az.us/dr/Pdf/Parenting_Time_Plan_Final.pdf
Oregon Judicial Department	http://courts.oregon.gov/OJD/OSCA/cpsd/courtimprovement/familylaw/parentingplan.page

---

tions and rules are unlikely to capture the complexity of each family's individual needs and especially the competing needs of disputing parents. A summary of common pitfalls follows in Table 7.8.

Table 7.8 Common Pitfalls in Parenting Plan Evaluations

Naming Pitfalls	*Explaining Solutions*
Use of cookie-cutter approach	Failure to consider uniqueness of a given family • Age and stage of development of each child must be considered. • Parents need to be flexible with their schedules to accommodate the unique and changing needs of the children. • Recommendations should not be static. Another common pitfall of evaluators providing recommendations is failing to consider the ages of stages of the children involved. Recommendations should not be static but should consider the growing needs of the children. Suggesting, for example, that a child should have supervised contact with a parent but without an end date to this arrangement or the steps required so that supervision would no longer be needed can leave children and parents in limbo. Recommendations may not be connected to the facts; that is, the content of the report may not match the conclusion of the report. There should be no surprises, and there should be no new information presented in the recommendations that has not been carefully considered in the analysis and synthesis section. For each and every recommendation in a parenting plan, there should be a specific and transparent connection made that connects the recommendation back to the data that was collected, analyzed, and synthesized.
Lack of use of community resources	Be familiar with community resources available to the family. Evaluators should be aware of the community resources available for parents and children (e.g., parent education programs, children group counseling services, substance abuse programs, parent coordination, etc.), the potential cost associated with these services, and the potential wait times for accessing these services. Developing a list of resources in the area where the evaluator practices will help in considering whether the recommendations are practical for location based on availability of services. Evaluators may also want to consider providing a list of services to families so that they can become linked more clearly to the services suggested.
Lack of consideration of costs	Be familiar with alternative sources for interventions that are not so costly.
Misuse of social science research	There is also a tendency for evaluators to rely on social science literature that lacks the scientific quality to make inferences to a broader population (based on small samples, selected sample settings, measurement errors, designs that do not support making inferences, etc.; see Appendix A on the use of research). It is therefore insufficient to simply state the findings of studies without providing a transparent opinion as to the quality of the study of which the findings are based on. By not being transparent about the quality of the evidence, the evaluator risks presenting factoids, which are sound bites of research studies with no verification of the credibility or validity of such claims. The evaluator must be cautious about overgeneralizing results and must resist trying to find research to support a predetermined point.

Table 7.8 Common Pitfalls in Parenting Plan Evaluations *(continued)*

Naming Pitfalls	*Explaining Solutions*
Use of labels	Given that PPEs take place in a legal context, often legal terms are used (e.g., sole custody, joint custody). Parents may not understand the full meaning of some of these terms. It is the responsibility of the evaluator to explain recommendations such that the parents will understand the impact of a given recommendation. The evaluator needs to be mindful of his or her responsibility to remain focused on the children in their cases.
	Recommendations developed within the context of an evaluation that is done in the shadow of the courts may place more emphasis on legal labels (e.g., sole custody, joint custody, parallel parenting) compared to parenting plans made outside of the context of the court (e.g., mediation, conciliation). It is the responsibility of the evaluator to explain recommendations such that the parents will understand the impact of a given recommendation. The evaluator also needs to be mindful of his or her responsibility to remain focused on the children in their cases.
	Further, some evaluators use diagnostic labels as a shortcut for describing a parent's pathology. The AFCC Model Standards (2006) recommend against use of diagnostic labels.

There are, though, a myriad of items that parenting plan evaluators have at their disposal. Those items include the following interventions: to assist with decision making, communication between parents, transitions of the children from one parent to another, and to provide recommendations for psychoeducational groups, interventions for parents, interventions for children, parenting coordination, and supervised access. A chart with these interventions more fully explained follows in Table 7.9.

At this point, it seems important to say something that most readers will have already thought about. The recommendations presented here are not different in elements or parts than those that most evaluators might think of for this family or for many other similar families. The point of the extra layer of methodology was not to lead to some new and miraculous solution to the intractable problems that these families face. The methods we propose using may, in fact, make a PPE slower and more laborious the first times that they are used. Like learning a new way to swing a golf club or a tennis racket, the initial change is likely to feel awkward and hard to master, but with experience, it becomes second nature and enjoyable. We believe strongly that if evaluators adopt the methods, adapt the tools to their own uses and practices, and use them for a few evaluations in a row, they will find that they are more clear and transparent in their evaluation processes and that they make decisions in a more clear and transparent way. An additional benefit is the ability to revisit a case after a few years have passed and to reconstruct the thinking that went into the decision made at the time of the evaluation.

Even the authors, who have worked with the models for some time, found that forcing themselves to use the grid led them to keep including facts and thoughts that otherwise might have been left out and led them to notice when high-level inferences were slipping into the descriptions of observations.

Table 7.9 Interventions in Parenting Plan Evaluations

Intervention Named	*Intervention Explained*
Making recommendations regarding decision making	Recommendations should address both day-to-day and major decisions. Day-to-day decisions can include: parent communication, exchange of information, extracurricular activities, telephone contact, childrearing routines, parent-teacher meetings, attendance at school events, field trips, hair cuts, purchasing of clothing, and temporary schedule changes (minor illness, special events, etc.).
	Major decisions, on the other hand, typically include school issues (choice of school and/or day care, psychoeducational testing, remediation, enrichment, tutoring); religious issues (practicing religious beliefs, formal religious education, involvement in religions rituals); and medical issues (medical emergencies, surgery, long-term medication, orthodontia, immunizations, therapy, counseling).
	In some situations of high conflict, parallel-parenting plans can be recommended so that each parent is responsible for the care and decision making of the child while he or she is in the parent's care. As stated by Janet Johnston (2006), "Rather than expecting communication and cooperative parenting that can instead lead to enmeshed hostility, sabotage, and further abuse in high-conflict and violent families, the protocols for parallel parenting need to be taught. Parallel parenting respects and supports each parent's relationship with the child free from interference from the other parent. Parallel parenting is coordinated by an over-arching explicit court order that governs the access schedule and essential health, education, and welfare decisions so there is minimal need for communication between parents" (p. 33).
	In some situations of high conflict, it may be best for one parent to make all decisions or for the decision making to be split. For example, one parent makes all medical decisions and the other parent makes all educational decisions. Those allocations of responsibility would, of course, need to be based on the qualities of the parent (skills, knowledge, judgment) that suggested that one parent would be qualified or that one parent would not be qualified to make major decisions.
Recommendations for families in high conflict	Based on the concerns and issues uncovered during the evaluation, evaluators may want to suggest that one, some, or all of the family members receive some additional services and interventions. There is a range of options for intervening with high-conflict families. Some options are focused on the need to provide structure around the conflict and to better monitor parents in order to address the conflict issues or risk management issues (violence and substance abuse for example).
Transitions	Transitions (the exchange of the children from one parent's home to the other) should be clearly outlined in the evaluator's recommendations to reduce the amount of stress that children can feel when their parents come into contact with each other. In low-conflict cases, suggestions about which parent transports the children to the other home may be sufficient. But in higher conflict cases, it may be necessary to have a third party intervene to facilitate this exchange to ensure that the parents do not have the opportunity to express their conflict in the presence of the children. Although libraries, restaurants, and the use of third party friends or relatives may be appropriate in some cases, evaluators should consider professional third party services (e.g., supervised exchange facilities). The transitions can also be scheduled to limit the contact between the parents altogether.

Table 7.9 Interventions in Parenting Plan Evaluations *(continued)*

Intervention Named	*Intervention Explained*
Transitions *(continued)*	For example, one parent brings the child to the school at the beginning of the day, and the other parent picks the child up at the end of the school day. Such plans should be in consultation with the school to ensure that it is aware of this arrangement and to ensure that the staff members are willing to accommodate such a transitional schedule.
Divorce psychoeducational groups	In some situations, it may be beneficial for parents to attend education sessions to learn how to better cope with the separation and to manage parenting duties after separation. There have been many studies to date that have looked at the effectiveness of divorce psychoeducational programs, but few have focused on the high-conflict divorce group. Other articles and reviews examine the effectiveness of mandated psychoeducational divorce programs for separated/divorced parents (Brandon, 2006; Criddle, Allgood, & Piercy, 2003; Faircloth & Cummings, 2008; Shifflet & Cummings, 1999; Yankeelov et al., 2003). These articles show mixed results and contain the same limitations as the aforementioned high-conflict group studies. Parents consistently report high levels of satisfaction; however, studies fail to demonstrate behavioral changes in the way that parents relate between themselves and their children, with no conclusive hard evidence showing whether these programs make a significant difference (Bacon & McKenzie, 2004; Goodman et al., 2004; Grych, 2005).
Intervention for parents	Some recently developed interventions are aimed at helping entire families in which there is a breach between one parent and one or more children that is determined to stem from complex hybrid causes (Friedlander & Walters, 2010; Walters & Friedlander, 2011). Other writers have outlined ways that therapists can work with the contentious high-conflict families who continue to be involved with the courts (Greenberg & Gould, 2001). A special issue of the *Journal of Child Custody* (Volume 9[1-2], 2012), with guest editors Matthew J. Sullivan and Lyn R. Greenberg, was published on Court-Involved Therapy. There is no research yet on the outcomes of these interventions, which include various, quite focused family therapy interventions. Other interventions for parents may include programs to address specific issues that are preventing the parents from providing optimal care after separation. Programs like anger management, substance abuse prevention, parenting skills, and mental health services can assist parents and can be integrated into a long-term plan for helping to restore, maintain, or enhance parent-child relationships.
Interventions for children	The path to reducing high conflict may include measures to help parents change behaviors or parenting practices or to help them receive interventions to address factors contributing to the conflict (e.g., mental health; Greenberg, Doi Fick, & Schnider, 2012; Greenberg et al., 2003; Sullivan & Greenberg, 2012). However, children may also benefit from participating in counseling services to help manage high conflict and to deal with its consequences. These programs are generally designed to help children adjust to the separation or divorce, to normalize their experiences (i.e., especially within group interventions), and to develop coping skills to manage the stress of being caught in the middle of their parents' conflict (Grych, 2005). In a review by Geelhoed, Blaisure, and Geasler (2001), the authors identified 46 different programs for children and adolescents who were experiencing a separation or divorce in the United States. The majority of these programs included one to four sessions for a total of 4 hours, with the majority of these interventions focused on providing information to children about common situations of being caught in the middle of high conflict.

Table 7.9 Interventions in Parenting Plan Evaluations *(continued)*

Intervention Named	*Intervention Explained*
Interventions for children *(continued)*	Children in high-conflict families may also attend mental health services, but they are often specific to the presenting problems identified by the parents (e.g., conduct problems, education problems, sleep disturbances, etc.) rather than specific to dealing with the emotional harm of being exposed to high conflict. Therefore, little is known about whether these interventions help children adjust from high conflict. Measures of success for these interventions are most often connected to the primary presenting problem (e.g., did the child reduce conduct disordered behaviors?), which may or may not be associated with adjustment to being caught in high conflict. There are intensive residential programs that involve the entire family, in which there are entrenched problems in the parent-child relationships. There is little or no research on their efficacy, but anecdotal information suggests that they can be helpful for families who are willing to engage in them (Sullivan, Ward, & Deutsch, 2010; Warshak, 2010).
Parenting coordination	A parenting coordinator is a professional with mental health, mediation, and/or legal training who is trained in a child-focused alternative dispute resolution process to help parents in high conflict after separation or divorce. Parenting coordinators may monitor compliance with the parenting plan and may mediate disputes as they arise over implementation of the parenting plan. Parenting coordinators also help parents to understand and apply strategies to minimize high conflict, disengage from each other emotionally, and learn about child development and children's issues in divorce (Coates et al., 2004; Kelly, 2008; Mitcham-Smith & Henry, 2007; Sullivan, 2008). The goal of parenting coordination is to potentially decrease court time and future litigation by helping parents solve day-to-day disputes stemming from parenting plans (Coates et al., 2004). Mental health professionals or experienced family lawyers usually take the role of parenting coordinator. Empirical research and evaluation on parenting coordination is limited. Parents have reported satisfaction with the use of parenting coordination, and some evidence suggests that parenting coordination may help in reducing litigation rates (Coates et al., 2004; Mitcham-Smith & Henry, 2007).

Summary

- This chapter provides the final steps in the overall structure of the proposed system for an evaluator to use to sort the factors that will inform his opinions and recommendations.
- The steps include clustering the issues into themes, organizing them into a new and probably final decision tree and list of hypotheses. This step was demonstrated for the case example.
- From those themes, a chart was proposed for explicitly laying out the conclusions about the connections between issues and the implications for the parenting plan and any interventions that might be recommended.

Annotated Bibliography

Ackerman, M. (2008). *Does Wednesday Mean Mom's House or Dad's? Parenting Together While Living Apart.* Hoboken, NJ: John Wiley & Sons.

Although written for parents, this text provides workable suggestions to consider when developing parenting plans. The suggestions provided by the author are both flexible and child-centered to optimally meet the needs of the children.

Austin, W. G., & Gould, J. W. (2006). Exploring three functions in child custody evaluation for the relocation case: Prediction, investigation, and making recommendations for a long-distance parenting plan. *Journal of Child Custody, 3*(3/4), 63-108.

The authors propose the four decisional alternatives facing the court and the evaluator in cases where relocation is being disputed. Different legal contexts for relocation are reviewed in terms of their implications for the custody evaluation. Complexities involved in the evaluator's function of making predictions for the court are presented. The need to conduct careful investigation on both risk and pragmatic factors is highlighted by case illustrations. The obstacles of crafting of long-distance parenting plans that will be in the best interests of the child are presented as governed by the goal of harm mitigation.

Bauserman, R. (2002). Child adjustment in joint-custody versus sole-custody arrangements: A meta-analytic review. *Journal of Family Psychology, 16*(1), 91-102.

The author reviews the empirical evidence of joint custody compared to sole custody and makes the argument that joint custody is the preferred option for children when there is low conflict and when the parents are able to cooperate.

Greenberg, L. R., & Sullivan, M. (2012). Special issue on therapy in court involved cases. *Journal of Child Custody, 9*(1-2), 91-102.

This double issue has a focus on the ways that treatment considerations, both ethical and clinical, are different in cases in which the courts are involved. It contains many articles about various aspects of treatment with these families. There are articles on ethical and professional treatment of children in high-conflict families, prudent therapy with adults in high-conflict families, issues surrounding privilege, informed consent, clinical risks in forensic cases, and more. The authors demonstrate the importance of the specific training and experience needed by mental health professionals who work in forensic areas.

Kelly, J. D. (2006). Children's living arrangements following separation and divorce: Insights from empirical and clinical research. *Family Process, 46*(1), 35-52.

Building on previous research, the author provides an updated review of the factors that should be considered when making parenting plans.

Kelly, J., & Lamb, M. E. (2000). Child development research to make appropriate custody and access decisions for young children. *Family and Conciliation Courts Review, 38*(3), 297-311.

The authors provide a review of the literature regarding optimal parenting schedules for children based on the ages and stages of children. The authors provide guidelines for consideration for parenting plans for young children.

Sanders, J. D. (2007). Age appropriate parenting plans: Using child developmental information. *American Journal of Law, 21*(3), 67-74.

The author considers the specific needs of children and how they should be applied to parenting plans to meet the best interest of the children.

Chapter 8
Review,
Revisit, Revise

This chapter serves both as a summary of the proposed framework and as a discussion for reviewing, revisiting, and revising the report and the evaluation process itself. Considerations and cautions for using the model within family law matters are also offered. This chapter discusses tips for writing reports and provides a checklist of activities that evaluators should think about in an evaluation before they file the report with the court.

Reviewing the Process and
Revising When Needed

Throughout the book, the authors have stressed the need for transparency. The proposed approach provides a structured and systematic method for ensuring that. By documenting the preliminary decision tree, the data collection sources, the steps taken for analyzing and synthesizing the data, and the process of developing recommendations (including the many matrices filled in), the evaluator creates a paper trail that documents the decision points through the evaluation process.

As described earlier, it is important for the data to be presented in the report in a way that follows the levels of inference from the concrete facts of Level I, to the interpretation and meaning attributed to those facts as the Level II inference, to the broader conclusions about those integrated opinions in Level III, to the conclusions about recommendations to the court in Level IV. Separating the levels of inference contributes to transparency and supports the thorough and rational thinking of the evaluator.

The Importance Of Crosschecking

The decision tree for systematic parenting plan evaluations emphasizes constant checking and cross-checking of the materials so that the evaluation is an integrated process of checks and balances. Vetting for bias and missing information are critical at all stages. Once preliminary hypotheses are developed, it is important to revisit them throughout the process of data collection and analysis and to revise hypotheses as new data are considered.

The constant interplay between data collection and analysis requires a fluid but systematic process of knowing what information is being collected, the reasons why certain information is being collected, and why certain data may or may not fit together. Given the complexity of PPEs, the systematic process proposed here allows for simple steps to deconstruct the complexity. Not taking the time to complete these critical steps can result in holes in the evaluation, and it is likely that a cross-examining attorney will find these holes, if they are not found first by the evaluator. Although there is no research proving it, the authors believe that parents are more likely to be satisfied with the process of the evaluation if they feel that the evaluator carefully considered their concerns as they relate to their children, even when they disagree with the outcomes. Studies that have explored settlement rates suggest that the majority of parents can reach an agreement regarding custody and access issues once they are informed of the evaluator's recommendations (Ash & Guyer, 1991; Maccoby & R. H. Mnookin, 1992; Simons, Grossman, & Weiner, 1990).

Writing the Report

Once the data have been vetted for biases, errors, and omissions, the evaluator needs to write the report. The report must be written in such a way as to be—and in such a way as to be perceived as—fair, unbiased, transparent, and focused on the best interests of the children (Pickar & Kauffman, 2013). Writing the report and putting all of the information together is perhaps the most difficult and time consuming of all activities of the PPE. The length of the report will vary depending on the complexity of the factors considered and on the local custom and court expectations. Bow and Quinnell (2001) found that custody reports averaged 21 pages, with a range of 4 to 80 pages. Bow and Quinnell (2002) also examined 52 child custody reports prepared by a national sample of doctoral-level psychologists, which ranged from 5 to 63 pages, with a mean of 24 pages.

Framing the Report to Avoid Shaming

When writing the conclusions and recommendations, it is possible (and helpful) to present them so that they represent an arrangement for the optimal functioning of the family system. These recommendations can be respectful of the parents' struggles as they attempt to re-establish roles and boundaries following separation rather than condemning or disparaging of them, while not avoiding areas of serious concern when there are such concerns. The balance can be difficult to reach, but it is possible to write in such a way that the family members are described in respectful terms but the facts are described openly so that the court has the necessary information to make decisions for the family.

One way to approach respectful writing is to write descriptions of a person's behavior and statements rather than to describe them with diagnostic terms or judgments. Describing the family in terms of the dynamics—what each person is doing in the family—and their motivations to the extent that those can be known, without blaming anyone, is less likely to lead to blaming statements about individual family members. The more that the descriptions are close to the experience of the person being described, the better.

Vetting the Report

Asking a peer to review the report can safeguard against bias, and it can serve as a good mechanism for debriefing to ensure that the tone and content are appropriate for the case and that each recommendation is connected to the major themes of the case. It is good practice for evaluators to vet their work, since we often learn from one another. A fresh pair of eyes is often able to see the small clues in the language used or in the choices of inclusion or exclusion of data that may point to bias.

Reporting the Limitations of the Evaluation

Although evaluators should be judicious in their attempts to collect all relevant data needed to form the analysis and synthesis to guide the recommendations of the parenting plan, it is not uncommon for there to be limits of the data collected in the PPE. Should there be holes in the data—or better said, limitations in the data—those need to be clearly articulated. For example, a parent's physician may refuse to provide information about his or her patient, and there will be no way of knowing whether the evidence from the physician would have changed the evaluator's weighting of the evidence. It is imperative that all limitations in the data collection phase and in the analysis are documented and that the evaluator provides the court with some comments about the implications of these limitations to the overall recommendations and proposed parenting plan. If the child custody evaluator has done a good job, he or she is not an advocate for either parent or for the child. The evaluator is an advocate for the data.

Practice Tips for Report Writing

Table 8.1 offers a number of practical tips for report writing so that evaluators are better able to discuss the complexity of the case in a simplified format.

Table 8.1 Tips for Report Writing

Tip	*Description*
Behavioral descriptions are superior to labels.	Describe the behaviors that would suggest the presence of problematic parenting rather than simply labeling the behaviors as, for example, Narcissism or Alienation. Rather than suggesting that a parent is "sabotaging" the child's relationship with the other parent, it is more helpful to the courts if specific examples are used that demonstrate both the behavior and the impact that the behavior has on the child. Behavioral descriptions are also superior to diagnostic labels, which usually provide little information in themselves about the implications of the diagnosis for the parenting issues before the court.
Parenting plan evaluations usually involve a multifactorial problem.	Recommendations should not reflect an all-or-nothing phenomenon. Consider all potential factors that may be influencing your views of the optimal parenting plan.
A parenting plan is a family issue, not an individual one.	Parenting plans should be viewed as a family relational issue rather than a matter of the individual pathology of one parent or child. This does not mean that both parents are always equally accountable; there are cases where one parent may have primary responsibility for the problems. Nevertheless, the complexity of these situations places the onus on custody evaluators to conduct an ecologically oriented and comprehensive assessment of the various factors that may impede or facilitate optimal parenting plans, rather than prematurely determining that the accountability rests specifically with one parent's individual pathology.
Use a systems perspective.	The evaluation should include a systems perspective, which includes an analysis of each family member (e.g., parents, children, grandparents) and the interactions and relationships among these members. Evaluators should refrain from being too quick to place blame on one factor (e.g., mental heath of one parent) until each factor is considered and assessed for its potential contribution to the dispute.
Use a decision tree.	To consider all potential factors, use a decision tree for brainstorming the potential presence of factors and the potential relationship among them. Using a multiple hypotheses approach will help to consider all potential factors and will help to avoid simplified attribution of blame based on a narrow focus of the problem.
Consider the level of severity and potential consequences.	Although there remains a lack of tools to quantify the severity, nature, and frequency of parental impairment, level of conflict, substance abuse, or strained parent-child relationships, it is important for evaluators to consider the level of severity of these behaviors and their potential consequences for children and families.
Be cautious to not overstate.	Empirical evidence can help to consider the potential factors that may be relevant to the unique case. It is important, however, that the research is not overstated to support a position.
A thorough assessment should come first—before interventions—and interventions should include accountability through timely follow-ups.	In the absence of these empirical data, individually crafted interventions need to be based on a thorough assessment of what appears to be causing or maintaining the problem, and timely follow-ups on progress should guide the continuation and direction of the interventions.

Table 8.1 Tips for Report Writing *(continued)*

Tip	*Description*
Recommendations should be child specific.	Providing recommendations to the court about optimal parenting plans should: (a) be based upon the needs of the individual child within his/her particular family situation, (b) address the factors that appear to be related to child well-being and adjustment, and (c) ensure a timely follow-up to review progress and determine the direction and need for further intervention if such follow-ups are supported by local rules.
Recommendations should thoroughly consider the expected benefits and risks for each family member and for the family as a whole.	Given the lack of evidence regarding treatment efficacy and effectiveness, recommendations for treatment should thoroughly consider the expected benefits and risks of family members participating in the intervention, the proposed factors that the treatment is intended to ameliorate, and the factors that the treatment may not improve. Recommendations should also include a discussion about the frequency, duration, and dosage needed to make the desired changes. Discussion about monitoring and reporting back to the court should also be considered. Attendance alone should not be considered an outcome.

Postevaluation

Testimony

When called to testify, the approach proposed in this book provides a good snapshot of the decisions that were made during the evaluation. Keeping copies of the decision trees and of the evaluation matrix can only strengthen the evaluator's credibility on the witness stand. Relying on these notes can demonstrate to the courts that the evaluator has carefully considered all evidence and that data and interpretations have been sufficiently vetted for bias and missed information.

Critiquing Others

One of the other benefits of this approach is that it creates a method for achieving the unbiased, clear, transparent, and comprehensive evaluation that meets the highest levels of professional practice that are set forth in the standards and guidelines for the field. These standards are ones that should be met in each completed evaluation, given the importance of the evaluations. Of course, not everyone needs to use the decision tree process that is proposed in the book to be systematic and transparent, but nevertheless they should strive to reach the same standard of clarity, transparency, comprehensiveness, and lack of bias. For a professional who is offering a critique of an evaluation conducted by someone else, these tools for clear and transparent analysis and synthesis provide a solid basis for such critiques by providing a framework comparing their work to established standards for PPEs such as the AFCC Model Standards, state requirements, APA guidelines, and so forth, rather than the personal opinion of the reviewer.

Considerations and Cautions

There are of course cautions and considerations that should be attended to when taking on this approach. They are listed below.

Time and Duration

By strongly discouraging cutting corners within the evaluation process, the authors understand that the proposed approach includes methods that will require additional time to prepare, develop, and perform. This time will need to be accounted for within the initial contract with the parties so that the evaluator has sufficient time to complete this comprehensive process. It is expected, however, that the extra time to complete the investigation in a comprehensive and systematic way can have huge savings (both financial and emotional) for families. Taking away the guesswork about how the evaluator came up with the recommendations can have the benefit of reducing the parents' suspicions of bias and improving the parents' comfort level that the evaluator followed all of the required steps to ensure that the recommendations were based on a solid understanding of the case situation. It may allow the parents to avoid the extremely costly process of hiring another expert to review the work of the evaluator and to testify about the report's inadequacies in court. Ultimately, it is proposed that parents who are unable to make decisions about parenting plans on their own due to conflict with one another want to ensure that plans for their child are being developed based on their child's interests and based on a fair, equitable, and transparent process; and they want to be heard.

There are two other ways that some evaluators take the extra step to make sure that they have done everything possible to ensure that each parent has his or her voice heard. One is to have the parents each review a near final draft of the data portion of the report, to allow them to comment on the draft in writing, and to include their final comments within the report, whether in the index or in the text itself. Such a review would take place only in the evaluator's office, would include only Level I data, and would occur before any kind of analysis or synthesis of the data occurs. And the final extra step to take in these evaluations is to give feedback to each parent, individually or together, depending upon the circumstances including whether there is a restraining order or not. The purpose of the feedback meeting is to let each parent know in person the evaluator's opinions, recommendations, and basis for these parenting plan suggestions.

These two procedures are not universal. The advantage of the former process is that the parent has the opportunity to know what has been written and to correct factual errors and for the evaluator to have more information about the parent's reaction to reading about himself or herself and the family before the final report is written. The advantage of the latter is that the parents are able to hear and discuss the evaluator's findings rather than reading them on their own without the ability to ask questions or discuss the conclusions. The possible disadvantage of these processes is that each will take extra time and could involve additional costs.

Cost

Evaluators following the decision tree approach for conducting PPEs will also need to consider issues of cost. An evaluator may not feel comfortable with billing for the extra time needed to think, sift, and sort through the data in the proposed comprehensive approach. It will be important for the evaluator to consider the issues of cost prior to accepting the case so that the parties are aware that the invoice will include the time it takes to think through these issues, if it will. The evaluator may also choose to not charge for the analysis, but this can devalue the importance of thinking clearly through the issues, and so evaluators should be cautious before choosing to simply "eat the cost" of thinking. Some evaluators charge a flat fee for analyzing data and writing the report, but they report in their billing the actual time spent. Either way, it is important that the evaluator clearly indicates the intentions at the beginning of the contract so that the parties are fully aware of the potential cost associated with using this comprehensive approach if the evaluator intends to charge them for it and so that they are aware of the time and effort expended even if they are not charged for it.

Capacity

In light of the well-researched fact that logical, analytical reasoning requires a thinker who is rested and fed and has enough time to think through the elements of their decision making in a step-by-step way, it is essential that the evaluator does not leave the final preparation of the report to the last minute. We have reviewed reports that are quite well reasoned through in the first half of the report and then deteriorate in quality toward the end. This is particularly problematic since the end of the report is ordinarily where the analysis, conclusions, and recommendations are found. It is also critical for evaluators to determine their capacity (e.g., expertise, training) to take on specialized issues in the dispute. Completing a self-assessment of the strengths or limitations of evaluation practice can help to determine whether the evaluator has the sufficient capacity to accept the case and/or to determine which cases should be accepted.

Ethical Responsibility of the Evaluator and the Use of Tools

There is convincing evidence on medical errors that checklists make a substantial difference in the competency of work done by even the most experienced and conscientious evaluators. Therefore it is suggested that evaluators make checklists for themselves for each case. Some checklists will be common to all evaluations, and some will be created for the specific evaluation in progress. These checklists can include lists of paperwork items that are delivered to the parties (contract, informed consent, questionnaires), as well as the dates that the documents were given to the sources and the dates they were returned to you. Another checklist should list paper and pencil measures that are administered in the evaluator's office, including detail about who provided the instruments to them, where they were completed, and whether the clients were supervised as they completed the measures. Yet another checklist should list psychological tests administered, including who administered and scored the tests. The evaluator should also include a list of collateral contacts, releases signed by both parents, dates contacted, dates interviewed, or when written responses were received if the collaterals were contacted in writing. By making a list of each contact, telephone call, interview, or observation, including who was present and how long it lasted, evaluators can keep better track of the activities in the case. If an appointment with a child is noted, the evaluator should also note which parent or other person brought the child to the office.

By using this Parenting Plan Evaluation Checklist, the evaluator can also double check the completeness of the file and can review the work that is completed (or outstanding) as part of the evaluation process. This checklist can also assist in reviewing the work of another evaluator.

Summary of the Decision Tree for Systematic Parenting Plan Evaluations

The decision tree for systematic parenting plan evaluations outlined in this book is a formal statement of procedures that many evaluators have done informally in their heads, without writing it down. There will have been parts that are recognizable to most evaluators. The goal of this book has been to make the process systematic, structured, transparent, and repeatable in the interest of improving the quality of evaluations and of the usefulness of these evaluations to the families and the courts that will read them.

The first step, after preparing in general and in particular with the necessary background knowledge, was to brainstorm about the possible explanations to account for the initial facts that were presented in the referral. These brainstormed thoughts were laid out in a page of sticky notes with different thoughts about what might be relevant. Those thoughts were then organized into lists of hypotheses and into a preliminary decision tree that provided some ideas about how the issues related to one another and how they were integrated.

The next step was to organize the data into issues, concerns, and/or allegations while noting the various sources of evidence and what light they shed on the issues named. Following that step and the gathering of all of the data, the approach called for organizing the issues into the themes that logically fit and then noting whether the factors are additive or antagonistic. The final step was to write the parenting plan implications for each theme and to think through what accountability is needed and how it can be achieved.

In this chapter, the authors have reviewed and summarized the major points made in the book and have provided additional suggestions for report writing and considerations about time and money. Additional suggestions were made for ways to manage the end of the evaluation process that might increase the acceptance of their work by the families who have been evaluated.

Annotated Bibliography

Gindes, M. (1995). Competence and training in child custody evaluations. *American Journal of Family Therapy, 23*(3), 273-280.

This paper recommends methods of training and the substantive areas to be mastered. Defining features of competence as well as ethical considerations relevant to this area of clinical practice are presented.

Gould, J. W. (2004). Evaluating the probative value of child custody evaluations: A guide for forensic mental health professionals. *Journal of Child Custody, 1*(1), 77-96.

In this paper, a detailed structure for reviewing the reliability and relevance of a child custody advisory report is provided in order to help these professionals produce a work product of greater weight and sufficiency to the court and a work product that is increasingly useful to the families evaluators seek to help.

Kirkpatrick, H. D., Austin, W., & Flens, J. (2011). Psychological and legal considerations in reviewing the work product of a colleague in child custody evaluations. *Journal of Child Custody, 8*(1/2), 103-123.

This article examines some important psycholegal and ethical considerations for work product reviews of PPEs and offers some suggestions about how and why a custody evaluator might derive some positive value from a competent and ethical review of his or her work product. The functions and ethics of this evolving role are discussed. The inherent tension between a retained reviewer's obligation to provide ethical and helpful testimony to the court while in the role of a retained expert is examined. The psychological perspectives of both evaluator and reviewer are presented.

Stahl, P. M. (2002). Child custody evaluations. In B. Van Dorsten (Ed.), *Forensic Psychology: From Classroom to Courtroom* **(pp. 171-197). New York, NY: Kluwer Academic/Plenum Publishers.**

This chapter focuses on four primary areas: considerations for starting a child custody evaluation practice, an integration of child development research into the concept of parenting plans, a way of understanding the special needs of the high-conflict population, and special ethical considerations for mental health professionals who work in the child custody evaluation field.

References

Ackerman, M. J. (1995). *Clinician's Guide to Child Custody Evaluations*. New York, NY: John Wiley & Sons.

Ackerman, M. J. (2001). *Clinician's Guide to Child Custody Evaluations (2nd ed.)*. New York, NY: John Wiley & Sons.

Ackerman, M. J. (2006). *Clinician's Guide to Child Custody Evaluations (3rd ed.)*. Hoboken, NJ: John Wiley & Sons.

Ackerman, M. J. (2006). Forensic report writing. *Journal of Clinical Psychology, 62*(1), 59-72.

Ackerman, M. J. (2008). *Does Wednesday Mean Mom's House or Dad's? Parenting Together While Living Apart*. Hoboken, NJ: John Wiley & Sons.

Ackerman, M. J. (2010). *Essentials of Forensic Psychological Assessment*. New York, NY: John Wiley & Sons.

Ackerman, M. J., & Ackerman, M. (1997). Custody evaluation practices: A survey of experienced professionals (revisited). *Professional Psychology, Research and Practice, 28,* 137-145.

Acklin, M. W., & Cho-Stutler, L. (2006). The science and art of child-parent observation in child custody evaluations. *Journal of Forensic Psychological Practice, 6*(1), 51-62.

American Psychiatric Association. (2012). *DSM (Diagnostic and Statistical Manual of Mental Disorders)*. Retrived from http://www.psychiatry.org/practice/dsm

American Psychological Association. (2011). *Specialty Guidelines for Forensic Psychology*. Retrieved from www.ap-ls.org/aboutpsychlaw/SGFP_Final_Approved_2011.pdf

Ariely, D. (2008). *Predictably Irrational: The Hidden Forces That Shape Our Decisions*. New York, NY: HarperCollins.

Ariely, D. (July 1, 2009). The end of rational economics. *Harvard Business Review*. Retrieved from http://hbr.org/product/the-end-of-rational-economics/an/R0907H-PDF-ENG

Ash, P., & Guyer, M. J. (1991). Biased reporting by parents undergoing child custody evaluations. *Journal of the American Academy of Child & Adolescent Psychiatry, 30*(5), 835-838.

Association of Family and Conciliation Courts. (2006). *Model Standards of Practice for Child Custody Evaluation*. Retrieved from http://www.afccnet.org/pdfs/Model%20Stds%20Child%20Custody%20Eval%20Sept%202006.pdf

Austin, W. G. (2002). Guidelines for utilizing collateral sources of information in child custody evaluations. *Family Court Review, 40*(2), 177-184.

Austin, W. G. (2011). Parental gatekeeping in custody disputes. *American Journal of Family Law, 25*(4), 148-153.

Austin, W. G., & Gould, J. (2006). Exploring three functions in child custody evaluations for the relocation case: Prediction, investigation, and making recommendations for a long-distance parenting plan. *Journal of Child Custody, 3*(3/4), 63-108.

Bacon, B. L., & McKenzie, B. (2004). Parent education after separation/divorce. *Family Court Review, 42,* 85-98.

Bathurst, K., Gottfried, A. W., & Gottfried, A. E. (1997). Normative data for the MMPI-2 in child custody litigants. *Psychological Assessments, 9*(3), 205-211.

Bauserman, R. (2002). Child adjustment in joint-custody versus sole-custody arrangements: A meta-analytic review. *Journal of Family Psychology, 16*(1), 91-102.

Bell, I., & Mellor, D. (2009). Clinical judgements: Research and practice. *Australian Psychologist, 44,* 112-121.

Benjamin, G. A. H., & Gollan, J. K. (2003). *Family Evaluation in Custody Litigation: Reducing Risks of Ethical Infractions and Malpractice.* Washington, D.C.: American Psychological Association.

Bow, J. N. (2010). Use of third party information in child custody evaluations. *Behavioral Sciences & the Law, 28*(4), 511-521.

Bow, J. N., & Boxer, P. (2003). Assessing allegations of domestic violence in child custody evaluations. *Journal of Interpersonal Violence, 18*(12), 1394-1410.

Bow, J. N., Flens, J., Gould, J. W., & Greenhut, D. (2006). Commentary: MMPI-2 readability. *Journal of Child Custody: Research, Issues, and Practices, 3*(1), 71-75. DOI:10.1300/J190v03n01_05.

Bow, J. N., Gottlieb, M., Gould-Saltman, D. J., & Hendershot, L. (2011). Partners in the process: How attorneys prepare their clients for custody evaluations and litigation. *Family Court Review, 49*(4), 750-759.

Bow, J. N., & Quinnell, F. A. (2001). Psychologists current practices and procedures in child custody evaluations: Five years after APA guidelines. *Professional Psychology: Research and Practice, 32,* 261-268.

Bow, J. N., & Quinnell, F. A. (2002). Psychologist current practices and procedures in child custody evaluation reports. *Family Court Review, 40,* 164-176.

Bradley, A. R. (2004). Child custody evaluations. In W. T. O'Donohue & E. R. Levensky (Eds.), *Handbook of Forensic Psychology: Resource for Mental Health and Legal Professionals* (pp. 233-243). New York, NY: Elsevier Science.

Brandon, D. J. (2006). Can four hours make a difference? Evaluation of a parent education program for divorcing parents. *Journal of Divorce & Remarriage, 45*(1/2), 171-185.

Butterfield, P. H. (2003). Issues in child custody evaluation and testimony. In C. R. Reynolds & R. W. Kamphaus (Eds.), *Handbook of Psychological and Educational Assessment of Children: Personality, Behavior, and Context* (2nd ed., pp. 493-507). New York, NY: Guilford Press.

Campbell, J. (1993). *Understanding Risk and Return* (Working Paper No. 4554). Retrieved from National Bureau of Economic Research website: http://www.nber.org/papers/w4554

Carter, K. C., & Carter, B. (1994). *Childbed Fever: A Scientific Biography of Ignatz Semmelweiss.* Westport, CN: Greenwood Publishing Group.

Centers for Disease Control and Prevention. (2013). Violence prevention. Retrieved from http://www.cdc.gov/violenceprevention/.

Chabris, C., & Simons, D. (2010). *The Invisible Gorilla: And Other Ways Our Intuitions Deceive Us.* New York, NY: Crown Publishing Group.

Clark, B. (1995). Acting in the best interests of the child: Essential components of a child custody evaluation. *Family Law Quarterly, 29,* 19-38.

Coates, C., Deutsch, R., Starnes, H., Sullivan, M., & Sydlik, B. (2004). Parenting coordination for high-conflict families. *Family Court Review, 42,* 246-262. doi:10.1177/1531244504422006.

Collins Dictionary of English. (2012). Retrieved from http://www.collinsdictionary.com/english-thesaurus

Connell, M. (2006). Notification of purpose in custody evaluations: Informing the parties and their counsel. *Professional Psychology: Research and Practice, 37*(5), 446-451.

Criddle, M. N., Jr., Allgood, S. M., & Piercy, K. W. (2003). The relationship between mandatory divorce education and level of post-divorce parental conflict. *Journal of Divorce & Remarriage, 39*(3/4), 99-113.

Cummings, E. M., & Davies, P. T. (1994). *Children and Marital Conflict: The Impact of Family Dispute and Resolution.* New York, NY: Guilford Press.

Darlington, Y. (2006). Experiences of custody evaluations: Perspective of young adults who were the subject of family court proceedings as children. *Journal of Child Custody: Research, Issues, and Practices, 3*(1), 51-66.

Drozd, L. M. & Olesen, N. W. (2004). Is it abuse, alienation, and/or estrangement? A decision tree. *Journal of Child Custody, 1*(3), 65-106.

Dutton, D. (2006a). Domestic violence: Different perspectives in domestic abuse assessment in child custody disputes: Beware the domestic violence research paradigm. *Journal of Child Custody, 2*(4), 23-42.

Dutton, D. (2006b). On comparing apples with apples deemed nonexistent: A reply to Johnson. *Journal of Child Custody, 2*(4), 53-63.

Ellis, E. M. (2000). *Rationale and Goals of the Custody Evaluation.* Washington, DC: American Psychological Association.

Elrod, L., & Dale, M. (2008). Paradigm shifts and pendulum swings in child custody. *Family Law Quarterly, 42*(3), 381-418.

Emery, R. E. (1994). *Renegotiating Family Relationships: Divorce, Child Custody, and Mediation.* New York, NY: Guilford Press.

Emery, R. E. (2011). *Renegotiating Family Relationships: Divorce, Child Custody, and Mediation (2nd ed.).* New York, NY: Guilford Press.

Emery, R. E., Otto, R. K., & O'Donohue, W. T. (2005). A critical asessment of child custody evaluations. *Psychological Science in the Public Interest, 6,* 1-29.

Erard, R. E. (2012). Expert testimony using the Rorschach performance assessment system in psychological injury cases. *Psychological Injury and Law, 5*(2), 122-134. doi:10.1007/s12207-012-9126-7

Erard, R. E., & Pickar, D. B. (2008). Countertransference bias: Self-examination, not cross-examination. *Journal of Child Custody: Research, Issues, and Practices, 4*(3/4), 101-109.

Evans, D. R. (1997). Custody and access assessments. In D. R. Evans (Ed.), *The Law, Standards of Practice, and Ethics in the Practice of Psychology* (pp. 201-231). Toronto, Ontario, Canada: Emond Montgomery Publications.

Faircloth, B. F., & Cummings, E. M. (2008). Evaluating a parent education program for preventing the negative effects of marital conflict. *Journal of Applied Developmental Psychology, 29,* 141-156.

Family Code, Section 3110-3118. (California Court appointed investigation of child sexual abuse.) Retrieved from http://www.leginfo.ca.gov/cgi-bin/displaycode?section=fam&group=03001-04000&file=3110-3118.

Fidler, B., Bala, N., & Saini, M. (2012). *Children Who Resist Postseparation Parental Contact: A Differential Approach for Legal and Mental Health Professionals.* New York, NY: Oxford University Press.

Flens, J. R. (2005). The responsible use of psychological testing in child custody evaluations: Selection of tests. *Journal of Child Custody, 2,* 3-27. doi:10.1300/J190v02n01_02

Flens, J. R., & Drozd, L. (2005). *Psychological Testing in Child Custody Evaluation.* Binghamton, NY: Haworth Press.

Fridhandler, B. (2008). Science and child custody evaluation: What qualifies as "scientific"? *Journal of Child Custody: Research, Issues, and Practices, 5*(3/4), 256-275.

Friedlander, S., & Walters, M. G. (2010). When a child rejects a parent: Tailoring the intervention to fit the problem. *Family Court Review, 48*(1), 98-111.

Galatzer-Levy, R. M., & Ostrov, E. (1999). From empirical findings to custody decisions. In R. M. Galatzer-Levy & L. Kraus (Eds.), *The Scientific Basis of Child Custody Decisions* (pp. 32-57). Hoboken, NJ: John Wiley & Sons.

Galatzer-Levy, R. M., Kraus, L., & Galatzer-Levy, J. (Eds.). (2009). *The Scientific Basis of Child Custody Decisions (2nd ed.).* New York, NY: John Wiley & Sons.

Garska v. McCoy, 278 S.E.2d 357 (W. Va. 1981).

Gawande, A. (2011). *The Checklist Manifesto: How to Get Things Right.* New York, NY: Metropolitan Books.

Geelhoed, R. J., Blaisure, K. R., & Geasler, M. J. (2001). Status of court-connected programs for children whose parents are separating or divorcing. *Family Court Review, 39,* 393-404.

Gindes, M. (1995). Competence and training in child custody evaluations. *American Journal of Family Therapy, 23*(3), 273-280.

Gladwell, M. (2005). *Blink: The Power of Thinking Without Thinking.* New York, NY: Little, Brown and Co.

Glancy, G., & Saini, M. (2009). The confluence of Evidence-Based Practice and *Daubert* within the fields of forensic psychiatry and the law. *Journal of the American Academy of Psychiatry and the Law, 37*(4), 438-441.

Goldstein, J., Freud, A., Solnit, A., & Burlingham, D. (1984). *Beyond the Best Interests of the Child.* New York, NY: Free Press.

Goodman, M., Bonds, D., Sandler, I., & Braver, S. (2004). Parent psychoeducational programs and reducing the negative effects of interparental conflict following divorce. *Family Court Review, 42*(2), 263-279.

Gould, J. W. (2004). Evaluating the probative value of child custody evaluations: A guide for mental health professionals. *Journal of Child Custody: Research, Issues, and Practices, 1*(1), 77-96.

Gould, J. W. (2005). Use of psychological tests in child custody assessment. *Journal of Child Custody: Research, Issues, and Practices, 2*(1/2), 49-69.

Gould, J. W. (2006). *Conducting Scientifically Crafted Child Custody Evaluations (2nd ed.).* Sarasota, FL: Professional Resource Press.

Gould, J. W., & Martindale, D. A. (2007). *The Art and Science of Child Custody Evaluations.* New York, NY: Guilford Press.

Gould, J. W., & Stahl, P. M. (2001). Never paint by the numbers: A response to Kelly and Lamb (2000), Solomon and Biringen (2001), and Lamb and Kelly (2001). *Family Court Review, 39*(4), 372-276.

Greenberg, L. R., Doi Fick, L. & Schnider, R. (2012). Keeping the developmental frame: Child-centered conjoint therapy. *Journal of Child Custody, 9*(1/2) 39-68.

Greenberg, L. R., & Gould, J. W. (2001). The treating expert: A hybrid role with firm boundaries. *Professional Psychology: Research and Practice, 32,* 469-478.

Greenberg, L. R., Gould, J. W., Gould-Saltman, D., & Stahl, P. (2003). Is the child's therapist part of the problem? What judges, attorneys, and mental health professionals need to know about court-related treatment for children. *Family Law Quarterly, Summer,* 34-69.

Greenberg, L. R., & Sullivan, M. (2012). Special issue on therapy in court involved cases. *Journal of Child Custody, 9*(1-2), 91-102.

Grisso, T. (1987). Psychological evaluations in divorce custody: Problems, principles, and procedures. In L. A. Weithorn (Ed.), *Psychology and Child Custody Determinations: Knowledge, Roles, and Expertise.* (pp. 157-181). Lincoln: University of Nebraska Press.

Grove, W., Barden, R., Garb, H., & Lilienfeld, S. (2002). Failure of Rorschach Comprehensive-System-based testimony to be applicable under the Daubert-Joiner-Kumho standard. *Psychology, Public Policy, and the Law, 8,* 216-234.

Grych, J. H. (2005). Interparental conflict as a risk factor for child maladjustment: Implications for the development of prevention programs. *Family Court Review, 43,* 97-108.

Gunsberg, L., & Hymowitz, P. (2005). *A Handbook of Divorce and Custody: Forensic, Developmental, and Clinical Perspectives.* New York, NY: Taylor and Francis Group.

Hammond, K. (1996). *Human Judgment and Social Policy.* Oxford, England: Oxford University Press.

Hardesty, J., Haselschwerdt, M., & Johnson, M. (2012). Domestic violence in child custody. In K. Kuehnle & L. Drozd (Eds.), *Parenting Plan Evaluations: Applied Research for the Family Court* (pp. 442-449).

Hodges, W. F. (1991). *Interventions for Children of Divorce* (2nd ed.). New York, NY: John Wiley & Sons.

Hynan, D. J. (1998). Interviewing children in custody evaluations. *Family and Conciliation Courts Review, 36*(4), 466-478.

Hynan, D. J. (2003). Forensic child evaluations. In L. VandeCreek & T. L. Jackson (Eds.), *Innovations in Clinical Practice: Focus on Children & Adolescents* (pp. 63-81). Sarasota, FL: Professional Resource Press.

In re Marriage of Seagondollar, 139 Cal.App.4th 1116, 43 Cal.Rptr 3d 575 (2006).

Institute of Medicine. (1999). *To Err is Human: Building a Safer Health System.* Retrieved from http://www.iom.edu/Reports/1999/To-Err-is-Human-Building-A-Safer-Health-System.aspx

Jaffe, P. G., Johnston, J. R., Crooks, C. V., & Bala, N. (2008) Custody disputes involving allegations of domestic violence: Toward a differentiated approach to parenting plans. *Family Court Review, 46*(3), 500-522.

Johnson, M. (2006a). Apples and oranges in child custody disputes: Intimate terrorism and situational couple violence. *Journal of Child Custody, 4*(2), 43-52.

Johnson, M. (2006b). A brief response to Dutton. *Journal of Child Custody, 4*(2), 65-67.

Johnston, J. R. (2006). A child-centered approach to high-conflict and domestic-violence families: Differential assessment and interventions. *Journal of Family Studies, 12,* 15-35. doi:10.5172/jfs.327.12.1.1

Johnston, J. R., Roseby, V., & Kuehnle, K. (2009). *In the Name of the Child: A Development Approach to Understanding and Helping Children of Conflicted and Violent Divorce (2nd ed.).* New York, NY: Springer Publishers.

Kahneman, D. (2011). *Thinking, Fast and Slow.* New York, NY: Farrar, Straus and Giroux.

Karras, D., & Berry, K. (1985). Custody evaluations: A critical review. *Professional Psychology: Research and Practice, 16,* 76-85.

Kelly, J. (2006). Children's living arrangements following separation and divorce: Insights from empirical and clinical research. *Family Process, 46*(1), 35-52.

Kelly, J. (2008). Preparing for the parenting coordination role: Training needs for mental health and legal professionals. *Journal of Child Custody, 5*(1), 140-159. doi:10.1080/15379410802070476.

Kelly, J., & Johnston, J. (2001). The alienated child: A reformulation of parental alienation syndrome. *Family Court Review, 39,* 249-256.

Kelly, J., & Lamb, M. (2000). Child development research to make appropriate custody and access decisions for young children. *Family and Conciliation Courts Review, 38*(3), 297-311.

Kirkpatrick, H. D., Austin, W., & Flens, J. (2011). Psychological and legal considerations in reviewing the work product of a colleague in child custody evaluations. *Journal of Child Custody, 8*(1/2), 103-123.

Kleinmuntz, D. N., & Schkade, D. A. (1993). Information displays and decision processes. *Psychological Science, 4*(4), 221-227.

Knapp, S., & Keller, P. A. (1993). Ethical issues in child custody evaluations. In L. VandeCreek, S. Knapp, & T. L. Jackson (Eds.), *Innovations in Clinical Practice: A Source Book* (Vol. 12, pp. 257-262). Sarasota, FL: Professional Resource Press.

Krauss, D. A., & Sales, B. D. (2000). The problem of "helpfulness" in applying Daubert to expert testimony: Child custody determinations in family law an exemplar. *Psychology, Public Policy, and Law, 5*(1), 78-99.

Kuehnle, K. F. (1996). *Assessing Allegations of Child Sexual Abuse.* Sarasota, FL: Professional Resource Exchange.

Kuehnle, K. F., & Connell, M. (2009). *The Evaluation of Child Sexual Abuse Allegations: A Comprehensive Guide to Assessment and Testimony.* Hoboken, NJ: John Wiley & Sons.

Kuehnle, K. F., & Drozd, L. M. (Eds.). (2012). *Parenting Plan Evaluations: Applied Research for the Family Court.* New York, NY: Oxford University Press.

Kuhn, T. (1962). *The Structure of Scientific Revolutions.* Chicago, IL: University of Chicago Press.

Lamb, M. E., Hershkowitz, I., Orbach, Y., & Esplin, P. (Eds.). (2009). Appendix: The NICHD investigative interview protocol. In K. Kuehnle & M. Connell (Eds.), *The Evaluation of Child Sexual Abuse Allegations: A Comprehensive Guide to Assessment and Testimony* (pp. 531-545). Hoboken, NJ: John Wiley & Sons.

Lamb, M. E., Orbach, Y., Hershkowitz, I., Esplin, P. W., & Horwitz, D. (2007). Structured forensic interview protocols improve the quality and informativeness of investigative interviews with children: A review of research using the NICHD Investigative Interview Protocol. *Child Abuse and Neglect, 31*(11/12), 1201-1231. doi:10.1016/j.chiabu.2007.03.021

Landrigan, C. P., Parry, G. J., Bones, C. B., Hackbarth, M. P., Goldman, D. A. & Sharek, P. J. (2010). Temporal Trends in Rates of Patient Harm Resulting from Medical Care. *New England Journal of Medicine, (363),* 2124-2134. DOI: 10.1056/NEJMsa1004404

Lebow, J., Walsh, F., & Rolland, J. (1999). The remarriage family in custody evaluation. In R. M. Galatzer-Levy & L. Kraus (Eds.), *The Scientific Basis of Child Custody Decisions* (pp. 236-256). Hoboken, NJ: John Wiley & Sons.

Lehrer, J. (2012, June 12). Why smart people are stupid. *The New Yorker.* Retrieved from http://www.newyorker.com/online/blogs/frontal-cortex/2012/06/daniel-kahneman-bias-studies.html

Lilienfeld, S. O. (2010). Can psychology become a science? *Personality and Individual Differences, 49,* 281-288.

Lilienfeld, S. O, Lynn, S. J., & Lohr, J. (2003). *Science and Pseudoscience in Clinical Psychology.* New York, NY: Guildford Press.

Maccoby, E. E., & Mnookin, R. H. (1992). *Dividing the Child: Social & Legal Dilemmas of Custody.* Cambridge, MA: Harvard University Press.

Martindale, D. A. (2004). Integrity and transparency: A commentary on record keeping in child custody evaluations. *Journal of Child Custody: Research, Issues, and Practices, 1*(1), 33-42. doi:10.1300/J190v01n01_03

Martindale, D. A. (2005). Confirmatory bias and confirmatory distortion. *Journal of Child Custody: Research, Issues, and Practice, 2*(1-2), 31-48.

Martindale, D. A. (2007). Setting standards for custody evaluators. *Journal of Psychiatry & Law, 35*(2), 173-199.

Martindale, D. A. (2013). Cognitive encapsulation: Thinking inside the box. *The Matrimonial Strategist, 31*(3), 3-5.

Martindale, D. A., & Gould J. W. (2008). Countertransference and zebras: Forensic obfuscation. *Journal of Child Custody: Research, Issues, and Practices, 4*(3/4), 69-75.

Martindale, D. A., Martindale, J. L., & Broderick, J. E. (1991). Providing expert testimony in child custody litigation. In P. A. Keller & S. R. Heyman (Eds.), *Innovations in Clinical Practice: A Source Book* (Vol. 10, pp. 481-497). Sarasota, FL: Professional Resource Exchange.

McKibbon, K. A., Wilczynski, N. L., & Haynes, R. B. (2004). What do evidence-based secondary journals tell us about the publication of clinically important articles in primary healthcare journals? *BMC Medicine, 2,* 33.

Melton, G., Petrila, J., Poythress, N., Slobogin, C., Lyons, P. & Otto, R. (1997). *Psychological Evaluations for the Courts: A Handbook for Mental Health Professionals and Lawyers (3rd ed.).* New York, NY: Guilford Press.

Meyer, G., & Archer, R. (2001). The hard science of Rorschach research: What do we know and where do we go? *Psychological Assessment, 13*(4), 486-502.

Mitcham-Smith, M., & Henry, W. (2007). High-conflict divorce solutions: Parenting coordination as an innovative co-parenting intervention. *The Family Journal, 15*(4), 368-373.

Mnookin, J., & Gross, S. (2003). Expert information and expert testimony: A preliminary taxonomy. *Seton Hall Law Review, 34,* 139-185.

Mnookin, R. H., & Kornhauser, L. (1979). Bargaining in the shadow of the law: The case of divorce. *Yale Law Journal, 88,* 950-956.

Mooney, K. C., & Nelson, J. M. (1989). Child custody evaluation. In M. C. Roberts & C. E. Walker (Eds.), *Casebook of Child and Pediatric Psychology* (pp. 176-191). New York, NY: Guilford Press.

Moran, J. A., & Weinstock, D. K. (2011). Assessing parenting skills for family court. *Journal of Child Custody, 8*(3), 166-188.

Munro, E. (2008). Lessons from research on decision-making. In D. Lindsey & A. Shlonsky (Eds.), *Child Welfare Research: Advances for Practice and Policy* (pp. 194-200). New York, NY: Oxford University Press.

National Institute of Child Health and Human Development. (2000, June 27). NICHD researchers improve techniques for interviewing child abuse victims [News release]. Retrieved from https://www.nichd.nih.gov/news/releases/Pages/interviewing.aspx.

Newmark, L., Harell, A., & Salem, P. (1995). Domestic violence and empowerment in custody and visitation cases. *Family Court Review, 33,* 30-62.

Newton, S. (2011). Obtaining and analyzing school-related data in a child custody evaluation. *Journal of Child Custody: Research, Issues, and Practices, 8*(3), 189-211.

Nmlawyer. (2012, January 17). Focus on the experts reasoning [Web log post]. Retrieved from http://www. standridgelawfirm.com/blog/page/4/

Otto, R.K. (2002). Use of the MMPI-2 in forensic settings. *Journal of Forensic Psychology Practice, 2*(3), 71-91.

Otto, R. K., Buffington-Vollum, J. K., & Edens, J. F. (2003). Child custody evaluation. In A. M. Goldstein (Ed.), *Handbook of Psychology: Forensic Psychology* (Vol. 11, pp. 179-208). Hoboken, NJ: John Wiley & Sons.

Pickar, D. B. (2008). Countertransference bias in the child custody evaluator. *Journal of Child Custody: Research, Issues, and Practices,4*(3/4), 45-67.

Pickar, D. B., & Kauffman, R. (2013). The child custody evaluation report: Toward an integrated model of practice. *Journal of Child Custody: Research, Issues, and Practices, 10*(1), 17-53.

Plous, S. (1993). *The Psychology of Judgment and Decision Making.* New York, NY: McGraw-Hill.

Powell, M. B., & Lancaster, S. (2003). Guidelines for interviewing children during child custody evaluations. *Australian Psychologist, 38*(1), 46-54.

Pruett, M. K., Arthur, L. A., & Ebling, R. (2007). The hand that rocks the cradle: Maternal gatekeeping after divorce. *Pace Law Review, 27*(4), 709-739.

Robb, A. (2006). Strategies to address clinical bias in the child custody evaluation process. *Journal of Child Custody: Research, Issues, and Practices, 3*(2), 45-69.

Rohrbaugh, J. B. (2007). *A Comprehensive Guide to Child Custody Evaluations.* New York, NY: Springer Science+Business Media.

Rubin, A., & Babbie, E. R. (2008). *Research Methods for Social Work.* Belmont, CA: Brooks/Cole.

Saini, M. A. (2008). Evidence base of custody and access evaluations. *Brief Treatment and Crisis Intervention, 8*(1), 111-129.

Sanders, J. D. (2007). Age appropriate parenting plans: Using child developmental information. *American Journal of Law, 21*(3), 67-74.

Schaul, B. H. (2005). Considering custody evaluations: The thrills and the chills. In L. Gunsberg & P. Hymowitz (Eds.), *A Handbook of Divorce and Custody: Forensic, Developmental, and Clinical Perspectives* (pp. 31-44). Hillsdale, NL: Analytic Press.

Schutz, B. M., Dixon, E. B., Lindenberger, J. C., & Ruther, N. J. (1989). *Solomon's Sword: A Practical Guide to Conducting Child Custody Evaluations.* San Francisco, CA: Jossey-Bass.

Semmelweis, I. (1999). *The Etiology, Concept, and Prophylaxis of Childbed Fever* (C. Carter, Trans.). Madison, WI: University of Wisconsin Press. (Original work published 1860)

Shifflett, K., & Cummings, E. M. (1999). A program for educating parents about the effects of divorce and conflict on children. *Family Relations, 48*(1), 79-98.

Simons, V. A., Grossman, L. S., & Weiner, B. J. (1990). A study of families in high-conflict custody disputes: Effects of psychiatric evaluation. *Bulletin of the American Academy of Psychiatry & the Law, 18*(1), 85-97.

Singer, J. (2008). Dispute resolution and the post-divorce family: Implications of a paradigm shift (Essay from University of Maryland School of Law). Retrieved from The Social Science Research Network Electronic Paper Collection: http://ssrn.com/abstract=1357330.

Singer, J., Hoppe, C., Lee, S. M., Olesen, N., & Walters, M. (2006). Child custody litigants: Rorschach data from a large sample. In C. B. Gacono & F. B. Evans (Eds.), *The Handbook of Forensic Rorschach Assessment* (pp. 445-464). New York, NY: Lawrence Erlbaum.

Stahl, P. M. (1994). *Conducting Child Custody Evaluations: A Comprehensive Guide.* Thousand Oaks, CA: Sage Publications.

Stahl, P. M. (1999). *Complex Issues in Child Custody Evaluations.* Thousand Oaks, CA: Sage Publications.

Stahl, P. M. (2002). Child custody evaluations. In B. Van Dorsten (Ed.), *Forensic Psychology: From Classroom to Courtroom* (pp. 171-197). New York, NY: Kluwer Academic/Plenum Publishers.

Stahl, P. M. (2010). *Conducting Child Custody Evaluations From Basic to Complex Issues.* Thousand Oaks, CA: Sage Publications.

Sullivan, M. J. (2008). Co-parenting and the parenting coordination process. *Journal of Child Custody, 5*(1), 4-24. doi:10.1080/15379410802070351.

Sullivan, M. J., & Greenberg, L. R. (2012). Parenting coordinator and therapist collaboration in high-conflict shared custody cases. *Journal of Child Custody, 9*(1-2), 85-107. doi:10.1080/15379418.2012.652571

Sullivan, M. J., Ward, P. A., & Deutsch, R. M. (2010). Overcoming barriers family camp: A program for high-conflict divorced families where a child is resisting contact with a parent. *Family Court Review, 48*(1), 116-135.

Tavris, C. (2003). The widening scientist-practitioner gap: A view from the bridge. In S. O. Lilienfeld, J. M. Lohr, & S. J. Lynn (Eds.), *Science and Pseudoscience in Contemporary Clinical Psychology* (pp. ix-xviii). New York: Guilford Press.

Tippins, T. M., & Wittmann, J. P. (2005). Empirical and ethical problems with custody recommendations: A call for clinical humility and judicial vigilance. *Family Court Review, 43,* 193-222.

Tumas, A. W. (2005). What judges want (and children dream). In L. Gunsberg & P. Hymowitz (Eds.), *A Handbook of Divorce and Custody: Forensic, Developmental, and Clinical Perspectives* (pp. 7-12). Hillsdale, NJ: Analytic Press.

U.S. CODE 42 - Title 42: The Public Health and Welfare. Retrieved from http://us-code.vlex.com/source/us-code-public-health-welfare-1041

Vertue, F. M. (2011). Applying case study methodology to child custody evaluations. *Family Court Review, 49*(2), 336-347. doi: DOI: 10.1111/j.1744-1617.2011.01375.x

Waller, E. M. & Daniel, A. E. (2004). Purpose and utility of child custody evaluations: From the perspective of judges. *Journal of Psychiatry & Law, 32*(1), 5-27.

Waller, E. M. & Daniel, A. E. (2005). Purpose and utility of child custody evaluations: The attorney's perspective. *Journal of the American Academy of Psychiatry and the Law, 33*(2), 199-207.

Walters, M. G., & Friedlander, S. (2011). Finding a tenable middle space: Understanding the role of clinical interventions when a child refuses contact with a parent. *Journal of Child Custody, 7*(4), 287-328.

Warshak, R. A. (2010). Family bridges: Using insights from social science to reconnect parents and alienated children. *Family Court Review, 48*(1), 48-80.

West, R. F., Meserve, R. J., & Stanovich, K. E. (2012) Cognitive sophistication does not attenuate the bias blind spot. *Journal of Personality and Social Psychology, 103*(3), 506-519.

Wood, J. M., Nezworski, M. T., Lillenfeld, S., & Garb, H. (2003). *What's Wrong with the Rorschach.* San Francisco, CA: John Wiley & Sons, Jossey-Bass.

Woodward Tolle, L., & O'Donohue, W. T. (2012). *Improving the Quality of Child Custody Evaluations: A Systematic Model.* New York, NY: Springer Publishing + Business Media.

Woody, R. H. (2000). *Child Custody: Practice Standards, Ethical Issues, and Legal Safeguards for Mental Health Professionals.* Sarasota, FL: Professional Resource Press.

Yankeelov, P. A., Bledsoe, L. K., Brown, J., & Cambron, M. L. (2003). Transition or not? A theory-based quantitative evaluation of families in transition. *Family Court Review, 41*(2), 242-256.

Appendices

Road Map for Using Research Within Parenting Plan Evaluations

The assistance of parenting plan evaluators in family law matters is generally considered beneficial because of the assumption that practitioners possess the necessary clinical wisdom and knowledge. This knowledge includes identification and delivery of assessments that are supported by rigorous scientific research and the integration of credible research evidence into recommendations for interventions. While parenting plan evaluators may use social science research to support their recommendations to the courts, the presentation and use of empirical evidence within these reports have not always been helpful to lawyers and judges.

Concerns have been expressed that the reliance on empirical evidence can be based on conclusions from studies that have questionable methodologies and lack empirical rigor, which may not be evident to legal professionals. It also may be a surprise to some that parenting plan evaluators are not always current on the best available evidence on issues influencing custody and access. Although there is no study that has considered the "research literacy" of parenting plan evaluators working within the courts, similar inquiries of the fluency of research knowledge by mental health professionals in general has demonstrated that practitioners do not consistently base practice decisions on empirical evidence.

Frustration about the overuse, overgeneralization, misinterpretation, and bias in the use of evidence to support parenting plan evaluations can lead to the legal community disregarding the importance of empirical evidence by casting research as irrelevant, of little value, and/or a source of support for advocacy claims. The critical question concerning the use of social science research within PPEs is not whether this evidence should play a role in family law proceedings but how to efficiently and effectively establish this role. It is logical, ethical, and necessary to integrate evidence-based principles into PPEs. The most important reason for integrating social science research into family law matters is to help guide legal professionals by identifying and promoting methods and procedures that are efficient and effective, while discarding those that are ineffective and potentially harmful.

We have developed a road map for the conscientious and explicit use of social science research within PPEs. We first introduce the various research designs that can help to inform the evaluator during the evaluation process. We also highlight seven interrelated phases of the evaluation process that are connected to the overall Decision Tree for Systematic Parenting Plan Evaluations and identify the various questions that can be answered from the empirical evidence at each phase. These phases include: Filling up the gas tank of knowledge; Preparation and Planning; Developing Preliminary Decision Trees; Data Collection; Analysis and Synthesis; Developing Recommendations; and Review, Revisit, Revise.

In this supplemental chapter, we also highlight common design flaws that can impact the interpretation and transferability of the results (e.g., ignoring the baseline, comparing apples and oranges, data snapshots of small samples, unrepresentative findings, data dredging, extrapolating the trend, and false causality). By identifying and discussing these common biases, we convey general knowledge about the quality and rigor of empirical evidence to provide the needed tools for developing research literacy. Within this section, we challenge the myth that "it's published so it must be good quality."

The third section of the supplemental chapter discusses strategies and approaches for managing and presenting research findings within evaluation reports. We focus on ways to present the findings to minimize the misrepresentation, overgeneralization, and biases in reporting these results. Using the airline industry example of checklists and manuals, we present guidelines for evaluators to report findings based on the judicious and systematic interpretation of the empirical evidence. We discuss how to present studies with small samples so that the evidence can inform the reader of both the implications and limitations of the findings. We also provide tips on how best to present the research to reduce the overgeneralization of findings (e.g., instead of "the research says," use more tentative language such as "the trend suggests"). Although the common line of "more research is needed" can frustrate the legal community looking for more certainty based on research findings, we provide tips on how best to convey, "it depends" by focusing on the factors that may influence how one should interpret the research results.

The ultimate goal of this supplement chapter is to help parenting plan evaluators to move away from simplified use of the empirical evidence and to help create a research literacy culture in the evaluation field that embraces the complexity both of the work and of the empirical evidence that helps to frame this work.

Filling up the Research Tank

The first step of the diagram is to "fill the research tank." We suggest that evaluators create folders (either electronically or in print) for the various factors/issues that are common across complex cases (violence, alienation, substance use, mental health, relocation, child development, etc.). To populate these folders with the most up-to-date research, we will discuss several strategies including:

- attending conferences specific to separation and divorce,
- updating one's library with recent books and peer-reviewed journal articles,
- joining listservs for discussions of recent books and articles,
- using AFCC access to the Family Court Review articles,
- looking for systematic reviews and topical reviews (e.g., Parenting Plan Evaluations: Applied Research for the Family Court includes many of the leading experts in the field and topical reviews of issues relevant to custody evaluations),
- being familiar with standards and guidelines relevant to this work,
- improving research literacy by taking basic research courses to know more about the strengths and limitations of research designs to become more critical of published works, and
- using research-quality decision trees to critically appraise evidence (with the understanding that not all published research is of good quality).

Data Planning

Here, parenting plan evaluators should ensure that they have the necessary knowledge from the social science research so that they can identify the tensions, debates, and factors to consider and can begin planning for the overall process for conducting the evaluation (see Chapter 2). Pertinent questions from the social science research should include the following.

- Are there any systematic reviews or topical overviews that can help identify the tensions, debates, and factors relevant to the issues?
- How common are the issues being considered?
- What is the prevalence, the base rate, and the etiology of the issues both for the normal population of separating families and for families involved in higher levels of conflict?
- What factors may be associated with the issues that the evaluator should be aware of and bring forward within the types of questions asked during interviews?
- What do we know about how best to assess, measure, and explore these issues?
- What tests, measures, and procedures would work best to explore these issues in a reliable and valid way?
- What is the quality of the social science research and how does this impact the weight given to the evidence in answering these questions?

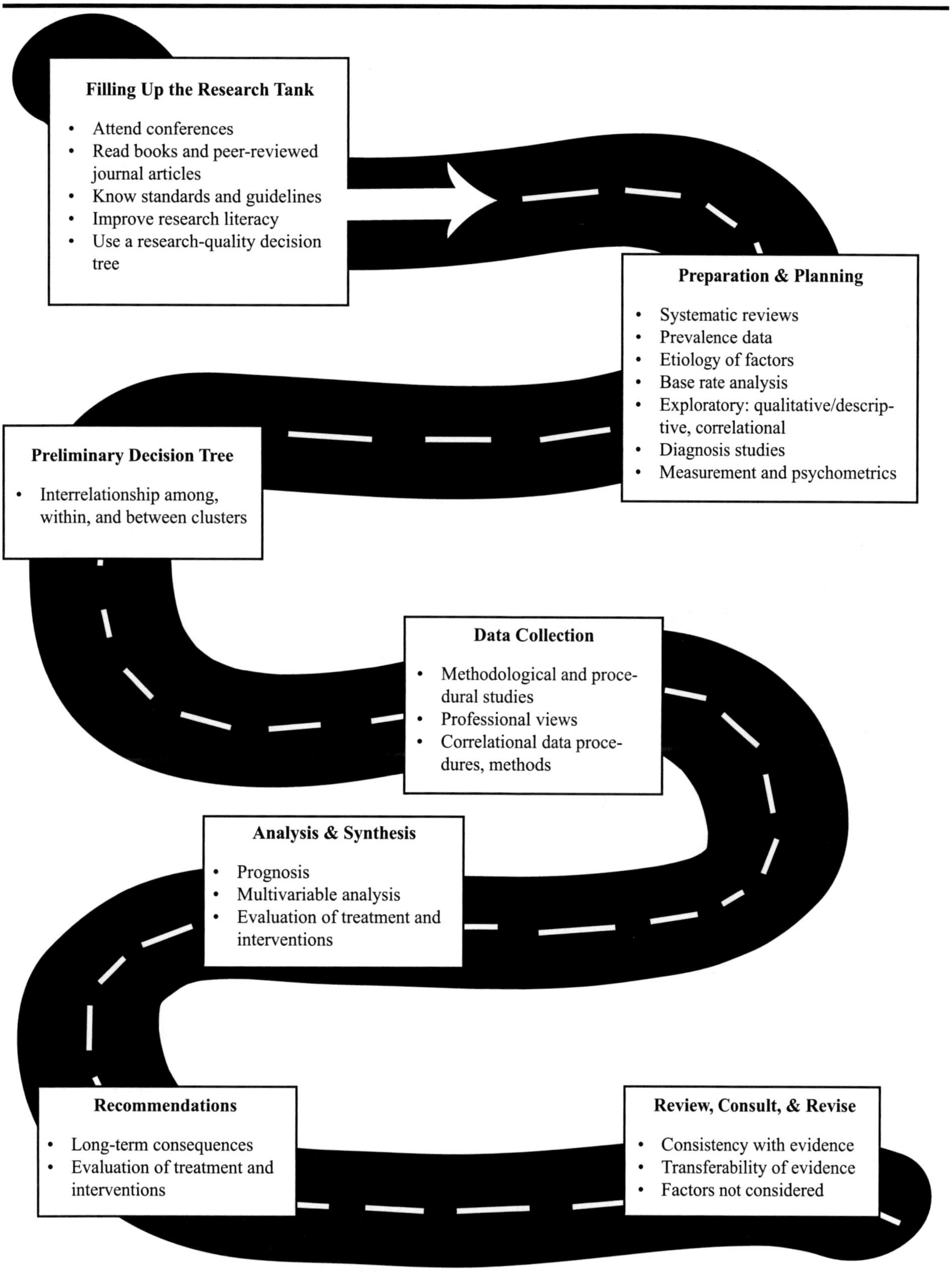

Filling Up the Research Tank

- Attend conferences
- Read books and peer-reviewed journal articles
- Know standards and guidelines
- Improve research literacy
- Use a research-quality decision tree

Preparation & Planning

- Systematic reviews
- Prevalence data
- Etiology of factors
- Base rate analysis
- Exploratory: qualitative/descriptive, correlational
- Diagnosis studies
- Measurement and psychometrics

Preliminary Decision Tree

- Interrelationship among, within, and between clusters

Data Collection

- Methodological and procedural studies
- Professional views
- Correlational data procedures, methods

Analysis & Synthesis

- Prognosis
- Multivariable analysis
- Evaluation of treatment and interventions

Recommendations

- Long-term consequences
- Evaluation of treatment and interventions

Review, Consult, & Revise

- Consistency with evidence
- Transferability of evidence
- Factors not considered

Figure A-1. Steps in Integrating Research Within Parenting Plan Evaluations

Preliminary Decision Tree

The focus of the preliminary decision tree (see Chapter 3) is to begin thinking about the interactional effects of issues and the ways that these factors can cluster together. Within this phase of the evaluation, social science evidence can help to inform the correlation/association among factors to begin mapping out these associations. For example, evidence could be sought to explore the relationship of the presence of alienation and domestic violence. Key questions to ask at this stage include:

- What are the relationships that have been found in the research regarding the presenting issues?
- How have these issues previously been clustered in the literature (e.g., alienation, estrangement, hybrid, etc.)?
- What are the variations both within and between the clusters of factors?
- Are there factors that have more weight in considering the relationship among these factors (e.g., is safety a stronger factor than well-being?)?

Data Collection

There are a variety of data collection methods that evaluators use within the evaluation process (see Chapter 4), and evaluators need to consider the empirical evidence to ensure that the methods and procedures chosen are based on sound scientific evidence. For example, in making the decision of whether to conduct the observation visit at the office or at the parents' home, it would be good to consult the literature to determine if the location has any impact on observation effect bias, testing effect bias, and so forth and whether there are any known strategies to control for confirmatory bias. Key questions to ask at this stage include:

- What does the research say about the various methods for conducting the evaluation?
- What can we learn from common practices in the field (professional views) regarding the various styles and procedures for data collection?
- Are some methods better than others for collecting reliable and valid information?
- Are there methods that do not provide the kinds of reliable and valid information that we are looking to collect?

Analysis/Synthesis

The analysis and synthesis of data can be the most challenging for evaluators as they attempt to make sense of an enormous amount of information (see Chapter 5 and Chapter 6). At this stage, the evaluator revisits the preliminary hypotheses developed within the decision tree and begins to consider the interactional effect of the various factors that have been identified. Considering the multivariate contribution of several factors is challenging and requires careful and systematic understanding of the potential impact of each factor included in the model. Empirical evidence can help to inform the evaluator about the kinds of relationships and interactional effects that have been found in the literature. This can help guide the weight provided to the various factors included in the hypotheses to be tested. Key research questions at this stage include:

- What does the research say about the interactions among the factors being considered?
- Do some factors carry more weight than others?
- What are the long-term consequences of these factors, both individually and as a group of inter-related factors?
- What are the protective buffers that have been identified that can help mitigate the negative results of the long-term consequences?

Recommendations/Parenting Plan

Recommendations regarding the parenting plan for the children should consider all of the issues and the interaction of the factors previously considered in the preceding steps (see Chapter 7). Key questions at this stage include:

- Are there parenting plan arrangements (e.g., sole custody vs. shared care) that generally work better for children in similar contexts?
- What factors (such as age, temperament, etc.) seem to be related to whether parenting plan arrangements work for children?
- What factors contribute to the parents' ability to make joint decisions?
- If a child/parent is amenable to receiving counseling, what evidence is there that would suggest that counseling would actually make a difference on the specified outcomes identified within the evaluation?

Building Research Literacy

Practitioners and Evidence

Social science research should be the foundation of mental health experts' conclusions and opinions (Kuehnle & Drozd, 2012), but mental health practitioners are not always current of the best available evidence, and practitioners do not consistently use evidence for making decisions.

Social science places a high value on "objective truths" based on systematic observations, and there is an explicit acknowledgement that subjective beliefs could be wrong. Scientific procedures are designed to protect the practitioner from relying on unfounded assumptions (Kuehnle & Drozd, 2012; Lilienfeld, 2010).

Judges, lawyers, and parents can be seduced by the expert who offers certainty in a context of uncertainty, but it is actually a downside to expert testimony that there is unwarranted confidence in the way that some mental health professionals express their opinions (Mnookin & Gross, 2003). Experts have the responsibility to inform the court of the multiple interacting variables that confound a linear decision (Kuehnle & Drozd, 2012).

Research Literacy

The volume of social science literature has increased dramatically over recent decades. To keep up with all research related to family law matters requires a significant amount of effort. In addition, it is challenging to apply social science research in family law matters, as contradictory research results may be difficult to interpret. Therefore evidence should be presented in a systematic, transparent, judicious, and ethical manner so that weight can be considered and appropriately distributed, and any limitation of evidence should be articulated and the grounds for any conclusion should be clearly spelled out (Glancy & Saini, 2009). A sample approach can be found in Table A-1.

"It's Published So it Must be Good Quality"

Based on a critical appraisal of 60,352 articles from 170 journals, McKibbon, Wilczynski, and Haynes (2004) found that only 6.8% of published articles were deemed "high-quality" studies. This is important given that published reports can make erroneous claims that may not be based on high-quality evidence, and contradictions in research findings may have more to do with the quality (or lack of quality) of the studies. Nowadays, and with the increased use of open-source publishing (e.g., publishing material on the Internet), it is not difficult to find at least one "study" to support just about any theory.

Table A-1. Questions to Ask Experts Regarding the Reliability and Validity of Research Studies

---

	Yes	*No*	*Unsure*

Design Issues

Are the reasons for the study clearly stated?

Are the objectives of the study consistent with the research design chosen?
    a) exploratory = qualitative; b) descriptive = survey;
    c) explanatory = experimental

Is there a clear statement of the hypothesis or expectation of outcome?

Has the research been conducted in such a way as to minimize bias and to
    increase trustworthiness and validity? For example: a) selection bias;
    b) measurement bias; c) attrition bias; d) performance bias;
    e) contamination bias

Sample Selection

Is the source of the sample appropriate (recruitment, setting) to recruit
    participants that represent the target population?

Are the sample characteristics appropriate for the research design (are they
    consistent with the intended target population)?

Is the eligibility of the participants sufficiently described?

Is the sample size adequately justified to find true differences in the results
    (e.g., based on sample power analysis)?

Measurement/Data collection

Are the proposed instruments/surveys/questions/interviews appropriate for
    measuring the expected outcome?

Does the outcome measure have sufficient reliability/validity?

Data Analysis

Does the data analysis seem appropriate and sufficient to report the findings
    (e.g., Do the numbers add up? Do the themes seem relevant?)

Results

Do any tables, graphs, or diagrams help in understanding the findings?

Are the results statistically/clinically significant?

Are the conclusions of the results justified?

Do the results on the same topic come to contradictory conclusions?
    If so, what may be the methodological issues impacting this difference?

Applicability of Findings

Are the demographic findings in the study similar to the particular client or
    context in which the decision is being made?

Do the results of the study help in making decisions/working with the client?

Common Research Flaws in Divorce Research

Ignoring the Baseline
A common error, whether accidental or intentional, is to compare raw numbers without adjusting for expected baseline differences. For comparisons to be valid, it is important to make some sort of adjustment.

Comparing Apples and Oranges
When making comparisons between two samples (e.g., court based versus population based), it is important to consider whether these samples are comparable or whether they are uniquely different from the other, thus making it impossible to make true comparisons.

Data Snapshots of Small Samples
Samples that are too small may not have sufficient power to detect an effect. Conversely, samples that are too large may find statistically significant differences but may not be clinically significant.

Unrepresentative Findings
Fallacy can occur when a statistic about a particular population is asserted to hold among members of a group for which the original population was not a representative sample. Nonrandom samples provide a rich description about the sample included in the study, but these descriptions should not be generalized beyond the sample.

Data Dredging
Also known as "data fishing" or "data mining," data dredging includes looking through data to find any relationships at all. Laws of Probability show that if one calculates a large number of correlations in data, there is a known likelihood of finding spurious significant relationships. Just because a relationship turns out to be statistically significant does not mean that it will be clinically relevant. Without forming a theory first of why the variables may be related, it is difficult to show the significance of why they are related, especially when several variables were included in the analysis at the same time.

Extrapolating the Trend
Extrapolation is about estimating data points outside the range of the current data, and therefore there need to be enough data points from the past to make an "educated guess."

False Causality
When a statistical test shows a correlation between **A** and **B**, there are usually five possibilities:

- **A** causes **B**
- **B** causes **A**
- **A** and **B** both partly cause each other
- **A** and **B** are both caused by a third factor, **C**
- The observed correlation was due purely to chance

Critical Appraisal of Evidence

Critical appraisal of evidence means making distinctions among "junk science," "pop science," and "scientific evidence." "Pseudoscience is particularly attractive because pseudoscience by definition promises certainty, whereas science gives us probability and doubt. Pseudoscience is popular because it confirms what we believe; science is unpopular because it makes us question what we believe" (Tavris, 2003, pp. xv-xvi). Critical appraisal is the judicious process of systematically appraising social science research to assess its trustworthiness and its value and relevance in a particular context. Using different kinds of evidence requires judgment, both about its validity and about its implications for practice in particular contexts.

Why So Many Study Designs?

There are so many research study designs because a chosen study design depends on the research question being asked by the researcher. Three common questions include: exploratory, descriptive, and explanatory.

Exploratory Questions = Qualitative Studies

To learn more about something that we know little about (e.g., youth's perception of the use of technology for parent-child communication), conducting qualitative interviews provides a method for gaining a rich understanding of these experiences and helps to explore the issues. The purpose is not to make inferences about these findings (e.g., not to make generalizations beyond the sample), but rather to explore the issues that may be important to consider.

Descriptive Questions = Surveys

To observe and then describe situations and events (e.g., the association between mental health problems and high-conflict divorce), it is often best to survey a random sample of participants from the population and then make generalizations back to the population. Random sample from the population provides the opportunity to describe situations and events without having to survey each participant in the population (e.g., all divorced individuals). The purpose is to describe relationships, associations, and patterns. These questions are not about making causal inferences about these relationships.

Explanatory Questions = Experiments

To explain whether an intervention works (e.g., do parent education programs reduce interparental conflict?), the sample receiving the intervention needs to be compared to a sample not receiving the intervention to assess whether the outcomes are different for the two groups. In the gold standard random control trial (RCT; see Figure A-2), the sample is randomly assigned to either a treatment group or a control group, and the outcome (e.g., conflict) is measured for both groups to assess whether the treatment group improved more (decreased conflict) than the control group not receiving the treatment.

Does sample size matter?

The inclusion/exclusion criteria: A high-quality study will clearly tell the reader all of the characteristics that people need to have had to be eligible for the study.

Sample selection: A good quality study specifies how the researchers selected whom to invite to be included in the study.

Random selection: Representative samples provide the best chance of the sample reflecting the population of interest.

Sample size: The number of participants included in a study should be based on "sample power calculations" to determine the number of participants that are required to achieve statistical significance for a given expected effect size.

Samples too small: "False negative effect" may occur where no significant findings are found despite the true relationship of the variables.

Samples too large: "False positive effect" may occur where a significant finding is found despite the

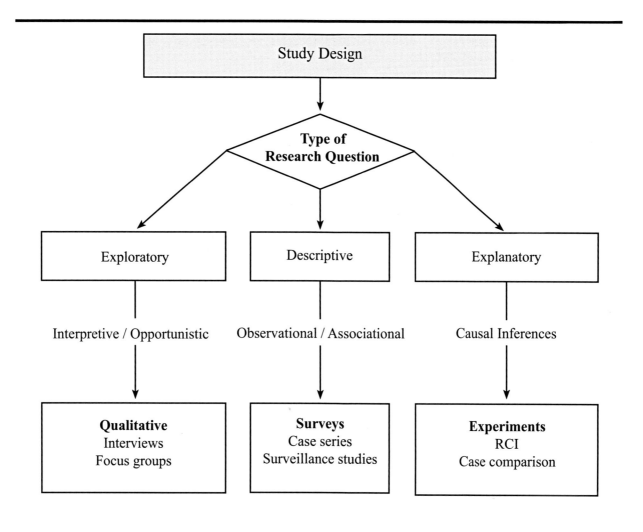

Note: RCT = Random Control Trial

Figure A-2. Determining the Best Research Design Based on Exploratory, Descriptive, and Explanatory Questions

fact that there is no true relationship of the variables, or the relationship is so small as to be meaningless.

Power of Test of Significance: To detect a large effect between two variables, a sample size of 30 is needed (Rubin & Babbie, 2008).

Qualitative samples: The purpose of qualitative studies is not to generalize findings so there is less emphasis on the size of the sample.

Tips on Literature Searching

- Be methodical in planning and conducting your search.
- Define and clarify your topic area. This means making sure that the area is neither too broad because you will be overwhelmed by information or too narrow because you will find it difficult to find information.

- Identify which databases you are going to search.
- Identify key words that best define your topic area (looking at key words contained in abstracts may be a helpful source).
- Set a time period for your searching. Would the last 5 years be sufficient, or do you need to go back further than that?
- Set exclusive and inclusive criteria—for example include all English-written articles from Europe, North America, and Australia.
- Keep a record of which databases you have searched as you go along. This helps to prevent you from repeating activity.
- Keep a record of all of your references as you search the literature. It may be tempting to skip this, but it is important that you write down the full reference accurately. It will save you time in the long run as you will not waste time hunting for a textbook or article months later when you do not have the full details.
- Be prepared to further narrow or widen you search if you identify too little or too much material.

Table A-2. The Research-based Practitioner Model

- Become adept at horizon scanning for evidence relevant to family law matters:
    - Start a journal club
    - Search research clearinghouses
    - Join listserves
- Enroll in additional training to make sense of social science evidence that can be contradictory.
- Be transparent about what research is guiding the creation of knowledge and the assumptions that underlie this knowledge.
- When new questions come up, search, explore, and appraise the best available evidence conscientiously and "judiciously."
- Lack of evidence should be articulated, and the grounds for any conclusion should be clearly spelled out.
- Consider the context and complexity of individual experiences of children and families by assessing the applicability of research findings.
- Push back from overgeneralizations and cookie-cutter approaches to solve complex problems.

Table A-3. Tips for Describing Research

---

1. Rather than stating, "The research demonstrates that . . ." it is better to be more tentative and state that "The trends suggest. . . ."
2. Do not throw out "little is known" or "it depends" without first considering the implications. On what does it depend? What factors are related and not related? For whom do the results apply?
3. "It depends" can frustrate, but it helps to talk about what it depends on (shared parenting depends on a number of factors: prior attachment, conflict, prior arrangements, development).
4. Be clear about describing small samples by reporting the size, setting, context, and implications for transferability and generalizability.
5. Focus your summary of the research on primary data rather than on summaries that others have made about the research.
6. If reviews are included (systematic reviews, meta-analysis), check for any selection bias of included studies.
7. Be clear in reporting results that you are referring to the probability (odds ratio) of an event occurring based on the research rather than predicting that the events will occur because of the results of the research.
8. There is no way to know perfectly, but you can focus on the potential risks (low, moderate, high) based on the research in a particular area.
9. Consider interconnected relationships among factors that may be related to the research question. For example, when looking at alienation, also consider research on child development, violence, maltreatment, parent-child relationships, attachment, and so forth. This will minimize the risk of presenting the research in silos.
10. Use rating systems to weigh the evidence. Do not assume that all research will provide the same results. Results can change depending on the methodological quality and rigor of the studies included.

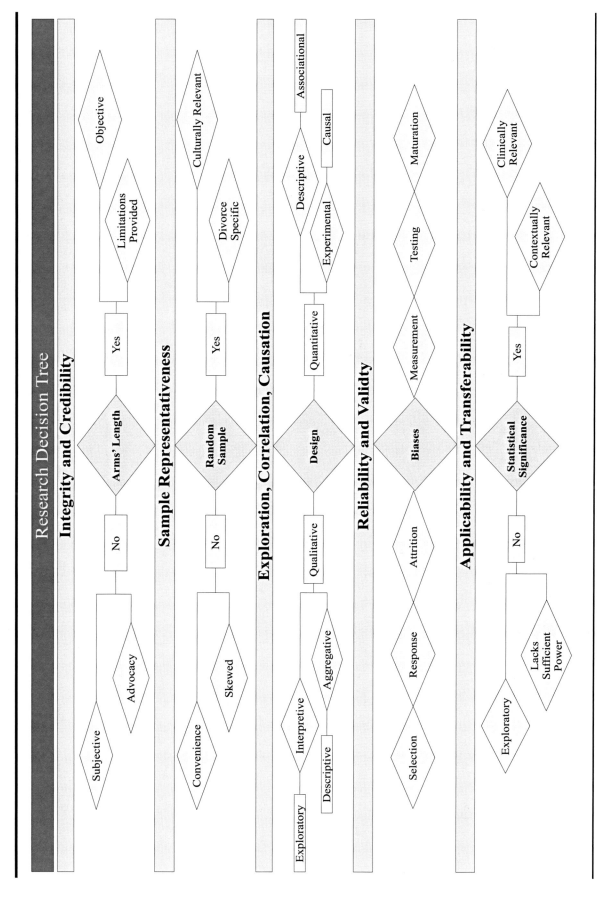

Figure A-3. A Research Decision Tree to Consider the Quality of Social Science Research

Tips For Using Google

- Use raw text logic: Unlike electronic databases that use controlled vocabulary, Google uses raw text searches, which means that Google matches the words in your search to the words appearing in pages on the Internet.

- Use only the important words rather than a full sentence or question. Generally, all of the words that you include in your search will be used to find matching content. Too many words will limit your results.

- By default, Google searches for your term throughout a web page. But if you just want it to search certain locations, you can use operators such as "inurl:", "intitle:", "intext:", and "inanchor:". Those operators search for a term only within the URL, the title, the body text, and the anchor text (the text used to describe a link).

- Keep it simple! Start by typing the name of a thing, place, or concept that you are looking for. Use the "funnel approach" by putting in terms one at a time to assess how the hits are being impacted by the addition of additional terms.

- Use of quotes: If you want to search for an exact phrase, use quotes. For example, ["this qualitative study"] will only find that exact phrase, and [alienation "this qualitative study"] will find pages that contain the word "alienation" and the exact phrase "this qualitative study." As another example [relocation "annotated bibliography"] will find pages that contain the word "relocation" and the exact phrase "annotated bibliography."

- Including methodological terms to find specific types of research designs can help to find specific examples of studies. Use of the terms ["parent education" "randomly assigned"] will find articles that included random assignment (usually RCTs) and the intervention identified within the searched pages that contain the word "parent education" and the exact phrase "randomly assigned."

- To increase the probability of locating peer-reviewed journals, limit the search by including "filetype:pdf" so that only .pdf hits are included in the hits. If you just want to search for .doc files (Word documents) use "filetype:doc." If you want to search for .ppt (Powerpoint presentations), use the "filetype:ppt."

- To search within a website (e.g., to search for research within clearinghouse websites), include the following in the search box: [site:cochranecollaboration.com parenting divorce]. That search will look for the term "parenting" and "divorce" only within the Cochrane Collaboration website.

- The "*" symbol is a wildcard. This is useful if you are trying to find research only in certain domains such as educational information: ["divorce" research *.edu].

If you cannot remember any of these operators, you can always use Google's advanced search (http://www.google.com/advanced_search).

Glossary

Accommodating	A cognitive coping strategy of disengaging and doing something different in the face of obstacles. It does not indicate whether the accommodation is effective or not (*see also* Tenacious).
Alienation	A cluster of commonly recognized behaviors in a child who rejects a parent and in a parent who undermines the child's relationship with the other parent.
Allegation	Refers to a claim or accusation of wrongdoing made by a party against another (*see* Substantiate).
Anchoring bias	A source of cognitive error involving the too heavy reliance on one piece of information (anchor), and making decisions by comparing this "anchor" to other information that moves decisions in ways that would not have been true without the anchor.
Attachment	Refers to the connections between individuals where at least one seeks proximity and security in times of distress. Although much attention has been paid to parent-child attachment patterns, growing research suggests the presence of attachment in adult couple relationships as well.
Attentional blindness	The cognitive error of not noticing or paying attention to certain types of observations because of the distracting attention paid to other observations.
Audit trail	The documentation of all steps taken during an evaluation (e.g., field notes, collaterals contacted, method for data reduction, etc.) so that a third party could review the work completed.
Best Interest Standard	Although there is no standard definition of Best Interest Standard for children, the term generally refers to the type of services, actions, and orders that will best serve a child's emotional, physical, and cognitive development. Many states have defined the factors that are considered as Best Interest Standards.
Bias	A predisposition to make observations that result in seeing what is being observed in a particular direction. Bias leads to distortions and misinterpretations.
Cause and effect	Established causal connections between variables (e.g., A causes B). Not to be confused with correlation (*see* Correlation).

Checklist	A written list of actions, steps, or activities that are to be completed when making a decision or starting an activity. A checklist ensures that all known preparations are made prior to making the decisions or beginning the activity.
Child-centered approach	An approach to evaluations in which the child's overall well-being is considered paramount and parents are seen in terms of their impact on the child, when making decisions that affect the child.
Child maltreatment	Sometimes referred to as child abuse and neglect, refers to all forms of physical and emotional harm, sexual abuse, neglect, and exploitation of children that may result in actual or potential harm to the child's health, development, and overall well-being.
Clusters	A stage of data analysis in which similar concepts are grouped together to form broader, integrated representations of factors.
Cognitive errors	Thought-process errors, or thinking mistakes, which lead to incorrect conclusions.
Collateral source	A person with knowledge about a family who can provide independent information to an officer of the court or parenting plan evaluator.
Complex child custody cases	Child custody disputes involving multiple, interacting factors.
Concept	1. An abstract idea. 2. A plan or intention.
Conceptualization	The mental formulation, the process of transforming an idea into a potential explanation.
Confirmation bias	The tendency to seek information and/or evidence that conforms to prior thinking or first impression, and to treat new information that does not conform to that thinking as irrelevant.
Confounding variable	In statistics, an extraneous variable, a factor that disguises the true relationship between variables.
Construct	A structured complex explanatory idea based in theory.
Convergent validity	The degree to which different measures agree with each other, lending support to the accuracy of the measurement.
Cookie-cutter	An expression to suggest a general and formulaic view or method, irrespective of contextual factors.
Coparenting	The process by which the parenting responsibilities of two parents who do not live together are jointly organized. It includes the parenting behaviors and the relationship between the parents as parents.

Correlation	The strength of association between two variables, but without indicating causality of the relationship.
Countertransference	A psychological process in which the evaluator projects his or her own unresolved issues onto the client and then perceives the client in those terms.
Credibility	When the findings make sense to, and can be accepted by, the reader or observer based on the data presented and the way it was presented.
Critical appraisal	A process of systematically examining evidence to establish its value and relevance.
Cross-sectional	A research design that measures a single group of subjects at a single point in time.
Cultural bias	A source of error stemming from ignorance or insensitivity to the meaning of cultural differences and the use of the larger group as the standard for human behavior.
Data analysis	The process of gathering, modeling, and transforming data by highlighting useful information, considering themes and identifying potential gaps in the evidence collected.
Data synthesis	Refers to the process of integrating multiple themes derived from data analysis to explore how the themes may converge and diverge in understanding the meaning of the evidence collected.
Decision Tree	1. A schematic tree-shaped illustration of multiple variables to be considered. 2. A method to determine a course of action in which each "branch" represents a possible decision or occurrence.
Descriptive research designs	Designed to describe situations and events, often including surveys of random samples to make generalizations back to the population (*see also* Exploratory research designs and Explanatory research designs). It does not indicate causality.
Determinism	The belief that all human acts are caused by something, and not by free will.
Dichotomous	A variable that has only two categories.
Dichotomy trap	A thinking error that simplifies a decision to only two possibilities, thereby excluding the middle ground or other possible categories.
Discriminant validity	The correspondence of measures such that they measure the same construct rather than different constructs.

Domestic violence
(Intimate partner violence)   Includes any use of physical or sexual force, actual or threatened, in an intimate relationship. It may include a single act of violence, or a number of acts forming a pattern of abuse through the use of assault, power, and control.

Empirical   An approach to knowledge based on the belief that only knowledge gained through direct observation is acceptable.

Enmeshment   A psychological relationship between two or more people in which personal boundaries are permeable and unclear.

Etiology   The causal pathway to explain events or outcomes.

Evidence-based practice   The integration of individual practice expertise with the best available evidence from science.

Explanatory research designs   To explain the causal relationship between some defined variables and a particular outcome.

Exploratory research designs   To learn more about something that we know little about in an open-ended, not explanatory way (*see also* Explanatory research designs and Descriptive research designs).

Extrapolation   To extend knowledge, generalizing from one context into another which was not directly studied.

Fabrication   Refers to the falsification of statements to suggest a different conclusion than the truth.

Facilitative gatekeeping   Refers to parents who are proactive in supporting the child's relationship with the other parent.

Fact finding   The process of conducting data collection, including interviews and observations to collect the evidence about a case.

Fast-thinking   Refers to System I or intuitive thinking (*see* Kahneman, 2011).

Forensic evaluation   A psychological evaluation with the primary goal of providing information to the court regarding the legal question at hand.

Gatekeeping   The influences of a parent in supporting (or not supporting) the relationship of a child with the other parent (*see* Facilitative gatekeeping and Restrictive gatekeeping).

Gender bias   1. The unwarranted generalization of evidence to the population as a whole when one gender is not adequately represented in the evidence.
2. A consistent preference for one gender over the other, often unconscious (*see also* Bias.).

Generalizability	The ability to make inferences to the larger population, not only the particular group studied.
Hybrid model	A term to describe the situation in which a child's rejection of one parent is caused by both alienating behavior from the preferred parent and some kinds of poor parenting from the rejected parent.
Hypothesis	A tentative and testable proposed explanation of the relationship between and among variables.
Hypothesis building	The method to develop and think about potential explanations that can be tested empirically.
Ideological	A closed system of beliefs and values that shape the understanding of the world for adherents.
Inferences	Tentative conclusions based on information examined.
Interactional	A research model that looks at the simultaneous interaction among more than one variable.
Intuition	Knowledge based on subjective meaning, perceptions, and personal experiences, as well as universal heuristics. Also known as one's "gut feeling."
Matrix	An organizing method for recording the variables under consideration.
Methodology	A series of steps taken to investigate, explore, and/or to acquire new knowledge.
Multidetermined	An event or behavior determined by more than one variable.
Multidimensional	Refers to the presence of more than one variable to measure a single concept.
Multifactorial	The simultaneous relationship among several variables or factors.
Outcome-based interventions	A method of intervening with particular goals in mind and then following up to determine whether these goals have been achieved.
Overnights	Refers to parenting arrangement where children stay at a parent's home throughout the night. Usually applied to the nonresidential parent.
Paradigm	A frame of reference that shapes our observations and understanding. When we change our reference point for observation and understanding, we call this a "paradigm shift."

Parallel parenting   Parenting arrangements in which each parent has an independent right to make decisions concerning the child while in that parent's care and control.

Parent capacity   Although no universal definition exists for parent capacity, there is general agreement that capacity normally includes the provision of resources for healthy development, sensitivity to the child's needs, appropriate sensory stimulation, positive emotional expression, and appropriate boundaries and limits in family interaction.

Parentification   A role reversal in parent-child relationships in which the child acts as the parent by providing emotional support, care, and sometimes safety.

Parenting Plan Evaluation   One term used to describe the method for evaluating custody disputes (others include custody assessments, child custody evaluations, etc.). The term is meant to emphasize the parenting role of the parents, rather than suggesting ownership (custody).

Parenting style   A specific parenting pattern and/or style (authoritative, authoritarian, lax, or permissive) that a parent tends to use most of the time with children.

Prediction   A statement that an event will occur in the future, often made with probability estimates included.

Probability   The mathematical description of the likelihood of an event occurring in the future.

Procedural errors   Errors occurring during the evaluation process stemming from deviations from the standards and best practices of a profession.

Protective gatekeeping   Restrictive gatekeeping behaviors for the purpose of protecting the child from harm.

Psychoeducational intervention   A program intended to provide education within a therapeutic context to alleviate presenting problems by giving the clients needed information about how best to deal with the issues they confront.

Questionnaire   A document that contains questions and other types of items that are designed to elicit information. Closed-ended questionnaires provide forced choices of predetermined categories for responses, while open-ended questionnaires provide the respondent with the opportunity to provide a narrative response to the question without selecting from a list of possible responses.

Recommendations   Guidance provided by the evaluator within the context of a parenting plan evaluation about the child's residency, visiting arrangements, decision making, and any suggested remedies for family problems.

Reliability	The quality of an observation that suggests that the same results would be found if the observation was repeated. This is not to be confused with validity (*see* Validity).
Restrictive gatekeeping	The process by which a parent tries to minimize the other parent's involvement with the child without justification (*see also* Protective gatekeeping).
Sabotaging	Refers to behaviors by a parent in an attempt to undermine the relationship of the child with the other parent. Often used to describe efforts by an IPV perpetrator to undermine the victim's relationship with the child.
Simple child custody case	A family presenting with a narrowly defined set of issues or problems.
Slow thinking	Refers to system II or analytical thinking (*see* Kahneman, 2011).
Social desirability bias	A source of bias based on the tendency of people to say or do things that will make them look good.
Social science	The scientific investigation of human behavior and social issues.
Spurious relationship	A relationship between two variables that is either coincidental or actually caused by a third variable.
Substantiate	To support an allegation with proof or evidence (*see* Allegation).
Synergistic	The quality of interaction among variables working together to create an outcome different than would be the result of any one variable or combination of variables taken independently.
Systematic method	A scientific approach based on a clearly formulated question and the use of transparent and explicit methods to identify, select, and critically appraise evidence.
Systematic parenting plan evaluation	The explicit and transparent method for conducting parenting plan evaluations based on a clear understanding of the presenting issues, the development of methods to collect and analyze data, and the development of recommendations that are explicitly connected to the collection, analysis, and synthesis of the data.
Systemic thinking errors	Consistent and predictable errors in thinking that result from bias in the thinker.
Tenacious	The quality of persevering in the face of obstacles (*see also* Accommodating).

Transferability

The ability to accurately generalize the results of one study to another similar individual, group, or setting (*see* Generalizability).

Transparency

The quality of openness by which observers can see the process, methods, and the decision making used by any person presenting opinions or conclusions.

Triangulation (Cross-Checking)

The process of using two or more sources of information to purposefully double-check facts or opinions.

Validity

The accuracy of measurement, the degree to which the instrument measures what it is intended to measure. Not to be confused with reliability (*see* Reliability).

Variable

The general term used to describe an element or feature of reality that may change or cause another element to change. Variable is used in describing research methods.

Vetting for bias

Appraising the methodology and the evidence to uncover any potential influence of bias on the overall results.

Weighting

A method to consider differential effects of different variables in influencing an outcome. It is used when different variables in a situation are not equal and there is at least some knowledge about the extent to which particular variables are salient.

Aerial Road Map

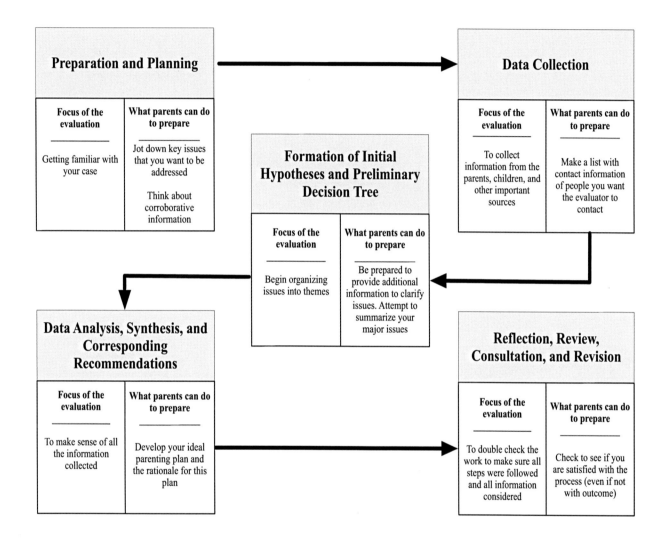

Parenting Plan Evaluation Data Matrix I: Data

Source of Concern	Mother's Evidence	Father's Evidence	Children's Evidence	Collateral Evidence	Evaluator's Evidence
Intimate Partner Violence or Domestic Violence					
Child Abuse/Maltreatment and/or Neglect					
Substance Abuse					

Source of Concern	Mother's Evidence	Father's Evidence	Children's Evidence	Collateral Evidence	Evaluator's Evidence
Mental Health					
Children's Adjustment					
Children's Preferences					

Source of Concern	Mother's Evidence	Father's Evidence	Children's Evidence	Collateral Evidence	Evaluator's Evidence
Parenting Competency					
Coparenting Capacity					
Relocation					

Source of Concern	Mother's Evidence	Father's Evidence	Children's Evidence	Collateral Evidence	Evaluator's Evidence
Other Issues					

Parenting Plan Evaluation Data Matrix II: Summary, Analysis, and Synthesis

Source of Concern	Summary of Evidence	Analysis of Evidence: Reliability & Validity	Synthesis of Evidence: Inferences
Intimate Partner Violence or Domestic Violence			
Child Abuse/Maltreatment and/or Neglect			
Substance Abuse			

Source of Concern	Summary of Evidence	Analysis of Evidence: Reliability & Validity	Synthesis of Evidence: Inferences
Mental Health			
Children's Adjustment			
Children's Preferences			

Source of Concern	Summary of Evidence	Analysis of Evidence: Reliability & Validity	Synthesis of Evidence: Inferences
Parenting Competency			
Coparenting Capacity			
Relocation			

Source of Concern	Summary of Evidence	Analysis of Evidence: Reliability & Validity	Synthesis of Evidence: Inferences
Other Issues			

Parenting Plan Evaluation Data Matrix III:

Themes, Analysis, Synthesis (Recommendations), and Accountability

Themes (Level II Inferences: Analysis)	Additive? Synergistic? Antagonistic? Direction? (Level III Inferences: Analysis)	Parenting Plan Implications and Recommendations (Level IV Inferences: Synthesis)	Accountability
Safety			

Themes (Level II Inferences: Analysis)	Additive? Synergistic? Antagonistic? Direction? (Level III Inferences: Analysis)	Parenting Plan Implications and Recommendations (Level IV Inferences: Synthesis)	Accountability
Child Issues			

Themes (Level II Inferences: Analysis)	Additive? Synergistic? Antagonistic? Direction? (Level III Inferences: Analysis)	Parenting Plan Implications and Recommendations (Level IV Inferences: Synthesis)	Accountability
Parent Issues			

Venn Diagram for Optimal Parenting Plan for Child Safety and Well-being

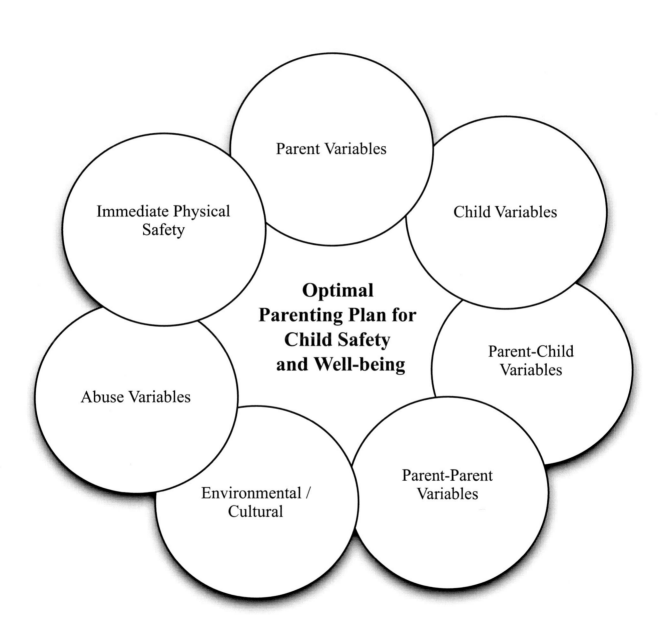

Parenting Plan Evaluator's Cognitive Error Checklist

✓		
	Self-interested biases	*Problem:* Is there any reason to suspect that the report contains recommendation of errors motivated by self-interest? *Solution:* Review the report with extra care, especially for overoptimism and/or harsh criticism.
	Any overcommitment to your recommendations	*Problem:* Have you fallen in love with your recommendations? *Solution:* Look for evidence that does not support your recommendations.
	Groupthink	*Problem:* Were there dissenting opinions within the sources of data? Were they explored adequately? *Solution:* Look for evidence from collateral sources that does not support the common views, and explore how these may impact your overall analysis.
	Bias of memorable data	*Problem:* Could your data analysis be overly influenced by an event or situation that you consider to be a memorable success or failure? *Solution:* Consider how your thoughts of the case may be guiding your analysis.
	Confirmation bias	*Problem:* Are credible alternatives included along with the recommendation? In California, the evaluation report must include information that does not support the conclusions of the evaluator. *Solution:* The presentation of differing information should be separated both in the analysis and in the presentation of findings.
	Anchoring bias	*Problem:* Do you know how the data was anchored? Can there be: • unsubstantiated numbers? • extrapolation from history? • a motivation to use a certain anchor? *Solution:* Re-anchor with figures generated by other models or benchmarks, and then conduct new analysis.

✓		
	Halo effect	***Problem:*** Are you assuming that a person, organization, or approach that is successful in one area (and is your favorite, perhaps) will be just as successful in another? ***Solution:*** Eliminate false inferences by seeking additional comparable examples.
	Ways that your professional history with similar cases may be impacting your analysis	***Problem:*** Are the recommendations overly attached to a history of past decisions/past behaviors? ***Solution:*** Consider the issue as if you were a new evaluator assigned to the case.
	Overconfidence and optimistic biases	***Problem:*** Are the recommendations overly optimistic about the future? ***Solution:*** Consider how the family will manage without court monitoring and/or involvement of professionals.
	Disaster neglect	***Problem:*** Is the worst case bad enough? ***Solution:*** Imagine that the worst has happened, and develop a story about the causes and potential solutions to mitigate the risks.
	Loss aversion	***Problem:*** Are the recommendations overly cautious? ***Solution:*** Realign recommendations to share responsibility for the risk or to remove risk.

Parenting Plan Evaluations Flaws

✓	*Name of Flaw*	*Description of the Flaw*
	"Pox on both their houses" flaw	The evaluator makes the competing claims of the parties equivalent, and dismisses both sides.
	"Everyone is like me" flaw	The evaluator does not account for personal, religious, ethnic, or cultural differences between the family and him- or herself.
	Pollyanna flaw	The evaluator gets weighed down by the seriousness of the problems and retreats into a superficial recommendation that does not account for the data in the report.
	Jerry Springer flaw	The evaluator focuses in detail on the parents and their allegations, with little or no attention on the child's needs or relationships.
	Tunnel-vision flaw	The evaluator considers one or two concerns and drops all others as though they never existed.
	Arrogance of Experience flaw	The evaluator uses training as a clinician in family systems or psychoanalytic theory, without looking at the psycho-legal issues and using forensic tools and understandings.
	This-Is-Probably-Good-Enough flaw	The evaluator lets pressures about time or money lead to limits on the necessary scope of the evaluation.
	No-One-Can-Influence-Me flaw	The evaluator does not control input from the attorneys, including attempts to frame the issues.
	Trust-Me! flaw	The evaluator does not maintain transparent methods and record keeping.
	It's not me, its you flaw	The evaluator has unexamined personal reactions to the issues or the people that interfere with objectivity.
	Confusion flaw	The evaluator fails to manage the complexity in the case and becomes overwhelmed.

Parenting Plan
Evaluations Checklist (PPEC)

Case Name: _____   Case Number: _____

Reviewer: _____

Date(s) of the Review: _____

Scope	Rating	Explain Rating
Has the scope of the report been delineated by the court order and signed stipulation by the parties?	❏ Yes ❏ No	
Cultural Competency Did the evaluator attend to the cultural, ethnic, racial, religious issues in the family and the case?	**Rating** ❏ Yes ❏ No	**Explain Rating**
Record keeping Is there a case file complete and transparent?	**Rating** ❏ Yes ❏ No	**Explain Rating**
Has there been reasonable care to prevent loss or destruction of records?	❏ Yes ❏ No	
Communication with litigants Has each party received all correspondence and documents associated with this case?	**Rating** ❏ Yes ❏ No	**Explain Rating**
Ex-parte communication Have steps been taken to minimize ex-parte communication?	**Rating** ❏ Yes ❏ No	**Explain Rating**
Review of policies Has each party been informed about the policies, procedures, and fees prior to commencing the evaluation?	**Rating** ❏ Yes ❏ No	**Explain Rating**
Informed consent of collaterals Have the collaterals been made aware of the potential use of information they are providing?	**Rating** ❏ Yes ❏ No	**Explain Rating**

Factors to be assessed	Rating	Explain Rating
Have all factors that are pertinent to the evaluation been included in the investigation?	❒ Yes ❒ No	
Use of diverse methods	**Rating**	**Explain Rating**
Has the evaluator used multiple methods and sources of information to provide multiple data points?	❒ Yes ❒ No	
Has the evaluator contacted all collateral sources identified by the parties? Or explained reasons for not contacting some?	❒ Yes ❒ No	
Use of a balanced process	**Rating**	**Explain Rating**
Has the evaluator used a balanced process in order to increase objectivity, fairness, and independence?	❒ Yes ❒ No	
Use of reliable and valid methods	**Rating**	**Explain Rating**
Have the methods for conducting the evaluation been based on empirically based procedures of data collection?	❒ Yes ❒ No	
Assessment of parenting	**Rating**	**Explain Rating**
Has the assessment included all adults who perform a caretaking role and/or live in the residence with the children?	❒ Yes ❒ No	
Assessment of children	**Rating**	**Explain Rating**
Has the evaluator followed generally recognized procedures when conducting interviews with children?	❒ Yes ❒ No	
Has the assessment included each child who is subject to the evaluation?	❒ Yes ❒ No	
Assessment of adult-child relationships	**Rating**	**Explain Rating**
Was the evaluator mindful of the fact that their presence in the same physical environment as those being observed may have created a risk that could influence the very behaviors and interactions that they are endeavouring to observe?	❒ Yes ❒ No	
Did the evaluator inform the parties the purpose for which observational sessions were being conducted?	❒ Yes ❒ No	

In-person meetings Has the evaluator conducted at least one in-person interview with each parent and with other adults who perform a caretaking role and/or are living in the residence with the child(ren)?	Rating ❐ Yes ❐ No	Explain Rating
Competency of the evaluator Has the evaluator conducted assessments in areas that they are competent?	**Rating** ❐ Yes ❐ No	**Explain Rating**
Incomplete, unreliable, missing data Has the child custody evaluator disclosed incomplete, unreliable, or missing data and the impact on the conclusions?	**Rating** ❐ Yes ❐ No	**Explain Rating**
Use of formal instruments Has the evaluator articulated the bases for selecting the specific instruments used.	**Rating** ❐ Yes ❐ No	**Explain Rating**
Team approach Are all of the mental health professionals competent to fulfill their assigned roles?	**Rating** ❐ Yes ❐ No	**Explain Rating**
Dual role issues Have reasonable steps been made to avoid multiple relationships with any and all participants of an evaluation?	**Rating** ❐ Yes ❐ No	**Explain Rating**
Weighing the evidence Has the evaluator explained how different sources and different types of information were considered and weighed in the formation of their opinions?	**Rating** ❐ Yes ❐ No	**Explain Rating**
Has the evaluator explained the limits and strengths of applying social science research to this case?	❐ Yes ❐ No	
Interim recommendations Has the evaluation refrained from making interim recommendations?	**Rating** ❐ Yes ❐ No	**Explain Rating**

Presentation of findings	**Rating**	**Explain Rating**
Has the evaluator striven to be accurate, objective, fair, and independent in their work? Does the report appear unbiased (neutral) on its face?	☐ Yes ☐ No	
Has the evaluator utilized high quality social science research to support his or her work?	☐ Yes ☐ No	
Has the evaluator refrained from including information in the report that is not relevant to the issue in dispute?	☐ Yes ☐ No	
Articulation of limitations	**Rating**	**Explain Rating**
Have the limits to the evaluation and the basis for making recommendations been provided?	☐ Yes ☐ No	
Overall Impressions:		

Parenting Capacity Assessment

Parenting Capacity is part of the Best Interest Standard factors included in most state statutes and in most evaluators' reports. What is lacking is an operational definition of what Parenting Capacity is and a way to measure it. Much of the published research and theoretical writing on the subject is focused on child welfare investigations, evaluating the minimum level of "good enough" parenting in the context of reducing risk of child abuse. Despite the different legal situations and the different standards of parenting being considered, there are some common factors described by many authors. After their review of the literature, Moran and Weinstock (2011) delineated three sets of skills involved in parenting competence: nurturing skills, teaching skills, and coparenting skills. These core parenting skills are thought to be highly correlated with children's healthy development. These skills are measurable and can be assessed by evaluators in parenting plan evaluations. These skill sets can be taught and hence, are the basis of parenting programs or therapy. It should be noted that the descriptions of these skills are not empirically derived, but come from the theoretical understanding of child development of Moran and Weinstock. They make sense at this point, given that there are no suitable empirical measures of parenting capacity.

Nurturing skills include shared affection. This is seen when the parent offers physical contact and affection, participates in activities with the child, and expresses enthusiasm and approval of the child. Nurturing skills also include the parent's responsiveness. How sensitive is the parent to the child's subjective experience and behavioral signals? How empathetic are the parent's responses? To what degree does the parent help the child identify and express emotions? And finally nurturing includes protection. Does the parent provide physical, emotional, and cognitive resources? Does the parent have developmentally appropriate expectations of the child? And does the parent ensure physical, emotional, and interpersonal security for the child?

Parenting competence also includes teaching skills involving communication, managing, discipline, and modeling. The communication aspect of teaching skills involves the clarity of the parent's expectations, rules, and values; the use of active listening; the minimal use of negative talk such as loud, demanding, threatening, or hostile speech; and the degree to which the parent teaches problem-solving and critical thinking skills. One aspect of the teaching skills component of parenting competence is management, which includes structuring routines, monitoring in a nonintrusive manner the child's academic progress, and social involvement. Management also includes the parent's appropriate exposure of the child to social environments including the media and the internet. Discipline is another aspect of teaching skills. Does the parent set developmentally appropriate goals? Does the parent establish clear and consistent limits, boundaries, rules, expectations and consequences; use praise and positive reinforcement; and use planned ignoring and time-outs? The final aspect of teaching skills is modeling, which in turn involves mood management, impulse control (e.g., anger, misuse of mood-altering substances), rule-compliance, conflict management, and time management.

The third major part of parenting competence involves a parent's coparenting skills. What is the parent's capacity to communicate with the coparent about the child's medical needs, school performance, recreational activities, friends, disciplinary incidents, daily routines, and the like. Also included in this concept of competent parenting is the degree to which the parent encourages the child's relationship with the coparent. This can be manifested in the parent refraining from criticism of the other parent, supporting the coparent's authority, providing flexibility for the parent in the timeshare schedule, acknowledging of the coparent's resources and benign intentions, and supporting of the relationship with the coparent's extended family and social network.

Areas to measure can be pulled from each of the three areas of parenting skills. Please find at the end of this section the table titled, Parenting Skills Assessment: Areas of Inquiry.

A given parent is not expected to reach all of these competencies all of the time. Progress, not perfection, is the goal. All parents and coparents have strengths and vulnerabilities. Competent parents teach honesty, responsibility, respect, kindness, and empathy through their actions and words. Competent parents treat their children with the respect they require that their children have for them. They both guide and encourage their child's uniqueness and their child's reaching of his or her potential.

It is also true that the inability to perform at least an adequate level of some of the parenting skills may, indeed, signal a source of potential harm to the child.

Parenting Skills Assessment: Areas of Inquiry				
Parenting Skill	**Mother**	**Source**	**Father**	**Source**
I. Nurturing				
A. Shared Affection				
• Hugging, holding, touching, kissing, tickling, other displays of affection				
• Participates in fun activities with children including sports, board games, card games, video games, paints, shopping, music, arts, and crafts				
• Offers verbal praise for child's specific behaviors				
• Uses playful voice tones and expresses enthusiasm for child's accomplishments				
B. Responsiveness				
• Examples of comforting unhappy, hurt, or sick child				
• Encouraging child to lead play activities, conversations				
• Talking to children about their feelings				
• Talking with children about their difficult thoughts				
C. Protection				
• Home safety standards, cleanliness, and organization				
• Use of safety devices, (e.g., seat belts, sun screen, etc.)				
• Exposing child to unsafe adults, domestic violence				
• Parent's history of safe driving practices				

Parenting Skill	Mother	Source	Father	Source
Parenting Skills Assessment: Areas of Inquiry *(continued)*				
II. Teaching				
A. Communication				
• Repeats to child what he/she said to demonstrate understanding				
• Does not use questions that put child on defensive				
• Does not use direct, harsh commands				
• Offers the child clear, specific instructions using soft voice tones				
• Uses kid-friendly prompts and questions to guide communication				
• Talks with child about problem behavior and better choices				
B. Managing				
• Providing stable home routines including meals, bedtime, hygiene practices, chores, pet care				
• Monitoring play activity, peer relationships, school performance, media exposure, computer use, cell phone use, diet, video games, TV time				
• Arranges child's physical and social environment for age-appropriate activities				
C. Discipline				
• Boundaries in home for nudity, profanity, TV time, video game time, curfew				
• Use of discipline practices including limiting repeated requests, time-out and quiet time, planned ignoring, logical consequences, behavior charts, and rewards systems				
• Discussion of correct behavior following rule breaking				
• Application of discipline in frequently problematic scenarios (e.g., wake-up time, leaving food mess, spending money, toys in common areas of house, fighting over TV)				
D. Modeling				
• Parent's successes and challenges with managing moods, anger, mood-altering substances				
• Parent's employment history including awards, advancements, and disciplinary actions				

Parenting Skills Assessment: Areas of Inquiry *(continued)*				
Parenting Skill	**Mother**	**Source**	**Father**	**Source**
III. Coparenting				
A. Communicating With Coparent				
• Parent's exchange of information about children (e.g., special activities at school, report cards, school pictures, school awards, medical reports, diet, incidents at school with peers, illnesses/events in extended family)				
• Keeping coparent informed about children's organized activities including sports activities and team schedules, daycare settings, tutors				
• Coparenting behavior at school events, medical appointments, exchanges of children				
• History of allowing children to take personal items between homes, clothing exchanges				
• Providing timely and detailed notice of travel plans				
B. Encouraging Child's Relationship With Coparent				
• Reports of supportive statements to child about coparent, reports of parent making critical comments about coparent				
• Parents' friendliness at exchanges, school, and extracurricular events; reports of children witnessing coparent anger				
• Encouraging child to call other parent, insisting child answer calls from coparent				
• Insisting child conform to court-ordered parenting schedule				
• If non-life-threatening crisis involving the other parent, calling the other parent before calling the police or involving the child				
• Expressing appreciation for gifts received by child from coparent				
• Assisting child to prepare gifts for coparent for holidays and celebrations				
• Encouraging the child's relationship with coparent's extended family and social network				
• Flexing the parenting schedule for coparent to take the child to special events				
• History of timeliness for exchanges				

Parenting Plan Evaluator's Self-Assesssment of Conducting Custody Evaluations

1. Name: _____

2. Date: _____

3. Number of cases in past year: _____

4. List of areas of specialized training and expertise

5. List of specialized training in the past year:

6. List of key journal articles that you have read in the past year:

7. List of key presentations you have attended in the past year:

8. Rate the degree to which you agree/disagree with the following statements. Please type in the number that corresponds with your answer in the box next to the statement.

1 = Strongly agree   2 = Agree   3 = Neutral

4 = Disagree   5 = Strongly disagree   9 = Don't Know

Statement	Answer
• I am confident about my knowledge of custody evaluations.	
• I can distinguish between focused reports and comprehensive evaluations.	
• I am confident that I can screen for violence when conducting custody evaluations.	
• I am familiar with the research relevant to custody evaluations.	
• I have skills in conducting interviews with children within the context of a custody evaluations.	
• I am clear on my decision to use or not use standard tests when conducting evaluations.	
• I am aware of my potential biases when conducting evaluations.	
• I believe continuing education regarding the basic skills in conducting evaluations will help me to be a competent evaluator.	
• It is important to use research to guide my practice when working with complex issues.	
• I can discern high quality research from those studies with serious methodological flaws.	
• I am able to identify the strategies that lawyers use to cross-examine witnesses.	
• I am able to identify limitations of poorly conducted custody evaluations.	
• I am confident that I can provide sufficient weight to various types of data when making recommendations to the court.	
• I am able to identify the various collateral sources that should be contacted during a custody evaluation.	
• I am confident that I can work through ethical dilemmas as they arise in the context of custody evaluations.	

9. Please indicate your learning needs in relation to evidence-based practice. Please choose all that apply.

Statements	Response	Additional Comment
• The context of divorcing families		
• The knowledge of law		
• The process of conducting custody evaluations		
• Knowledge of best practice guidelines and model standards for conducting evaluations		
• Introduction to special topics relevant to evaluations (e.g., domestic violence, alienation, high conflict, etc.)		
• Case-based discussions		
• Starting your own private practice		
• Other:		
• Other:		

10. Goals for the next year:

Sample Table of Contents:
E.C. 730 Evaluation (Report A)*

Judge and Attorneys
The Honorable _____
Superior Court of _____,
County of _____
Department _____
P.O. Box _____, _____, _____
Phone: _____
Attorney for father:_____
Attorney for mother: _____

---

* This Table of Contents is an illustration of how to present the data collection, data analysis, and synthesis in a manner in which it is mostly included in the text of the report. Miscellaneous data appears in the Appendix of the report.

Sample Table of Contents:
E.C. 730 Evaluation (Report B)*

Judge and Attorneys

The Honorable _____
Superior Court of _____,
County of _____
Department _____
P.O. Box _____, _____, _____
Phone: _____

Attorney for father: _____
Attorney for mother: _____

---

* This Table of Contents is an illustration of how to present the data collection, data analysis, and synthesis in a manner in which the body of the report includes an introduction and then an analysis of the data and a synthesis of same leading to recommendations with the entire data collection section being found in the Appendix of the report.

Parenting Plan Evaluator's
Information Template

Case Name: _____   **Date:** _____

1. **Date of Appointment:**

    First contact:
    Case #:
    Case name

2. **Names of the parties:**

    a. Petitioner:
    b. Respondent :

3. **Contact information for the attorneys for the parties:**

    Petitioner's attorney:
    Name:
    Firm:
    Street address/suite:
    City, State, Zip Code:
    Phone:
    Fax:
    E-mail:

    Respondent's attorney:
    Name:
    Firm:
    Street address/suite:
    City, State, Zip Code:
    Phone:
    Fax:
    E-mail:

4. **Contact information for the parties:**

    Petitioner
    Address:
    Home/work/cell phone #'s:
    E-mail address:

    Respondent
    Address:
    Home/work/cell phone #'s:
    E-mail address:

5. **The evaluation shall include the following people (DOB's):**

    a.   Father:

    b.   Mother:

    c.   Minor Children (including DOB's):

    d.   Step-parents (significant others):

6. **Fees to be paid by:** _____ (per order)   **Hourly rate:** _____

                                                                                        (to be filled out by evaluator prior to this form being sent out)

7. **Purpose of the evaluation:**

    <u>Per Father</u>:

    <u>Per Mother</u>:

8. **Scope of the evaluation:**

    <u>Per Father</u>:

    <u>Per Mother</u>:

9. **Issues to be investigated/evaluated:**

    <u>Per Father</u>:

        1.

        2.

        3.

        4.

    <u>Per Mother</u>:

        1.

        2.

        3.

        4.

10. **Court information:**

    a.   Name of Judge:

    b.   Address:

    c.   Phone Number:

11. **Police or Child Abuse Reports.** Are there any police or sheriff's department or child abuse reports on file for any member of this family and if so, how many, for whom, and where?

12. **Next court date** (report to be completed and to the court and counsel xx days prior to this date):

Parent's Relationship Timeline

Case Name: _____ **Date:** _____

Timeline. Please put together a timeline of the relationship with the other parent – from the time you met to the present. Include in that timeline any things that stand out in the history of this relationship (e.g., met x date, dated exclusively beginning x date, lived together x date, engaged x date, married x date, children born, moved, separated, plus any events that stand out since the separation). Include in this timeline the dates or approximate dates of any things that happened that have become allegations against or by you.

Please have this timeline to me no later than _____ .

Date	*Description*

Date	Description

Collateral Contact Sheet*

Name	Contact Information (Phone/Address/Email)	Relationship to Parties	Consent Form Completed (Yes/No)	Date(s) Contacted	Date Interviewed	Time of Interview

* This form is to be filled out by the parenting plan evaluator.

Parent's Collateral Contact Sheet*

Name: _____
Date: _____

Please provide a list of no more than 5 people (collaterals) who might have information that either backs up claims or accusations that you have/are making and/or people that can defend you against accusations that have/are being made against you and/or anyone who has personal information about your caregiving and parenting. Please fill in the blanks in the chart below for each collateral. In most cases, the answers that each collateral provides will be reviewed and the collaterals will not be spoken to. Phone interviews will be conducted with some collaterals. This list is due _____. Thank you.

Name of Collateral	Email Address for Collateral	Street Address	Phone: Day Night Cell	Relationship to You	Information You Expect This Person to Provide	Questions You Suggest Be Asked if They Are Interviewed on the Phone

* This form is to be given to the parents and their counsel to fill out.

Police and Child Abuse Reports Form
_____ Case

Instructions. Please list below any and ALL child abuse reports and/or police reports involving any member of this family. This is due _____. Thank you.

Report #/City Filed In/ Agency Filed With/Address and Phone Numbers of Agency	Date Filed	Name/Description of Report

Decision Tree for Child Physical Abuse

Does the child need to be protected from a parent due to the risk of physical abuse?
(restriction of contact and/or contact supervised)

Safety Issues	Children's Strengths and Weaknesses	Parenting Capacity and Mental Stability
Child Abuse Child abuse has been verified.	**Adjustment and Resiliency** The child's temperamant impacts the child's vulnerability for the risk of future abuse.	**Allegations** A parent is fabricating allegations of abuse for the litigation.
Child Protection There is a risk of child abuse in the future.	**Child's Perspective** The child is afraid of the abusive parent.	**Mental Health** A parent's mental heath affects parenting.
Child Treatment for Abuse The child is not receiving individual treatment for the abuse.	**Ages and Stages** The child's age and stage impacts the child's vulnerability for the risk of future abuse.	**Substance Abuse** The parent's abuse of substances affects parenting.
Parent Treatment for Abuse The perpetrator of abuse has not received individual treatment.	**History of the Child's Relationships** The child's relationship with the abusive parent has typically been strained.	**Parenting** The parent lacks strategies for appropriate and effective discipline per the child's age and stage of development.

Decision Tree for Relocation

**Should a child be allowed to move with a parent?
(Factors to consider in cases of relocation)**

Safety Issues*	Child's Strengths and Weaknesses	Parenting Capacity and Mental Stability	Practical Matters
IPV There are no issues of IPV that affect the family.	**Adjustment and Resiliency** The child's temperamant protects the child from distress.	**Communication** The parents are able to communicate and cooperate flexibly.	**Distance between Residences** The distance provides the opportunity to maintain contact.
Child Abuse There are no issues of child abuse and/or risk of abuse that affect the child.	**Child's Perspective** The child favors the move.	**Parenting** Both parents are effective in their parenting.	**Travel Cost** The cost associated with travel is reasonable.
Child Neglect There are no issues of child neglect and/or risk of neglect that affect the child.	**Ages and Stages** The child's age and stage allows the child to adjust to changes and transitions without serious disruptions.	**Parents' Homes** The parents both have appropriate living arrangements for the child's age & needs.	**Reasons for Move** The move provides opportunities for growth and development.
Substance Abuse There are no substance abuse issues that affect parenting.	**History of the Child's Relationships** The child has a good enough attachment relationship with the nonresidential parent.	**Gatekeeping** Facilitative gatekeeping will ameliorate challenges resulting from the move.	**Social Capital** The move provides additional support and resources.

* In extreme cases of abuse, relocation to a safe unnamed location may be indicated.

Decision Tree for Child Under Age of 5

What is the optimal parenting plan for a child under the age of 5 years of age?
(limited contact, frequent contact, overnight contact with nonresidential parent [NRP])

Safety Issues	Children's Strengths and Weaknesses	Parenting Capacity and Mental Stability	Stability
IPV There are no issues of IPV that affect the family.	**Adjustment and Resiliency** The child's temperamant protects the child from changes and transitions.	**NRP Contact** NRP has been consistently available to the child.	**Routine** Both parents provide similar routines for the child.
Child Abuse There are no issues of child abuse and/or risk of abuse that affect the child.	**Child's Caregivers** The child has been in the care of different caregivers (e.g. grandparent) without significant discomfort.	**Mental Health** Both parents' mental heath are positively affecting parenting.	**Consistency of the Schedule** The parenting plan schedule has consistency and stability.
Child Neglect There are no issues of child neglect and/or risk of neglect that affect the child.	**Siblings** Siblings provide a protective buffer during times away from the residential parent.	**Adult Relationships** The parent-parent relationship historically has been positive.	**Living Arrangements** Both parents' homes are safe and appropriate for the child.
Substance Abuse There are no substance issues that affect parenting.	**Child's Relationships with NRP** The child has a good enough relationship with the nonresidential parent.	**Gatekeeping** Facilitative gatekeeping positively affects parenting .	**Proximity** Parents live in close proximity to support frequent transitions.

Decision Tree for
Optimal Sharing Time of Parenting

What is the Plan that is Best for the Sharing of Parenting

Safety of Child
The Abuse Hypothesis

Parent-Child Relationship: *The Gatekeeping Hypothesis*

Parenting Problems: *The Parenting Hypothesis*

Safety of Child	Parent-Child Relationship	Parenting Problems
Intimate Partner Violence	Facilitative Gatekeeping	Hypervigilant
		Intrusive
Child Abuse/Neglect	Restrictive Gatekeeping	Too Lax / Too Rigid
		Alienating/Sabotaging
Substance Abuse	Protective Gatekeeping	Self-Centered
		Enmeshed

Decision Tree for
Safety and Well-being of Children

What is the optimal parenting plan for the safety and well-being of the children in this family?

Safety Issues	Children's Strengths and Weaknesses	Parenting Capacity and Mental Stability
IPV There are no issues of IPV that affect the family	**Adjustment and Resiliency** The child's temperament protects the child from distress and maladjustment	**Mental Health** There are no parental mental heath problems affecting parenting
Child Abuse There are no issues of child abuse and/or risk of abuse that affect the child	**Child's Perspective** The child's views and preferences influence the optimal parenting plan	**Allegations** The parents are not fabricating allegations for litigation purposes
Child Neglect There are no issues of child neglect and/or risk of neglect that affect the child	**Ages and Stages** The parent's attunement to the child's needs protects the child from distress and maladjustment	**Adult Relationships** Historically the parent-parent relationship has been positive
Substance Abuse There are no substance abuse issues that affect parenting	**History of the Child's Relationships** Historically the child's relationships with his/her parents have been positive	**Gatekeeping** Facilitative gatekeeping positively affects parenting

Gatekeeping Formation, Patterns, and Responses Following Divorce

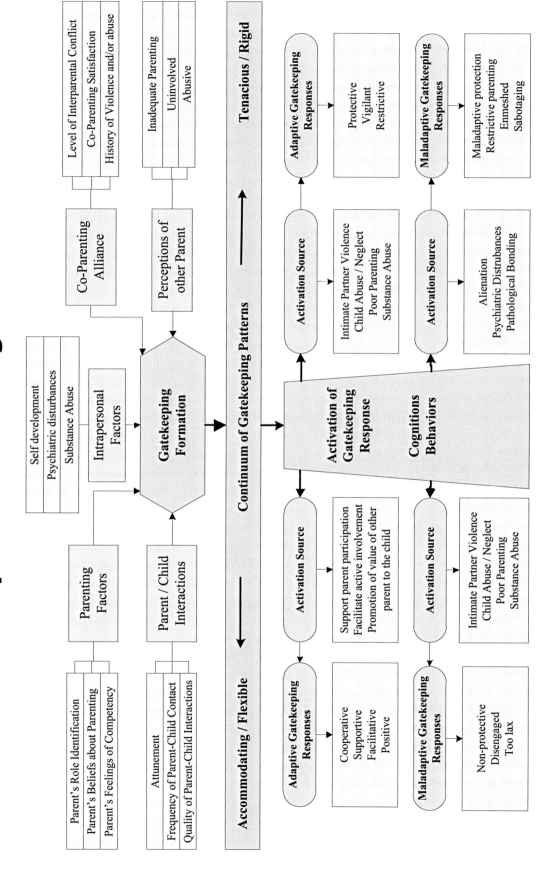

Decision Tree for Assessment of Allegations of Intimate Partner Violence (IPV/Domestic Violence)

Assessment of Allegations of Intimate Partner Violence (Domestic Violence)

Risk Factors
Previous Violence
Substance Abuse
Major Mental Disorder
Threat Assessment Factors
• Making a threat
• Obsessive following
• Weapons

Kind of Aggression
Physical
Emotional or Psychological
Sexual Coercion
Coercive Control

Frequency, Severity, Active v. Remote, Pattern, Children's Exposure
Frequency
Severity
Active v. Remote
Pattern
Children Exposed / Children Witnessed

Instigator
Primarily Male Partner
Primarily Female Partner
Mutual
Defensive or Reactive
Others

Children's Well-Being & Adjustment
+
Parenting/Co-parenting
+
Violence Risk
↔
Predicted to a Parenting Plan

Categories of Intimate Partner Violence (Domestic Violence)

Mental Disorder Associated (MDA)

Conflict-Instigated, Situation- Specific (CISS)

Separation Associated (SA)

Substance Abuse Associated (SAA)

Coercive Control, Intrusive, Authoritarian (CCIA)
➤ Control with violence
➤ Control without violence

The variables in each of these categories are continuous, and are to be assessed independently, and described in behavioral terms. The size of each part of the circle is an estimate.

From Intimate Partner Violence and Child Custody Evaluation, Part I: Theoretical Framework, Forensic Model, and Assessment Issues (William Austin & Leslie Drozd, *Journal of Child Custody, Vol. IX(4)*, December, 2012). Reprinted with permission.

Leslie Drozd, Ph.D.
lesliedrozd@gmail.com
William Austin, Ph.D.
wgaustinphd2@yahoo.com

Subject Index

A

Abuse,
    risk of, 191, 193, 197
    sexual, 9, 12, 18, 115, 136
Accountability, vii, 65, 74-78, 90-97, 107, 110, 121, 153-155
Accuracy, v, 7, 21, 49-50, 136, 142
Accusations, 31, 69, 96, 135, 185
Activities, children's school, 42
Additive, 74-78, 90-95, 153-155
Admissibility issues, 49
Adult-child relationships, 164
AFCC (Association of Family and Conciliation Courts), 2, 16, 83, 113
AFCC Model Standards of Practice for Child Custody Evaluation, 2
Aggression, 35, 42, 45, 47, 58, 66, 82, 87, 201
Alcohol abuse, 35, 40, 47, 66, 70, 73, 76, 82, 86, 90-92, 95
Alienation, 15-16, 20, 27-28, 32, 45, 107, 115, 124, 126, 132, 134-135, 173, 199
Allegations, viii, 12, 34, 38, 42, 45, 48, 55, 58-59, 61, 69-70, 72-73, 85-86, 141, 201
    fabricating, 35, 47-48, 66, 82, 189, 197
    supporting domestic violence, 27
Allegations of abuse, 16, 19
Allegations of domestic violence, 27-28, 114, 117
American Academy of Child and Adolescent Psychiatry, 49, 113
American Academy of Psychiatry, 12, 116, 119-120
American Psychological Association (APA), 2, 10, 16, 40, 63, 113-114
Analysis, transparent, 108
Anchor, 9, 135, 159
Anger, 42, 58, 60-61, 74-78, 83, 89-93, 95-96, 167, 169
Antagonistic, 74-78, 90-95, 110, 153-155
Anxiety, 44, 48, 74, 77, 87, 92
Anxiety issues, 44
APA (*see* American Psychological Association)
Applicability, 97, 128, 132-133
Approach,
    child-centered, 117, 136
    comprehensive, 27, 50, 109
    evaluator's, 38
    evidence-based, 12
Assertion errors, 4
Assessment, viii, 2, 16, 18, 26, 28, 55, 67-68, 107, 117, 121, 123, 164, 201
    adult-child relationships,   164
    children, 164
    parenting, 164
Association of Family and Conciliation Courts (*see* AFCC)
Attachment, 4, 6, 27, 37, 77, 132, 135
Attentional blindness, 6, 135
Attorneys, v, 3, 6, 8-9, 11-12, 16-17, 19, 26, 29-32, 38, 40, 55, 96, 175, 177

R

Randomly assigned, 134
RCTs, 130-131, 134
Recommendations, 15, 25-28, 50, 53-55, 65, 74-78, 80-81, 83, 90-100, 105-106, 108-109, 123, 140-141, 153-155, 159-161
    appropriate, 65
    developing, 105, 123
    evaluator's, 54, 100, 106
    making, 54, 100, 103, 113, 166, 172
    nonobjective, 11
    suggested, 97
    ultimate, 54
Records, 4, 16, 29, 40, 46, 55, 59, 76-8, 91-6, 118, 132, 161, 163
Referral, 15, 17, 19, 30, 38, 44, 110, 175, 177
Relationship history, 34-36, 47, 66, 82
Relationship issues, 60
Relationship quality, 23-24
Relationships, 3, 20-21, 25, 30, 32, 42, 77-78, 80-81, 92-93, 95, 126, 129-131, 136-139, 141, 181
    children's, 32, 37, 45, 81, 83
    child's, 107, 135, 138, 167, 170, 189, 197
    parent's, 100
Reliability, 8, 39, 55, 66-73, 84-86, 88, 111, 128, 133, 141-142
Religious issues, 100, 163
Relocation, viii, 15-16, 27, 56-57, 68, 89, 103, 121, 124, 134, 147, 151, 191
Research, 3-4, 7-8, 10-11, 16-20, 27-28, 40-41, 49-51, 74, 98, 101-103, 113-119, 124, 126-128, 132, 134
    published, 124, 167
    scientific, 26, 123
Research bias, 8
Research designs, 124, 128, 134, 137
Research knowledge, 123
Research literacy, 123, 125, 127
Residence, 164-165, 191
Resiliency, 27, 33-36, 47, 66, 82, 189, 191, 193, 197
Resistance, 7, 28, 92
Resources, v-vi, 15, 25, 96, 98, 140, 191
    community, 98
    coparent's, 167
Restrictive parenting, 199
Risk, 9, 18-19, 23, 27, 31-32, 53-54, 63, 74, 79, 87, 103, 108, 132, 160, 189
Risk factors, 25, 28, 116, 201
Risk management issues, 100
Road Map for Using Research, vii, 121, 123
Role, caretaking, 164-165

S

Safety, viii, 6, 20-21, 31-32, 34-35, 37, 47-48, 65-67, 74, 76-77, 82, 89-92, 121, 126, 197
    child's, 32
Sample size, 128, 130-131
Schedule, 42-43, 45, 98, 193
    regarding optimal parenting, 103
Schedule parenting time, 97
School, 24, 43, 59, 70, 72, 79-80, 85, 95, 100-101, 170
Separation, 13, 27-28, 35, 37, 47, 57-58, 66, 74, 77, 82, 92, 96-97, 101-103, 106, 117
    parental, 45
    parent's, 79

Parenting Plan & Child Custody Evaluations